D1597350

ARCHITECTS TO THE NATION

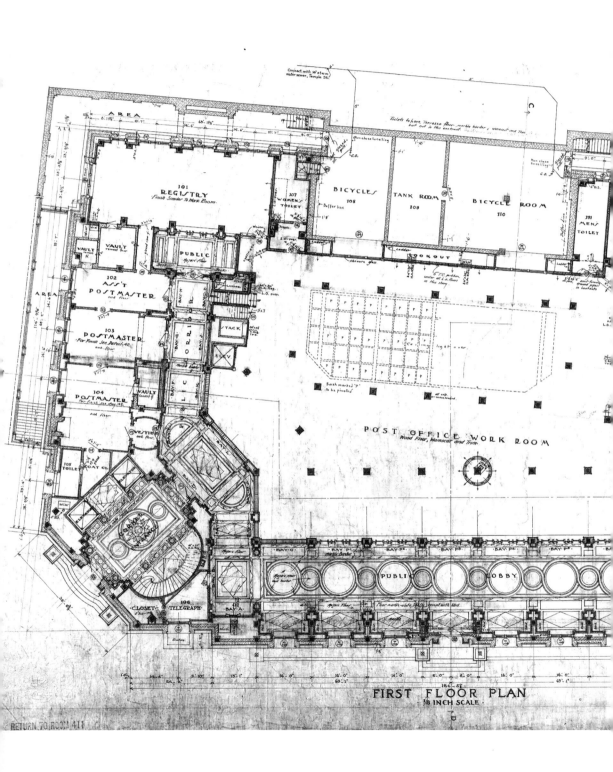

FIRST FLOOR PLAN
1/8 INCH SCALE

ARCHITECTS
TO THE NATION

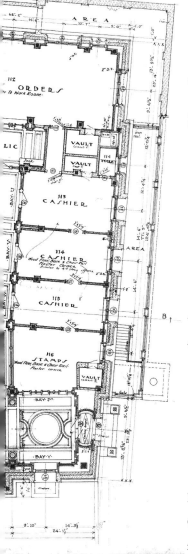

The Rise and Decline of the
Supervising Architect's Office

ANTOINETTE J. LEE

with Foreword by William Seale

New York   Oxford
Oxford University Press
2000

Oxford University Press

Oxford   New York
Athens   Auckland   Bangkok   Bogotá   Buenos Aires   Calcutta
Cape Town   Chennai   Dar es Salaam   Delhi   Florence   Hong Kong   Istanbul
Karachi   Kuala Lumpur   Madrid   Melbourne   Mexico City   Mumbai
Nairobi   Paris   São Paulo   Singapore   Taipei   Tokyo   Toronto   Warsaw

and associated companies in
Berlin   Ibadan

Published by Oxford University Press, Inc.
198 Madison Avenue, New York, New York 10016

Oxford is a registered trademark of Oxford University Press.

Library of Congress Cataloging-in-Publication Data

Lee, Antoinette J. (Antoinette Josephine)
Architects to the nation : the rise and decline of the
Supervising Architect's Office
Antoinette J. Lee with introduction by William Seale.
p.   cm.
ISBN 0-19-512822-2
1. United States. Dept. of the Treasury. Office of Supervising
Architect.   2. Public buildings—United States—Designs and plans.
I. Title.
NA4421.L44   2000
725′.1′0983—dc21   99-13565

The murals of Harold Weston (1894–1972) depicting "Architecture
Under Government—Old and New," Regional Office Building,
General Services Administration (formerly the Procurement Building),
1936–1938, Washington, D.C.

9 8 7 6 5 4 3 2 1

Printed in the United States of America
on acid-free paper

Dedicated to the memory of Karel Yasko

FOREWORD

William Seale

This book presents a unique view of a strata of American architectural history seen heretofore only in glimpses. It is the story of a bureaucracy, which, somewhat like our National Endowments today, long ago assumed a significant role in art—in this case architecture—but unlike the endowments, which stimulate production in the arts and humanities, the Office of the Supervising Architect of the U.S. Department of the Treasury was actually in the business of design and construction, employing professional architects to provide public buildings all over the nation.

From his headquarters at the Treasury Building in Washington, the supervising architect, presiding over a large staff, exercised nearly exclusive control over federal government buildings. He was close to the Congress, which funded him, and he carried out its wishes with considerable freedom. Few traces remain. The great drafting rooms in Treasury, long abandoned, their skylights painted over, recently fell to the wrecking ball. Records of the Office, numbering in the hundreds of thousands of documents and drawings, were transferred long ago to the able care of the National Archives. No other historical record of American architecture is as vast and detailed. These papers are the basic resource from which Antoinette J. Lee's history is written.

The production of the supervising architect's office, from birth in the early 1850s to weakening before political fire in the 1890s and eventual death a half-century later, was both remarkable and widespread. Some of the buildings the office built are icons in American architecture. In Carson City, Nevada, Ammi B. Young's United States Mint stands on the desert, a beacon whose Italianate light shines in the subsequent Nevada State Capitol up the street. The State, War, and Navy Building, Supervising Architect Alfred B. Mullet's mighty granite pile west of the White House, is perhaps America's best expression of the French Second Empire mode.

Supervising Architect William Appleton Potter gave us the high-towered Post Office and Courthouse in Nashville following his Gothic ideas. Under Supervising Architect James Knox Taylor, Cass Gilbert designed and built New York City's superbly neo-Renaissance customhouse, an ideal of Beaux-Arts civic beauty, with its elliptical rotunda and sumptuous art program. Potter's was a traditional Treasury product designed in-house, while Gilbert won his commission under new rules, in a competition among private firms.

In addition to monuments, the supervising architect of the Treasury enriched the American landscape with hundreds of lesser buildings—post offices, custom houses, courthouses, and marine hospitals. These buildings form a vernacular of public architecture for the late nineteenth and early twentieth centuries that cast long shadows regionally. A few were even "restorations," such as the remodeling of the early seventeenth-century adobe Palace of the Governors at Santa Fe for federal use, and the transformation of the eighteenth-century Spanish Governor's Palace at St. Augustine into a post office. Still it was the new construction that made the most profound imprint. Distributed from Washington, D.C., as neat, detailed drawings on oiled linen, these buildings rose in brick or stone and announced the federal government, often in far-flung places. They were likely to be the best buildings in town. For the strength of their presence today, many are the objects of historic preservation.

Design forms the spine of Lee's study. Did the Office produce great architecture? Was that its objective in fact, or simply to build useful and permanent housing for governmental functions? Certainly the supervising architect could take credit for the rapid transfer of style over the nation. Since then *The Fountainhead* and the idea of the architect-as-hero has come to pervade our architectural histories. The institution of the supervising architect has not heretofore been well remembered.

Founded in the early stages of the development of the architectural profession in the United States, the Office of the Supervising

Architect of the Treasury first represented an expediency. After the Civil War, the Office was institutionalized into an organized machinery and carried the legacy of the Army engineers.

The Office flourished until 1893—the year, not inconsequentially, of the World's Fair in Chicago—when the Tarsney Act of Congress, ardently supported by the American Institute of Architects, opened up federal building to private enterprise. Competitions eventually became a permanent feature of federal design and construction, with much of their character and specifications shaped by the AIA. The tables turned. Federal contracts being some of the largest available, private architects now scrambled directly to the lawmakers for favor, while also laboring in the beginning to create handicaps that would reduce the number of competitors. Political patronage, thus rechanneled, remained a major influence on the practice of public architecture throughout the twentieth century.

Lee's study unearths what came before, which is a missing and vitally important story. The volumes of architectural history that line our library shelves rarely give any reference at all to the Office of the Supervising Architect; when they do, it is usually not to the Office itself, but to a notable building the office produced. A few of the supervising architects have been allowed to join the heroes, but most are little known. Lee's book opens up a panorama. Architectural historians will find here a new perspective on American architecture and a valuable resource to keep close at hand.

Few architectural organizations have enjoyed the scope and durability of the Office of the Supervising Architect of the U.S. Treasury Department. Between the mid-nineteenth century and the end of the 1930s, the Office designed numerous federal government buildings that were located in the nation's capital city, Washington, D.C., and in thousands of communities nationwide. Despite its great longevity, the Office was as artistically vigorous and prolific near the end of its existence in the late 1930s as it was at its inception in the early 1850s.

The Office developed within the U.S. Treasury Department because that agency collected the customs duties and other fees, and it seemed natural that the same department should handle the design of the edifices that housed its functions. As the federal government's role evolved, the addition of other federal government agency and bureau activities to these buildings seemed a logical step. By the end of the Depression era, when federal government responsibilities had increased markedly, the Office was moved out of the Treasury Department and into a public works agency.

The Office took root in a period when the architectural profession was only barely defined. The Office employed government architects who undertook the design of federal government buildings and were compensated with civil service salaries. The Office grew to prominence as private architects became organized into a powerful lobbying force. Its scope was abruptly cut short when the nation began preparations for World War II, and it never regained its standing when the nation returned to peacetime. It endured decades of intense scrutiny and negative public attacks by private architects, who sawed away at the Office's foundations and prerogatives.

Today, the Office is barely known, even to architectural historians. But its architectural patrimony has not been forgotten. Many of the Office's buildings have been identified and documented as part of historic resources surveys and are designated as landmark buildings. Many continue to play vital roles in serving the public. Others have been demolished and their records are available only in paper and photographic files. Still others have been emptied of federal government functions and turned over to new uses.

Although the Office as a whole is little known, its name recurs time and time again when studying the architectural development of Washington, D.C., and other cities. However, while studies have been undertaken on groups of federal government buildings or on specific architects who worked in the Office, never has a single work been devoted to the overall development of the Office.

This project occurred to me on several occasions when I was conducting research on the architectural and planning history of Washington, D.C. The imprint of the Supervising Architect's Office can be seen in Ammi B. Young's Georgetown Custom House (now post office) of 1857–1858, in the Old Post Office of the 1890s at 11th and Pennsylvania Avenue designed under Willoughby Edbrooke's tenure as Supervising Architect, the 1915–1917 Old Interior Office Building (now the General Services Administration Building) in the West End, and in the Internal Revenue Service Building of 1928–1935 in the Federal Triangle. These Washington, D.C., buildings are just the tip of the veritable national architectural iceberg.

Clearly, there was a much larger story to be told. The important work of Bates and Isabel Lowry and Pamela Scott during the early years of the National Building Museum brought to light the exceptional cache of architectural drawings of the Office, which were then housed in a National Archives storage facility. Sarah Bradford Landau's study of William Appleton Potter, supervising architect from 1875 to 1876, was another signal of the significant story waiting to be told. Other articles, monographs, and publications presented enticing glimpses of the Office's power and scope.

A comprehensive study of the Office based on written correspondence and other records seemed a logical next step. Over a period of several years at the National Archives, I read seemingly endless rolls of microfilm containing the general correspondence of the Office. This chronological record forms the backbone of my study. In addition to these microfilm records are the numerous boxes of construction documents for individual building projects; these were too voluminous to research for this project, but they are invaluable for detailed studies of individual buildings. In order to understand how the Office fit into the larger picture of the evolving architectural profession, it was necessary to review records at the American Institute of Architects Archives and scour articles in the leading architectural periodicals of the time. Few architectural institutions left such a large quantity of written and graphic documentation as the Supervising Architect's Office.

While vilified by many private architects over the years, the Office represented a center of culture and design in the federal government well before there were National Endowments for the Arts and the Humanities and before the Smithsonian Institution served as a national force for learning. The location of the Office in the U.S. Treasury Department provided the financially based agency with a strong cultural flavor. The buildings were regarded as not only facilities to house federal government services, but also as architectural ornaments to their communities and as inspiration for civic consciousness in a young nation.

The story of the Supervising Architect's Office also runs contrary to the image of the architect as "hero." Most of the office's staff architects toiled virtually anonymously in the offices of the Treasury Department without credit or national recognition. In most cases, only the name of the supervising architect is recorded on the architectural drawings or on the building cornerstone. But, clearly, one architect could not have served as the artistic designer of every building that emerged from the Office. It is only through architectural publications and from American Institute of Architect membership records that architects claimed credit for a building.

This book was envisioned as a national framework against which the contributions of individual architects and of singular buildings could be better evaluated and appreciated. With the passage of time, the Supervising Architect's Office and its buildings have moved beyond the contemporary architectural debates of their era and are instead now the focus of judgments about the protection of significant cultural heritage in cities and towns across the nation. With this publication, I hope that many more buildings and government architects will capture the attention of researchers, scholars, and citizens. Only then will the legacy of this important government institution be secured for future generations.

ACKNOWLEDGMENTS

Many individuals have had a hand in this publication. William Seale, author of the Foreword, stands above all others. He suggested the project as one that might interest the National Endowment for the Humanities (NEH). We earlier had discussed the Office of the Supervising Architect of the U.S. Treasury Department while he was preparing the massive study of the history and architecture of state capitol buildings. He was a cooperative partner throughout this venture and was correct about the significance of the subject.

The National Endowment for the Humanities supported the research and manuscript preparation. NEH program officers Dorothy Wartenberg and David Wise guided the project through its early years. The U.S. Customs Service provided a welcome supplement to the NEH grant; I owe special gratitude to William von Raab, Commissioner of Customs in 1982. The Historical Society of Washington, D.C., under the directorships of Perry G. Fisher and Jane North, generously agreed to sponsor and house the project.

Much of the research was conducted at various offices of the National Archives. The assistance of numerous National Archives staffers—who daily show researchers through the maze of finding aids—is much appreciated. Their dedication and knowledge are a credit to all government employees. For the private sector side of this story, the American Institute of Architects Archives was indispensable. Its former Archivist, Tony P. Wrenn, was a loyal and steadfast supporter of this project and made the AIA's voluminous files and scrapbooks available to me. His successor, Sarah Turner, helped me tie up many loose ends.

Over the years, many other historians reviewed and critiqued chapters and the whole manuscript. They include project consultants Robert Ennis of Philadelphia (an expert on Thomas U. Walter) and Wayne Morgan of the University of Oklahoma; Pamela Scott, Daniel Bluestone, Richard Guy Wilson, Stephen N. Dennis, James M. Goode, and C. Ford Peatross. In its final months of editing, Joe Wallis reviewed the manuscript and made valuable editorial and organizational suggestions.

From the project's start and through its early years, the late Karel Yasko, the former assistant commissioner of design and construction and later the fine arts counselor of the General Services Administration, cheered it along. Those fortunate enough to have met Mr. Yasko during his years at the General Services Administration could not have failed to leave his presence without being convinced that the history of federal government architecture was the most worthwhile subject for research. He greeted visitors from behind tilting stacks of reports and files and proceeded to pull out relevant papers as if they had been filed according to the most orderly and logical system. This project likely would not have existed without his contagious enthusiasm. It is only fitting that this publication is dedicated to his memory.

CONTENTS

1

[T]o the future historian of American art,
the succession of the Government Architects
will be nearly as important as that of the
kings of England in British secular history.
(American Architect and Building News, 22
[July 30, 1887], p. 45)

When this prophecy was written in 1887, comparing the succession of supervising architects with that of the kings of England, the "Government Architects" were those who headed the Office of the Supervising Architect of the U.S. Treasury Department. The prophecy was not borne out and only a few of the fifteen supervising architects are remembered: Ammi B. Young, Alfred B. Mullett, William A. Potter, James G. Hill, and James Knox Taylor are the most prominent. The names of Mifflin E. Bell, Jeremiah O'Rourke, and Oscar Wenderoth are obscure at best, even in the relatively restricted field of architectural history.

The Supervising Architect's Office was a bureau located within the U.S. Treasury Department, which for nearly a century designed custom houses, courthouses, post offices, and other buildings that housed federal government functions. Established in 1852, the Office blossomed at a time when the U.S. Congress appropriated funds to design and construct a large group of federal buildings in communities east of the Mississippi River and in the South. The Office grew and expanded through the 1930s, when it addressed the economic crisis caused by the Great Depression. Efforts by private architects to wrest control of federal building design finally bore fruit in the post–

World War II era. The Supervising Architect's Office was, however, unlike any private architectural firm, because Congress and the secretary of the treasury played important roles in shaping this national building program. The Office's legacy is evident in federal government buildings that serve as the political and architectural anchors of thousands of communities nationwide.

The rise and decline of this federal government bureau paralleled the development of the nation and of the architectural profession. When the Office was established in 1852, the American Institute of Architects (AIA) had not yet been organized. Architects were so scarce that the federal government had difficulty in locating them in the increasingly far-flung places in which federal buildings were to be built. It was perfectly natural that a central architectural organization should have been developed to handle the growing number of architectural projects. Nearly a century later, by contrast, when the Supervising Architect's Office was removed from the Treasury Department in 1939, the architectural profession had mushroomed and profited from a healthy national lobby in the AIA. The profession had become an important force and architects were located throughout the nation, wherever the demand existed. The AIA could reflect on a long record of lobbying the U.S. Congress and the federal agencies to open more architectural projects to private practitioners.

The building program that ultimately evolved for the federal government out of the colonial, Federalist, and national periods was one of amazing extent. The factors that led to the establishment of the Supervising Architect's Office had their roots in the governmental system that the U.S. Constitution created. Two hundred years' hindsight makes it possible to assess the full magnitude of the impact of the Constitution upon the development of the U.S. landscape. However, in the summer of 1787, the effects could barely be perceived. The task before the group of 55 delegates who gathered in Philadelphia was to form a stronger central government than that provided in the Articles of Confederation adopted during the Revolution six years before. The largest cities at that time were New York with 49,000 inhabitants, Philadelphia with 28,000, Boston with 18,000, and Charleston, South Carolina, with 16,000. A network of trade with Europe and its colonies linked coastal port cities along the Atlantic coast and major inland waterways. Beyond that a vast frontier beckoned.

What the nation would look like ten, fifty, or one hundred years hence was unknown. What was clear was that the Constitution, outlining the powers of the federal government, would play a significant role in facilitating the physical development of the nation. Nearly all the provisions of the Constitution affected government architecture; the new federal functions would require bureaucracies to be housed in structures of some kind. Two provisions in Article 1, Section 8, provided a legal basis for a federal building program. One of these was the power of Congress "to establish Post Offices and post Roads" (Clause 7). The other was legislative authority to create a capital city and "to exercise like Authority over all Places purchased by the Consent of the Legislature of the State in which the Same shall be, for the Erection of Forts, Magazines, Arsenals, dock-Yards, and other needful Buildings" (Clause 17). The first provision was later interpreted to allow the condemnation of land and other powers related to the construction of the physical infrastructure that facilitated the transport and delivery of mail. The second provision served as the basis for the acquisition of land for military and civilian buildings.[1]

What examples of public building construction could the young nation look to in 1787? The statehouses, colony houses, and courthouses reflected the diversity of colonial settlements in America. Early gatherings of citizens frequently took place in private homes, taverns, and churches. Although not part of the nation at that time, the Palace of Governors in Santa Fe, New Mexico, built in 1610, is often regarded as the first building in North America designed for governmental purposes. It served as a combined residence and executive office for New Mexico under the successive regimes of Spain, Mexico, and the United States.[2]

The New Mexico Palace example of accommodating public functions was not immediately replicated in the British colonies. The first meeting of an assembly of burgesses in Jamestown, Virginia, in July 1619, took place in a "framed, cedar-interior trimmed church."[3] A church was considered appropriate because of the "ample space, and it was the most convenient place."[4] The assembly continued to meet there and later at the governor's house in Jamestown. In April 1641, the Jamestown colony purchased the residence of Governor Sir John Henry for use as a statehouse. Over the next fourteen years, the building was used for General Assembly meetings, with part of it occupied by Virginia governors. The 1641 statehouse burned and was succeeded by three more residential-like statehouses in Jamestown. After the fourth statehouse burned in 1698, the capital was moved to Williamsburg where a new statehouse, now called a capitol, was constructed between 1700 and 1703. Although in a new location, the plan for the Williamsburg Capitol resembled the doubling of the Jamestown Statehouse.[5] Elsewhere in the British colonies, the City Hall of New York City was built in 1699, the Boston State House in 1712, and the Colony House in Newport, Rhode Island, in 1739.

For an administrative model for the management of a public buildings program, the new nation might have looked to Great Britain. Since the restoration of the monarchy in 1660, various departments of the royal household were consolidated into the Office of Works with a Surveyor of the King's Works at the helm. One of the best known of the surveyors, Sir Christopher Wren, served as the administrative and design head of this bureau from 1669 to 1719. During his half-century tenure as surveyor, Wren produced designs for cathedrals, churches, hospitals, custom houses, theaters, observatories, libraries, and university buildings, mostly in the London area. Wren's notable successors included Sir William Chambers, who served from 1782 to 1796, and James Wyatt, who served from 1796 to 1813.[6]

Public buildings of the pre-Revolutionary period represented architectural tastes derived from European precedents found in town halls, county buildings, and large residences in Great Britain. The grander of these early buildings, such as the Capitol at Williamsburg, also symbolized the authority of the Crown. Others served as the setting for the colonial legislatures that eventually broke with the Crown. These buildings represented the aspirations of a transplanted Old World culture, tempered by local conditions. This collection of buildings provided little architectural foreshadowing of the stirrings of democracy that would unify the thirteen colonies into a single nation.

There are many ways to examine this complex (and ultimately large) federal government program because of the program's magnitude and factors that guided its destiny. Before the mid-nineteenth century, the number of federal buildings designed and constructed numbered only a few dozen, but the program undertaken by the Supervising Architect's Office from 1852 to 1939 included thousands of buildings—custom houses, federal courthouses, post offices, marine hospitals, mints, and, in the early twentieth century, a large numbers of federal office buildings. They were built in all sizes of communities across the country. Only a few other governmental departments—most notably the U.S. Corps of Engineers—rivaled the virtual monopoly over federal building design and over the actual design and construction of a large number of projects held by the Supervising Architect's Office in Washington, D.C.

The evolution of American public architecture paralleled and reflected the development of the country itself and the cities and towns contained within it. From a collection of single building projects, a unified program for federal building construction emerged by the mid-nineteenth century. The design of federal buildings represented democratic ideals, reflecting a growing sense of national identity. Because such federal buildings as custom houses and federal courthouses usually were located in expanding urban centers, their construction signaled the arrival of that particular city into the community of major U.S. cities. The placement of federal buildings also portended excellent prospects for continued growth and prosperity. This aspiration was reflected in the painted views of cities done in the early nineteenth century by artists who captured on canvas America's pride in its growing cities and harbors.[7]

Congressmen argued both the present and future growth of cities within their districts as a means of justifying expenditures for federal building construction. Federal buildings were regarded as such coveted items of federal patronage that their realization was often a monument to a politician's effectiveness in securing the project for his jurisdiction.

When federal buildings represented an ideal architecture, they became models for other public buildings. In the first four decades of the nineteenth century, the various architects called upon to design federal buildings provided variations upon the classical style. Symbols drawn from Greece and Rome provided a unified republican image.[8] Once the federal design responsibilities were centralized in the Supervising Architect's Office in 1852, the architectural language became more economical nationwide. Financial constraints as much as architectural taste encouraged the trends toward standardization and economy. A policy of consistency in federal building design prevailed during a succession of design episodes, from the Italian Renaissance palazzo of the 1850s, the French Second Empire of the 1860s and 1870s, the picturesque eclecticism of the 1880s and 1890s, and the academic classicism of the early twentieth century. The responses to these buildings were both laudatory and negative, and these reactions provide a level of understanding on a human scale of how well the Office did its work.

Another theme intertwined with the Supervising Architect's

Office is the procession of men who served as head of the bureau from the creation of the position in 1852. Some of the nation's best-known architects with private practices, such as Isaiah Rogers, William Appleton Potter, and James Windrim served for brief intervals as supervising architect. Others, such as Alfred B. Mullett and James Knox Taylor, achieved national stature through the job itself. Still others, such as Will. A. Freret and Jeremiah O'Rourke, were never nationally prominent, nor did they achieve national recognition for their government work. Whatever their reputation or length of tenure, each supervising architect wished to leave his own legacy in architectural design to the nation. To the man who held the position, it represented the grandest opportunity of his career.

Supervising architects were highly political men, with skills far beyond those of their chosen profession. The appointments of men who would serve as supervising architect were frequently bold acts of political patronage. Nationally, the position did not attract architects with flourishing private practices; the demands of bureaucratic administration did not appeal to them. The heavy workload also precluded the supervising architect from maintaining a private practice concurrently. He was dependent upon his government job for a livelihood. A number of men who were later to be leading architects on the national stage occupied staff positions in the Office. Upon leaving the Office, they established private architectural firms that became nationally recognized. Identifying these individuals requires reference to personnel lists of the Office and other sources, since the supervising architect was most often the only name publicly identified with federal architecture projects.

The growth in political influence of the professional private architect, as represented by the evolution of the American Institute of Architects, was another potent force in the operation of the Supervising Architect's Office. Professional criticism of the quality of public building design and of the abilities of the men who occupied the position of supervising architect led to an intense public debate regarding the authority of the governmental bureau within the Treasury Department. Private architects first challenged the power of the supervising architect in the mid-1870s and resumed the attack in the mid-1880s.

It was not until 1893, however, coincident with the World's Columbian Exposition in Chicago, that the first congressional legislation was passed that allowed private architects to seize control of a portion of the approved building projects. Control of federal architecture bounced back and forth between government and private architects for the next forty years, but the eventual outcome in favor of the private sector was predictable. Moreover, as the political savvy of the private sector grew, the complexity and scale of the federal architecture program became so great that it far exceeded the ability of a single governmental entity to keep up with the demands for new construction, alterations, additions, and maintenance.

Federal buildings served as major architectural icons in the urban landscape. During the nineteenth century, these buildings were often the largest buildings in the commercial centers of towns and cities. Monumental bell and clock towers accentuated their height and importance. After 1900, federal buildings often became elements of large scale "City Beautiful" plans that joined together public buildings, civic spaces, and formal landscape settings. In the next phase, following World War I, federal buildings were increasingly dwarfed by rising skyscrapers whose tall profiles proclaimed the dominance of commercialism on the city. In smaller communities, federal buildings were proudly regarded as ornaments to the community and frequently attracted substantial attention from the press.

Since architecture is a highly visible manifestation of American material culture, federal government buildings embody social proclivities at particular periods in a society's history. Federal buildings incorporated functional requirements for space, shelter, and the spatial needs of mail handling, customs collections, and judicial proceedings. The treatment of the building reflected both the design preferences of the architect, in the form of the Supervising Architect's Office, and the requirements of the client, here the federal government.

The appearance of federal buildings also mirrored the emotional needs of a society for unifying symbols that reflected authority and stability. For example, federal buildings of the 1880s, generally of the Romanesque style, exemplified an "official" style for public buildings nationwide that lacked immediate associations with wealth and splendor. At the turn of the century, by comparison, federal buildings in their Beaux Arts garb bespoke the power, influence, and self-assurance of a nation on the brink of world leadership.

This study presents a history of the Office of the Supervising Architect. It centers on the period from the creation of the Office in 1852 to 1939, when the Treasury Department was relieved of its architectural responsibilities. Although the derivation of the Office can be traced far back into the early days of the American nation, this study will not dwell at length on the architects who worked in Washington, D.C., on the Capitol, the White House, and other federal buildings; who assumed the title of "Architect of Public Buildings"; or who worked on federal building projects scattered throughout the nation during the first half of the nineteenth century. It will not cover the architectural works carried out under military auspices or under independent governmental bureaus such as the Smithsonian Institution.

Rather, the study will trace the evolution of the Office of the Supervising Architect of the U.S. Treasury Department—its development over nearly a century through the various prisms previously suggested. It presents the story of a single government bureau that served as the central design agency for civilian government architecture in the United States—an agency that was responsible for some of the most important architectural commissions of the day.

2   NO BLUEPRINT FOR THE NEW NATION

1789–1851

Experimentation and creativity in the art of governing marked the
first six decades of nationhood under the Constitution. Executive departments, offices, and bureaus were established to implement the
provisions of the Constitution and the wishes of Congress. No man-
ual existed to guide the development of a new federal government,
and each step required discussion and clarification as to the limits of
legislative mandates. The administration of public buildings projects
was no exception. Like the development of the nation itself, federal
building activities evolved from one of localized, piecemeal administration to a highly centralized program managed from the nation's
capital city.

In the early part of this period, federal government functions outside of the capital city were housed in rented buildings that were originally constructed for some other use. As time passed, however, it became clear that many governmental functions were unique and
required accommodations built and tailored specifically to these special functions. By the mid-nineteenth century, the growth of governmental responsibilities across the nation had reached a level that required the construction of dozens of federal buildings.

In these early years, the response of the federal government to its
growing architectural needs was cautious and hesitant. The extent of
a national public works program was the initial dilemma—how

many buildings? How could they be justified? As early as the 1790s, the Treasury Department, which collected custom revenues and administered the hospital fund for the nation's seamen, saw the need for custom houses and marine hospitals. Responsibility for public building design and construction fell to the Treasury Department because of these collection and administrative tasks. Custom houses and marine hospitals could be justified based on the amount of revenues collected at each location.

As congressional demands increased for buildings in locations where current revenue levels alone could not justify construction costs, public buildings were then justified largely on projections of growth in revenues at some future date. As a result, the federal building program grew and prospered. Cautionary statements issued by successive secretaries of the treasury were considered by Congress and then usually discarded as it continued to appropriate funds for federal building construction.

Closely tied to the question of the commitment of the federal government to a national building program was the issue of architectural symbolism. Were governmental functions so similar to other commercial and administrative tasks that they could be housed in any standard functional building? Or were the functions so unique that they required special accommodation? Beyond housing governmental functions, public buildings played other roles. As symbols of strength and stability, such buildings inspired confidence in the federal government on the part of the local citizenry. If properly designed, public buildings could also serve an educational purpose in art, beauty, and culture that would make for a more civilized society and uplift the level of cultural aspirations in a community.

The question of a suitable architecture for federal buildings was thus a recurrent theme in the development of a public building program at the national level after 1789. The debate was initially concentrated in Washington, D.C., with the laying out of the federal city and the design and construction of the President's House and the Capitol. The designs of monumental buildings for the president and the Congress contrasted with those for the growing departments of the executive branch, which were housed initially in modest brick buildings. As federal buildings were constructed in other cities and towns, the debate concerning suitable architecture became one of national dimension.

The question of how the program should be administered also developed during this period. Should the program be run on a project-by-project basis by federal officials resident at the locality where the building was required? Once the designs were procured, who should supervise the construction of the building—the customs collector, a contractor, the architect, or a member of the U.S. Army Corps of Engineers?

The closest model for the administration of a public buildings program, that of Great Britain during the early nineteenth century, may have bestowed a stamp of approval on the role of architects as administrators. However, in the early years, the United States had few architects. Solicitations for architectural designs attracted scant submissions. The modesty of the public building construction program envisioned by the executive branch at that time would not have warranted the employment of such a professional on more than a consulting basis. The general public usually did not understand the profession of architecture, adding to the unlikelihood that the Treasury Department would have employed a full-time government architect. In fact, during the early years of the nineteenth century, on-site supervision of public buildings most often fell to customs collectors who were to occupy the completed building. Later, Army engineers who had experience with the supervision of far-flung civil and military construction projects were assigned to superintendency responsibilities.

The role of the private architect in the federal building program in these early years was a limited one. Architects were requested to produce plans for custom houses and marine hospitals. When the designs were completed and approved by the customs collector and the secretary of the treasury, the federal government occasionally protested the architect's fees and, at times, paid no fee at all. In many cases, the architect did not superintend the construction of his own building. In the early years of nationhood, no one could have imagined that the architectural profession would grow in large numbers and political influence, both factors that would characterize the federal government building program later in the century and into the next.

The First Generation of Custom Houses

No centralized administrative structure existed to handle the first wave of federal government custom houses that accompanied the development of the nation under the Constitution. The secretary of the treasury served as the focal point of guidance on how to implement congressional appropriations for new custom houses buildings. However, locally situated federal officials oversaw the design and construction process. Several key projects illustrate the ad hoc, piecemeal nature of federal building activities during this period.

With the exception of the Postal Service, the formation of the governmental agencies important to a future federal architecture program took place in 1789. In that year, the Treasury Department and the Customs Service were established and legislation was passed establishing a marine hospital fund. The Postal Service had been in operation since 1775, but its diffused services throughout the nation did not require any more than rented space for many years to come. In 1790, the Residence Act was passed, providing for the capital city in a ten-mile square to be located along the Potomac River. Thus, the stage was set for the introduction of a public architecture that reflected the values of the new nation.

The creation and administration of the Customs Service drew upon the colonial experience with customs collection under the British Empire that dated back to the Navigation Acts of the 1660s and 1670s. The British had established ports of entry and appointed collectors. With the creation of the U.S. Customs Service, fifty-nine customs districts were established in eleven states, with each customs collector appointed by President George Washington. The collection of customs duties was viewed as an important function in the new nation because the income generated constituted a major portion of the federal government's budget. The customs collector reported directly to the secretary of the treasury and was a person of considerable influence in his community.

The customs collector not only collected duties on imported goods, but also served as the eyes and ears of the federal government at the local level. For example, in 1809, each customs collector provided information to the secretary of the treasury on the status of manufacturing, roads, and canals in his district. The collector also was the agent for the marine hospital fund, which meant that he collected the tax and disbursed funds to seamen requiring medical attention. In their districts, the customs collectors also superintended the operation of lighthouses and served as the caretaker for bonds and other public papers. Because he served as the representative of the federal government at the local level and occupied whatever premises were provided, the collector, with the approval of the secretary of the treasury, obtained designs for new buildings from architects and subsequently often supervised their construction.

One of the earliest buildings that was designed specifically for customs purposes was built in New Orleans between 1807 and 1809 after designs by Benjamin Henry Latrobe. Born in England and educated there and in Europe, Latrobe emigrated to the United States in 1796 and engaged in an active architectural practice in Philadelphia and Washington. Latrobe's New Orleans building was located on the site of an earlier wooden custom house. The new custom house, along with the lighthouses at Cape Lookout, North Carolina, and at the mouth of the Mississippi, were Latrobe's major commissions from Secretary of the Treasury Albert Gallatin in 1807. He designed them from a distance. Unfortunately for the building, it was constructed hastily and with masonry footings in place of the customary wooden logs in the trenches. In addition, a poor quality of brick was used, causing cracks in the walls. By 1817, the custom house was ready for replacement.[1]

Another great port city of the period, Baltimore—which emerged as a great commercial power during the Federalist era—was the site of a unique custom house designed to harmonize with a major commercial edifice. In July 1816, Customs Collector James H. McCulloch wrote to Secretary of the Treasury Alexander J. Dallas, recommending that the custom house be located adjacent to the new Exchange building, then under construction and designed by French-born architect Maxmilian Godefroy and Latrobe. Because of the flourishing nature of trade in Baltimore, McCulloch wanted the new building to be "sufficiently commodious and extensive for the growing commerce of Baltimore for many years to come." The design for the building, according to McCulloch, should be in "conformity to the rest of the place with as much solid plainness as consists with the carracter [sic] of a structure designed for the use of public purposes of wealth and commerce." The design should also be compatible with the Exchange to "preserve the unity of design."[2] The custom house, as designed by Godefroy and Latrobe, formed the southern wing of the Exchange building (figure 2.1).

Latrobe's negotiations with Dallas regarding the integration of the custom house into the Exchange building persuaded him that he would be commissioned to design the custom house in Philadelphia.[3] This expectation was not fulfilled, however, as Dallas resigned his position in October of 1816 and was succeeded by William H. Crawford.

Figure 2.1
U.S. custom house,
Baltimore, Maryland,
designed 1816–1817,
Maximilian Godefroy and
Benjamin Henry Latrobe.
Courtesy National
Archives.

Instead, one of Latrobe's former apprentices, William Strickland (1788–1854), who was already actively engaged on several public building projects in Philadelphia, was selected. Strickland was probably the choice of the Philadelphia customs collector, John Steele.

Strickland began his career as an apprentice to Latrobe. Between 1808 and the mid-1840s, Strickland designed many buildings in Philadelphia, including the Philadelphia Custom House, the Second Bank of the United States, and the U.S. Naval Home. He also designed the U.S. Mint buildings in Philadelphia; Charlotte, North Carolina; and New Orleans. On the bank project, Strickland met Thomas U. Walter, son of one of the bricklayers, and served as his mentor in his early career.

The Philadelphia custom house project began in 1816 with an appropriation from Congress "for the hire, purchase, or building, of Custom Houses, warehouses, and stores."[4] As Steele reported to his superiors, the current accommodations were crowded, making the measurement, examination, and validation of merchandise difficult. He also did not know of any appropriate buildings that were for sale.[5] Steele recommended that a parcel of land large enough for any anticipated growth in customs business be acquired because "the improvement, that will naturally follow in the vicinity of public buildings, would render it impracticable, afterwards to enlarge the bounds without paying an 'extravagant price' for the ground as well as for the improvements which most probably would be of no use for public purposes."[6]

In July 1818, Strickland was poised to enter into a contract to supervise the erection of the new custom house in Philadelphia. Crawford instructed Steele to require Strickland to provide a bond "with security for the faithful performance of contract."[7] If the architect refused, Steele was at liberty to seek another contractor. Strickland's fee for superintending the construction was judged by Crawford to be "inadvisable," leading him to inquire about his fees for preparing the design. As Crawford noted, "very extravagant prices have been asked for drawings plans of Custom Houses in other districts."[8]

Despite these misgivings, the contract for construction was signed by August 1818 and the work proceeded. As a building designed to stand on its own, the custom house exhibited a Greek Revival robustness that contrasted with the more restrained lines of Latrobe's custom houses. The design of the building also appeared to defy Congressional wishes for a functional, rather than an ornamental, custom house. In 1844, this custom house was superseded by Strickland's redesigned Second Bank of the United States for custom functions.

Strickland's work as both designer and superintendent of the Philadelphia custom house impressed Secretary Crawford sufficiently that he asked him to prepare a plan for a new customs house at New Orleans. Although a replacement for Latrobe's failed 1807–1809 customhouse building was eventually designed by New Orleans architect Benjamin Buisson, Crawford was drawn to Strickland's ideas because, as he wrote to Steele, he was "desirous of availing myself of the knowledge which Mr. Strickland and yourself have acquired in such matters."[9]

The Second Generation of Custom Houses

By the early 1830s, the federal government could claim a modicum of experience in the construction of public buildings to house its functions. The role of architects was better understood as well. Now the executive branch was ready to invest in major federal buildings that attested to a confidence in the stability of the young nation and its governmental institutions. This period brought to prominence a new generation of architects associated with federal government building projects. These figures included Robert Mills, Ammi B. Young, Ithiel Town, and John Norris. The federal buildings they designed remained important fixtures on the urban scene for many years, and indeed, some of them have survived to the late twentieth century. The custom houses of this era were constructed in the great seaport cities as well as in smaller mercantile strongholds and resembled Greek temples near the waterfront.

One of the first buildings of this new crop of federal buildings was the New York custom house. The busy port of New York generated such a workload for federal officials that Customs Collector Samuel Swartwout described the need for a new custom house: "The increase in the Revenue and the immense increase in the labors of the Appraisers' Department, call for more space to do business in and better accommodations."[10] By 1831, the accommodations, described as "ordinary and inconvenient buildings," had become so crowded that new space was leased.[11] Secretary of the Treasury Louis McLane questioned the propriety of leasing new space "while the strong possibility exists that in the course of two or three years, Congress may see proper to provide buildings for the permanent accommodation of all of the Offices connected with the collection of the Revenue at New York."[12] In June 1832, Swartwout called for a "spacious, safe, secure" building."[13]

Architect and engineer Ithiel Town wrote to Secretary McLane describing the design for the new custom house in New York City that he had prepared with architect Alexander Jackson Davis. As Town wrote, the new building was nearly in proportion with the Parthenon in Athens. The design exhibited antae (square columns) on the side, each separated by windows. The dome and vaulted ceiling provided light and air to the building. When compared with granite buildings in New York and Boston, Town estimated that the new custom house would cost $250,000. If the best brick, masonry, and marble were used, Town estimated the cost to be $320,000 to $350,000. He advised against using the dark Quincy marble for the building, preferring a lighter colored material for Grecian-style buildings. Quincy marble, according to Town, "does not admit the most favorable and rich effect of light and shade."[14] In a letter of August 1833, Secretary of the Treasury William J. Duane wrote to Customs Collector Swartwout indicating that Town and Davis's plan had been adopted.

Once under construction, Town and Davis's plan fell asunder. Samuel Thomson, who served for a year as superintendent of construction, took it upon himself to modify the plans, especially in the interior. When Thomson resigned in 1835, he carried off all the plans for the building. His successor, John Frazee, a successful sculptor, made heroic efforts to reconstruct the designs based on the building materials that had already been cut and that were arriving at the building site. Frazee's own contributions to the building design rest primarily with the working out of the details and in designing ornamentation. Disagreements with the new customs collector, Jesse Hoyt, and one of the building's commissioners, Walter Bowne, caused Frazee's dismissal in 1840. Reinstated in 1841, Frazee continued to superintend the building until its completion in 1842.[15] In the end, the cost was $928,312, the costliest federal building of its day.[16]

Another expensive building constructed in the 1830s and 1840s was the Greek-revival Boston custom house. Designed by Ammi B. Young (1800–1874) in 1838, the custom house remained a conspicuous presence in Boston harbor until the extension of the shoreline by fill construction and subsequent development on the landfill blocked the view. The origins of the Boston custom house go back to 1835 when the initial appropriation was made. Three commissioners, one of whom was the customs collector, were appointed to oversee the design and construction of the building. Young entered a model in the competition and won first prize. His model was placed on exhibit in the window of a local insurance company and, as Young noted, "received the approval of the merchants and all others who viewed."[17] In a letter to the commissioners, Young urged them to approve the acquisition of the full parcel of land required for his design in order to accommodate the broad steps of the portico. The steps were an integral part of his design that "has all the architectural character necessary to render it [the building] pleasing to the cultivated mind"[18] (figure 2.2).

With this important commission in hand, Young quickly emerged as a rising star in the constellation of architects engaged in federal government building activities. A native of Lebanon, New Hampshire, he gained national recognition in the 1830s for his design of the domed Vermont State House in Montpelier. A monumental Doric pile in granite, it was praised as one of the finest examples of Greek architecture in the United States.[19] The building, which was designed with a cruciform floor plan and pedimented portico, stood against a mountainside that had been cut out to accommodate it. The Ver-

Figure 2.2
U.S. custom house,
Boston, Massachusetts,
1837–1847, Ammi B.
Young. Courtesy
National Archives.

mont State House served as the model for the Boston custom house, which was the commission that likely ensured Young the appointment in 1852 as supervising architect in the Bureau of Construction in the Treasury Department.

Young acted as superintendent of construction for the Boston Custom House, making also several trips to Washington, D.C., to discuss aspects of the building's design and construction with Treasury Secretary Levi Woodbury. This link was significant. After a visit in late 1840, Young was impressed with Woodbury's "lively interest in its [the building's] success" and "strong desire that we should have a building which as a specimen of good taste in Architecture should not be inferior to any and as an example of scientific skill in construction and mechanical art in Building should equal anything in the United States."[20] Young requested of the commissioners and Secretary Woodbury that he be permitted to make a six-month visit to Europe in order to obtain information on the heating and ventilation of the building and on the construction of the stone dome, and to inspect marble from European suppliers.

The matter of Young's proposed European trip and its proposed cost of $1,000 was referred by Woodbury to Robert Mills, who was engaged on the new Treasury Building in Washington. Born in Charleston, South Carolina, Mills (1781–1855) was one of the first American-born architects. Mills served as an apprentice to James Hoban on the President's House in 1801 and later to Benjamin Henry Latrobe on the Capitol and other projects. He established an independent architectural practice in Philadelphia in 1809; from this base he designed buildings in Philadelphia, Richmond, and Baltimore. In 1815, he moved to Baltimore and established an enormously successful practice. Mills was invited back in 1820 to his home state where he served as "Acting Commissioner" of the state Board of Public Works (later renamed Superintendent of Public Buildings), a position that made him responsible for the design and construction of all state and district public buildings. Mills's work succeeded that of English architect William Jay, who between 1817 and 1819 had prepared six stock architectural plans for courthouses and jails. Mills remained in South Carolina until 1829 when nearly all state construction projects ceased.[21]

In 1830, Mills left South Carolina for Washington, D.C., where he remained until his death in 1855. Apparently, he went to work as a draftsman in the Land Office, which was then part of the Treasury Department. The position gave him access to the secretary of the treasury and he was called upon to advise him on architectural matters as they arose, although not in an exclusive capacity.[22] Because of Mills's role in the Treasury Department, his frequent assignment on matters associated with federal buildings, and his title of "Architect of Public Buildings" starting in 1836, Mills is often referred to as the first in the line of supervising architects. He reinforced this notion in March 1843 when he presented himself to Secretary of the Treasury John C. Spencer as "being professionally employed by your department for many years back to furnish plans etc., for all the Custom Houses, Marine Hospitals (being eight in number) erected during the last twelve years."[23]

In his response to Secretary Woodbury about Young's proposed trip, Mills regarded the possibility of European travel at government expense as of benefit primarily to the architect rather than to the government. Mills also thought such a trip would set a bad precedent "as every architect or undertaker of a public building would consider himself entitled to improve his knowledge in his Art at public expense, and thus a privileged order might grow up."[24] On the matter of European marble, Mills felt that the American material was less expensive and was bountiful, and artisans were available to dress it. Mills added:

> It is to be regretted that works of sculpture have been so often sent to Europe for execution, when we have artists among ourselves highly talented and capable of the undertaking, for the opportunity for our youth to improve their taste, and learn the art, is lost, and thus the public interest suffers.[25]

Mills concluded his letter by stating, "I should certainly prefer seeing our own materials used in our public buildings."[26]

The construction of the Boston custom house proceeded over a period of ten years. Young recommended annual amounts from the commissioners in order to complete the building. However, the amount appropriated usually covered only the next annual phase of building activity. By 1843, the stone walls had barely risen above the basement story. To show good faith, the commissioners opened the gates to the site so that the public could enter and observe the progress of the work. A contemporary account anticipated that the structure would be "one of the most substantial buildings erected in modern times." Its eastern front would look over the commercial activity of the harbor "which, we hope, will soon rise to a pitch of prosperity that will not be surpassed by many of the marts of trade in this western world."[27] In the end, it cost nearly $900,000, a staggering investment in a building at that time.[28]

Another major federal project of the time was the custom house at Wilmington, North Carolina. New York architect John Norris was selected to design and superintend the construction of the building. The secretary of the treasury, John C. Spencer, likely selected Norris because he too was from New York and he knew of Norris's practice throughout the southern states, in particular, at Savannah, Georgia. Norris's active business in far-flung locations caused problems for him as he was frequently absent from the Wilmington site, and his role as an outsider caused resentment among Wilmington's building tradesmen and politicians who coveted the position of superintendent of the building's construction.

The Wilmington building was one of the earliest custom houses to provide accommodations for customs collectors, postal services, a courtroom, and offices for other federal functions. It was an early "federal center." Norris forwarded his plans to Secretary Spencer in

July 1843, with an estimate of the cost for the custom house and ad-
joining warehouse of $38,000.[29] Later in the year, however, Norris in-
creased the estimate of the cost by an additional $28,000 and assured
Spencer that the custom house would be completed by early 1844.[30]
By early 1845, however, Customs Collector M. V. Jones wrote to
Spencer's successor, George M. Bibb, that the work was "neatly and
handsomely executed, but it appears to me that the progress of the
building is very slow, the roof is not yet commenced, tho [sic] the
walls are nearly ready for the securing of it, and there seems to be little preparation for the inside work."[31]

Customs Collector Jones later related to Secretary Bibb that as
Norris was paid on a per diem basis, the architect hindered the
progress on the building "by frequently calling off the workmen
thereon employed, on private business, and of retaining a very small
number of operations for the sake of spinning out the time to as great
a number of days as possible."[32] By late 1845, portions of the building were ready for occupancy, and although Jones felt the work could
have been expedited, he thought the buildings' workmanship was
"not to be surpassed by any in the state and the structures does credit
to the skills of the architect."[33] When the custom house and warehouse were completed in May 1847, Jones, together with other federal officials occupying the custom house, had special praise for the
courtroom, which they felt "was not to be surpassed [in] style or
finish by any in our state"[34] (figure 2.3).

While America's major seaports were beneficiaries of new federal
buildings, Robert Mills designed custom houses for several smaller
mercantile strongholds. These towns included Middletown and New
London, Connecticut, and New Bedford (figure 2.4) and Newburyport, Massachusetts, all designed and constructed between 1834 and
1835. These projects followed earlier assignments to provide designs
for the marine hospitals at Mobile, Alabama, and Charleston, South
Carolina. In 1833, Mills prepared a report on the destruction by fire of
the Treasury Building. William J. Duane, who served briefly as secretary of the treasury in 1833, asked Mills to examine various building proposals in Middletown, New London, New Bedford, and
Newburyport and to report to him as to how costs might be lowered
and how the buildings could be made more fireproof.[35] It appears
that Duane relied upon Mills for other public building matters, because Mills also reported to Duane on the alterations to the custom
house at St. Augustine, Florida.[36]

Figure 2.3
U.S. custom house, Wil-
mington, North Carolina,
1844–1846, John Norris.
Courtesy National
Archives.

The departure of Duane, and his replacement by Roger B. Taney for a brief period and later by Levi Woodbury as secretary of the treasury, caused Mills's relationship with the national public building program to become more tenuous. By 1834, Mills requested of Woodbury that he be authorized to superintend the completion of the contracts for the four New England custom houses. Mills maintained that few mechanics were familiar with his fireproof construction methods and that he would be able to save the federal government thousands of dollars. He added the postscript, "I am at present not professionally employed."[37]

To this pleading, Woodbury returned a terse reply, "As before mentioned to you verbally, the collectors are now deemed competent for that duty."[38] The continuing correspondence between Mills and Woodbury in 1835 underscored the former's peripheral role in the execution of his designs for the New England buildings. Even after his appointment in 1836 as "Architect of Public Buildings," which in-

cluded primarily the Treasury Department and the Patent Office
building, Mills continued to write to Secretary Woodbury offering his
services on marine hospitals. Woodbury fended off these requests
but, as already described, did refer to Mills the matter of Ammi B.
Young's request to embark on a European trip.

Figure 2.4
U.S. custom house, New
Bedford, Massachusetts,
1833–1836, Robert Mills.
Courtesy National
Archives.

Early Marine Hospitals

Forerunner of the Public Health Service hospitals, the marine hospitals resulted from the 1789 legislation that was intended to provide
temporary medical assistance for "officers, seamen and marines of
the navy of the United States, and masters, marines and seamen employed in private and merchant vessels."[39] This care was financed
through the collection of duties on the wages earned by all potential
beneficiaries of the program. At first, the fund covered the cost of
temporary care in local private hospitals and with local physicians
who also served the general population. Later, marine hospitals were

built to circumvent the charges of private hospitals and doctors, whose fees varied greatly.

Given the demands upon the marine hospital fund, it is not surprising that the marine hospital was an early federal building type and that the first such hospital should be located in Boston, one of the nation's great seaport cities. In May 1802, Secretary of the Treasury Albert Gallatin wrote to the customs collector Benjamin Lincoln, reporting that Congress had appropriated $15,000 for a marine hospital in Massachusetts. Gallatin directed Lincoln to "communicate such general information on the proper situation and probable expense of ground and buildings as may enable the President to take the steps necessary to carry the law into effect."[40] A site was obtained at the Boston Navy Yard.

As to the plan for the building, Gallatin suggested that Lincoln insert an advertisement in a local newspaper offering a $50 premium for the "most appropriate plan of a hospital of 4,000 square feet area . . . the convenient distribution of the rooms and economy of space and construction will be principally regarded in the decision."[41] Gallatin instructed Lincoln to transmit the plan, elevation, and section to Washington, D.C., for his approval. The newspaper advertisement for the Boston Marine Hospital elicited only one plan, that of Asher Benjamin. Benjamin was best known as the publisher of American buildings guides, which influenced building design nationwide. After reviewing the submission, Gallatin described Benjamin's plan as "not possessed of any great merit," but in the absence of any alternatives, he decided that it would be used with a few modifications. Gallatin directed that the construction of the marine hospital would follow the "mode adopted for lighthouses, that of a public advertisement will be more eligible."[42]

Asher Benjamin's marine hospital at Boston served the naval and merchant shipping community in the Boston area until 1826 when the establishment was moved to Chelsea, Massachusetts. Alexander Parris drew the plan for the new building at Chelsea. Customs collector H. A. S. Dearborn received construction contract proposals and recommended that Joseph D. Emery receive the contract for furnishing the building materials. Dearborn also suggested to Secretary of the Treasury Richard Rush that Parris be retained to superintend the construction. Secretary Rush judged Parris's request for $1,000 in compensation for superintending the work to be "higher than was expected," but he permitted the work to proceed.[43]

The Engagement of the Corps
of Engineers on Marine Hospital Projects

Although the federal government commissioned several dozen federal buildings during the early decades of the nineteenth century, the management of a national building program was not universally recognized as an objective of the federal government. In fact, the fate of the program was closely tied to political attitudes toward the role of the federal government in internal improvements in general. The U.S. Army Corps of Engineers and Bureau of Topographical Engineers carried out the initial efforts in federally sponsored improvements. Army engineers served as geographers and surveyors and fostered the location of roads and the improvement of rivers and harbors. They were also assigned to duty with the Coastal Survey and the Lighthouse Board and to numerous public works projects in Washington, D.C. The construction of the federal buildings followed on the heels of the Army-sponsored pioneering efforts and carried symbols of civilization and culture into the newly settled areas of the country.

The secretary of the treasury's annual report for 1829 reflected ambivalence regarding the authority for an expanding federal building program. Secretary of the Treasury Samuel D. Ingham likely reflected President Andrew Jackson's own aversion to federally sponsored internal improvements by describing duties associated with repairs to custom houses and warehouses as an "exercise of powers not sufficiently defined by law" that were "derived from usage, rather than statutes." Ingham feared that such powers might be "enlarged by successive gradations . . . without legislative sanction."[44] In contrast, a surplus in the Treasury in 1836, due to the sale of large tracts of public lands, encouraged Secretary of the Treasury Levi Woodbury to suggest that the extra monies be applied to "erecting, where needed, appropriate custom and warehouses, as well as suitable marine hospitals, court-houses, and post offices." The state of the finances justified that "the great works heretofore deemed useful and constitutional, and which are intimately connected with the duties and powers of the General Government, should be more hastened."[45]

An expansion in the number of marine hospitals was anticipated in 1837 with a Congressional resolution directing the Treasury Department to submit information relative to the "plans most suitable for several marine hospitals."[46] The demands upon the marine hospital fund had always been greater than the level of contributions provided by the fund's beneficiaries. By a law passed in 1843, contributions to the fund were now required of owners of all registered vessels, which increased the ability of the federal government to build more marine hospitals.[47] In 1849, Secretary of the Treasury William M. Meredith viewed the increased number of marine hospitals as a justifiable government expense in support of the "men, who, by their labor and perth in peace and war, contribute so largely to the wealth and power of the nation."[48]

The ample appropriations for marine hospitals that began in the mid-1840s provided an opportunity for the Army engineers to become engaged in their erection as part of the Treasury Department's construction program. When the Treasury Department was charged with the construction of a marine hospital in Louisville, Kentucky, in 1845, the Treasury Department "applied for the services of an officer of the corps of topographical engineers, stationed at that place, to superintend the work."[49] Lt. Col. Stephen H. Long of the Bureau of Topographical Engineers was assigned to supervise this work. With an increase in the number of marine hospitals authorized by Congress in 1848, "it was decided, after due conference and consideration of all effects and consequences, that officers of the Corps were not to be detached for such purposes, but the bureau could take the direction of the Treasury Department in reference to them and carry them into effect." In a letter of agreement, the Army engineers attached to the Bureau of Topographical Engineers took charge of the construction of marine hospitals in Chicago; Paducah, Kentucky; Napoleon, Arkansas; and Natchez, Mississippi. Later Pittsburgh and St. Louis were added to the list. Long took over superintendency of these buildings and carried the title of Superintendent of Marine Hospitals. Other officers of the corps were stationed at each location as superintendents of construction. The construction unit of the topographical engineers became a "bureau of the Treasury Department for these buildings."[50] The stage was set for the creation in the following decade of the Bureau of Construction in the Treasury Department and the continued association of Army engineers with the national building program.

The relatively large number of architects associated with the federal government's building program and the administration of the program on a project-by-project basis precluded much standardization of public buildings during this period. Robert Mills's New England custom houses of 1834–1835 are an exception. However, the surplus in the federal Treasury in 1836 and the prospect of applying the extra funds to the construction of public buildings encouraged the first concerted efforts at standardization. Mills's designs for marine hospitals "on the Western Waters" to accommodate one hundred patients and fifty patients were specific enough that they likely served as models for the marine hospitals built in the 1840s under the superintendence of the Army engineers.[51] To execute each building, the Army engineers may have provided additional design work themselves, or they may have contracted out with private architects for this work.

In an 1850 report, the chief of the Bureau of Topographical Engineers, J. J. Abert, noted that his bureau "engaged itself in preparing the plan for the [marine] hospital at Chicago."[52] As the bureau wished to confirm its estimates of the cost of the Chicago building, it sent the plan to the Baltimore architectural firm of Niernsee & Neilson, a firm of men Abert described as "among the most accomplished architects of our country—of great experience as builders, and highly celebrated for the accuracies of their estimates, which have been always found to accord with great nicety to actual expenditures."[53]

Early Federal Government Buildings in the National Capital City

While the Treasury Department was managing the building projects across the nation, the design of federal buildings in the national capital city was handled in a different fashion. The scale of the capital city's projects far overshadowed any that could be found elsewhere in the United States. The large scope called for several architectural "establishments" within the capital city, for example, the U.S. Capitol, the Treasury Department, and projects handled by individual departments of the executive branch. Many of the architects who designed federal buildings outside of Washington, D.C., also participated in the capital city's new building projects and, at times, represented one or another of these architectural establishments.

The public buildings built to house functions unique to the federal city were overseen by appointed commissioners. It was unlikely that the President's House and the Capitol would have served as models for public buildings elsewhere. The massive scale of these public buildings can be more fully appreciated when they are compared with public buildings that were located in other cities. The dimensions of these structures, as well as their orientation and location, had been established by Pierre L'Enfant in his 1791 design for the capital city and were given greater detail by Andrew Ellicott in his 1792 engraved map based on L'Enfant's drawings. The inspiration for the scale and design of the President's House and the Capitol were derived from the Old World, although the ultimate details and symbolism were linked to the aspirations of the new American republic. There was also no precedent in the Old World for the executive, legislative, and judicial functions that would be housed in these buildings.

In 1792, competitions were held for the President's House and the Capitol. Thomas Jefferson likely encouraged the holding of competitions, but it was a practice for which there was no long tradition in the United States. Competitions were held for the Pennsylvania State House in 1732 and for the Philadelphia Library Company building in 1789. The small number of competitions for major buildings may be due more to the difficulty in securing any submissions from creditable designers. The early federal building projects, such as the marine hospital at Boston's Navy Yard by Asher Benjamin, is testimony to the lack of success with competitions. The President's House and the Capitol represented the first major competitions in the United States.[54]

James Hoban of Charleston, South Carolina, won the competition for the President's House, the premium for which was $500 and a gold medal. Hoban was appointed superintendent of construction for the building, which proceeded at such a slow pace that the building was far from complete in 1800 when the federal government moved from Philadelphia to the new capital city. The design of the President's House resembled more an English country house of the eighteenth century than residential traditions of the United States. But it was what Jefferson desired: "the building was unlike anything in the United States at the time and had the overtones of European grandeur."[55]

The design of the Capitol followed a much more circuitous path. The Capitol competition, which offered a prize of $500 and a city lot, produced no designs that were satisfactory to the commissioners, or to George Washington or Jefferson. Dr. William Thornton, a physician who had won the Philadelphia Library Company competition, submitted a later design. Thornton's design, which had a central dome modeled after the Pantheon at Rome with two wings derived from Palladian examples, was received enthusiastically by all concerned and was awarded the first prize. Stephen Hallett, who had produced the most satisfactory of the previous Capitol designs, was hired to oversee the construction of the Capitol. When he attempted to alter Thornton's design to conform to his own ideas, Hallett was dismissed in 1794. George Hadfield worked briefly as superintendent of construction but resigned in 1789. From 1789 to 1802, James Hoban was superintendent of the Capitol as well as the President's House. By 1800, the north wing of the Capitol was complete, which held space for the Senate, House of Representatives, and Supreme Court. Under Benjamin Henry Latrobe, who served as "Surveyor of Public Buildings" between 1803 and 1817, the Capitol's central section and south wing were constructed. A wooden dome and the east and west fronts were completed in 1824 under the supervision of Latrobe's successor, Charles Bulfinch.

Besides the President's House and the Capitol, two other buildings awaited the removal of the federal government to the new capital city on the banks of the Potomac River in 1800. Two executive office buildings, one on either side of the President's House, were built of brick with stone trim after designs of George Hadfield in 1797. The building on the east was for the Treasury Department, while the one on the west was for the War and Navy Departments. After the British destroyed the buildings in 1814, they "were rebuilt using the original walls and probably followed the original design."[56]

After the federal government moved from Philadelphia, other less monumental buildings were constructed to house federal functions. One of these was a jail, designed by Hadfield in 1803. As compensation for design, specification, and superintendence work, Hadfield agreed to the sum of $200. After completing the work, however, Hadfield estimated that the sum was too small for seven months of work. The government representative on the project, Daniel C. Brent, thought Hadfield's work to be "attentive" and requested an additional $200 as compensation. The jail, according to Hadfield, was "plain, but the work is strong, substantial, and firm."[57]

By 1818, the federal government functions had become so voluminous that President James Monroe asked the Committee on Public Buildings to look into the requirements for new public buildings. Committee chairman Albion K. Parris declared the public offices to be insufficient for the transaction of government business and that the Treasury, War, and Navy Departments had already resorted to renting space in private buildings. Parris felt it "expedient to place the buildings about to be erected near those now occupied as public offices," possibly at the northwest and northeast corners of the President's square "to be placed on a line parallel with the other offices." The commissioner of public buildings, Colonel Samuel Lane, was directed to provide an estimate of the "expense of erecting and finishing fit for occupation two buildings, similar in structure to those at present occupied by the Treasury and War Departments." Hoban, still employed as superintendent of the President's House, provided an estimate of $90,380.50 for:

> a building to contain forty rooms on two floors, exclusive of the garret and basement stories, to be built in a substantial manner of brick and stone, with a portico of six columns of the Ionic order, with a pediment and flight of steps, with a cornice round the building, all of cut stone, and the basement story to be arched, every room and passage with brick, and to be covered with slate, thereby rendering the building as secure from fire as the nature of such a building will admit.[58]

The new Treasury Building, built to the south of the executive office building along Fifteenth Street, stood for less than two decades before it was engulfed by fire.[59] Planning for the rebuilding of the structure on its old site took place over the next three years. Both Robert Mills and William P. Elliott, a draftsman at the Patent Office, produced plans for the new Treasury Building. Elliott spoke eloquently of the folly of considering the rebuilding of the previous structures. Urging the use of granite for the new building, Elliott stated, "the public edifice in the capital of our confederated republic ought not to be inferior to those erected for federal or State purposes in our large commercial cities; and if not in advance of public opinion, they ought at least to keep pace with it."[60] However, Mills's designs for the Treasury were selected, along with Elliott's plans for the Patent Office Building, and Mills was hired to superintend the construction of both buildings.

The construction of the four wings of the Treasury Building took place over a period of more than thirty years. The east wing along Fifteenth Street was the only wing to be constructed under the superintendence of Mills. It was attached at the south of the old Executive Office Building, which later became the site of the north wing of the new Treasury Building. The building was constructed of

Aquia sandstone, judged by Mills to be an inferior building material (which in fact did ultimately have to be replaced by granite in 1909). The Mills wing was made fireproof not only by the use of masonry in the construction of the building, but also by the use of brick-lined groined arches which permitted the carrying of the floor weights without wood. A heroic file of Ionic columns lined the facade along Fifteenth Street. The south wing was constructed under the superintendence of Ammi B. Young between 1855 and 1860; the west wing by Isaiah Rogers between 1862 and 1864; and the north wing by Alfred B. Mullett between 1866 and 1869.

The stern Patent Office building with Doric columns and entablatures was constructed on the site that L'Enfant envisioned for a national church and later the Treasury Department. Mills superintended the south facade, while Capitol Architect Thomas U. Walter and Walter's successor, Edward Clark, oversaw the east, west and north wings. Across F Street from the Patent Office, the Post Office building with Corinthian pilasters was constructed of marble and superintended by Mills and later Walter, Clark, and Montgomery C. Meigs.

The need for a new building for the War and Navy Departments on the west side of the President's House did not go unnoticed. In 1843, Colonel J. J. Abert of the Corps of Topographical Engineers submitted a report to the House of Representatives along with written remarks on the subject from William Strickland, John Notman, and Mills. According to Abert, it was not intended that the new building for the War and Navy Departments would be similar to the Treasury Building. Abert observed, "the position [of the two buildings] are too distant from each other, and are not visible, as a whole, from any point." Differing buildings would also be "without violence to architectural effect" and provide for "better accommodations of the War and Navy Departments." Mills objected to Abert's statements, urging the retention of the same lines of placement, same order of architecture, and a general "unity of design in the corresponding buildings." Submitting designs for the War and Navy Departments, Mills stated:

> As the character of a nation is judged of by the character of its public buildings, I consider it my duty, as an American, having the honor of his country at heart, to recommend nothing that would compromise its honor. Where imperious necessity compels to

economize the public expenditures in its necessary works, we
should not lose sight of giving that final finish to it which will
prove creditable to the country.[61]

William Strickland's report the following year, 1844, on the building for the War and Navy Departments provided a preview of the national architectural program of the 1850s. Whether Strickland's views
were uniquely his or were strongly influenced by his association with
the U.S. Army Topographical Engineers is not clear. However,
Strickland's report represented the attitudes toward architectural
style and construction superintendence that would reign in the following decade.

Strickland "set out with the idea of plainness in the character of
architecture both within and without," introducing windows in the
building's frieze so that the fourth floor would provide light for the
draftsmen and topographers who would be located on that floor.
The frontispiece of the building would be a simple Ionic colonnade.
The building would be constructed of Sing Sing marble, the same
material used in the Post Office building, and of cast iron from the
West Point Foundry. The plainness envisioned was in keeping with
the desire of the War and Navy Departments for a "workshop, not a
palace." The proportions of ancient architecture were not compatible with "modern purposes of utility." As Strickland wrote, "Look
around you—in your Hall of Representatives. Look at the show.
Where is the utility? You cannot hear yourself nor your colleagues
speak. No sir; usefulness first, and ornament made to bend to the propriety of the purposes of the building." Strickland concluded his report with the recommendation that the War Department handle construction of the building and that Colonel Abert, "who knows
perfectly well all the theory and practice of the building art" be appointed superintendent of construction.[62]

Appended to Strickland's report on the War and Navy Departments was a statement by W. H. Ward, proprietor of the Washington
City Foundry, who recommended the use of cast iron columns,
beams, window frames, and arches. The extensive use of cast iron in
the new buildings, according to Ward, would make it fireproof and
less expensive than other fireproofing methods.[63] Ward's enthusiasm
for cast iron was not only in the interest of improving his business,
but it also reflected a growing national fascination with the many possible uses to which cast iron could be applied in architecture. This interest reached a peak in the 1850s when the Corps of Engineers played

a large role in the construction of federal government buildings around the nation and championed the use of cast iron in their construction. Despite the extended discussions on the War and Navy Building, plans to initiate its construction were postponed until the late 1860s.

Federal Government Architecture at Midcentury

Studies conducted on the War and Navy Departments building brought into focus a cast of architectural characters who played an important role in the evolution of the federal government's architecture program. As the nation approached midcentury, Robert Mills could claim the title of architect of public buildings (figure 2.5). However, his services for individual buildings or groups of buildings represented the old piecemeal method of procuring designs for federal buildings; thus they were not comparable to the scope and continuity of the supervising architect in later decades. Ammi B. Young represented the future; his architectural accomplishments foretold a prominent role for him in a centralized administration. Despite William Strickland's best efforts to gain a foothold in Washington, D.C., his services were confined largely to federal buildings outside the capital city.

As architect of public buildings, Mills was "an independent officer of the Government, drawing his authority from the President."[64] Between the time of his appointment in 1838 and the completion of his work on the Patent Office in 1842, Mills worked on buildings primarily in Washington, D.C. Buildings outside Washington were handled between the secretary of the treasury, the customs collectors, and the architects who designed them. Mills's claims overlooked the separate and independent role of the Army engineers in superintending the construction of federal buildings, which was an important factor in the evolution of the national building program.

Young is sometimes cited as the successor to Mills, but his Treasury Department appointment followed the conclusion of Mills's appointment by ten years. During the 1850s, Young's work with the Treasury Department covered federal buildings throughout the nation; his position was subordinate to the chief of the Bureau of Construction, who was a member of the Army Corps of Engineers.

Although never successful in obtaining a major federal building

Figure 2.5
Robert Mills and his wife,
ca. 1851. Courtesy
National Portrait Gallery,
Smithsonian Institution,
Washington, D.C., gift of
Richard Evans.

commission in the capital city, William Strickland was nonetheless a key figure in the development of public architecture in the United States during the first half of the nineteenth century. In the early 1840s, Strickland's career slipped into a lull, and with the exception of residences for the governor and medical officers on the grounds of the U.S. Naval Home in Washington, his strenuous lobbying for federal government commissions fell flat. His 1844 report on the War and Navy Departments building was prophetic. He echoed the sentiments of many politicians and citizens who favored buildings that bespoke economy over those that could be described as ornamental. In the following year, Strickland retired from the national debate and moved to Nashville, Tennessee, in order to design and superintend the state capitol building.[65]

By 1850, the major paths leading to the creation of a centralized design service had been blazed. The volume of public building construction had increased rapidly in the 1840s, creating a level of administrative responsibility that went far beyond the ability of the secretary of the treasury to manage the program by dealing directly with the customs collector and the architect. Mills's design of four custom houses in New England in the 1830s and the Army engineers' supervision of several marine hospitals in the 1840s were precursors to the consolidation of design and construction responsibilities in Washington, D.C., in the early 1850s. The volume of construction work also encouraged the trend toward standardization, at least among buildings for like functions and serving similar population numbers. The full implementation of standardized design required a centralized administrative entity. The period from 1789 to 1851 was a time when the federal government experimented with various approaches to a national building program and, in the process, gained the experience sufficient to propel the effort into its centralized phase.

3

THE BUREAU OF CONSTRUCTION
AND THE CORPS OF ENGINEERS

1852–1865

The 1850s witnessed a tremendous growth in the nation's cities and governmental institutions. Thriving urban settlements located along major water routes became centers of revenue collection, postal distribution, judicial proceedings, and other federal functions. The scope and scale of these activities required physical accommodations beyond rented or adapted buildings. The expansion of the national building program provided an opportunity for the federal government to provide more than mere shelter. The federal government's limited experience with public building construction prior to 1850, plus the growth of the architectural profession, contributed to the development of a public architecture replete in symbols of nationalism. The national building program of the 1850s, as administered under a newly centralized governmental bureau, produced buildings that were highly standardized and consistent in their architectural language. This unity of federal government architecture from one city to another appeared to contradict other national forces of the decade that led to disunion and the Civil War.

The management of the booming national building program required the consolidation of the civilian architectural functions of the federal government. The increased scope of the federal program is reflected in the numbers. Prior to 1850, it was estimated that the federal government had built or purchased forty-one custom houses and marine hospitals. Between 1850 and 1858, eighty-eight additional buildings were constructed or were in the course of construction.[1]

These buildings included custom houses, courthouses, post offices, marine hospitals, mints, a miscellany of territorial buildings, an appraisers store, and an assay office. Presiding over the early phase in this public building boom was Secretary of the Treasury Thomas Corwin, who served from 1850 to 1853. Although Corwin's successor, James Guthrie, is most often credited with consolidating public building responsibilities into the Bureau of Construction, it was Corwin who took the first steps in this direction.

Secretary Corwin's Decision to Centralize

In early 1851, Secretary Corwin continued to administer the building program personally, maintaining direct lines of communication with building superintendents, customs collectors, and local three-man commissions that oversaw the design and construction of federal buildings. Some of the plans for federal buildings were acquired by competition; other plans were secured by the direct hiring of an architect. The New Orleans custom house, designed by A. T. Wood, was under construction and being superintended by James Dakin, architect of the Louisiana State Capitol. John W. Kerr provided plans for the new custom house in Pittsburgh and was hired to superintend its construction. Architect of the Wilmington, North Carolina, custom house, John Norris was chosen as the architect and superintendent of the new custom house at Savannah, Georgia. "Colonel" Edward B. White was architect and superintendent of the new custom house at Charleston, South Carolina. All of these new buildings were located in cities and towns in "reference to future commerce and business of the city."[2] Local businessmen were frequently consulted in the identification of building sites.

Out of the cluster of architects associated with federal buildings, Ammi B. Young emerged as the first among equals. In June 1851, Young was dispatched to inspect and report on a shipment of granite for the New Orleans custom house. Later that year, Young joined a team of architects and engineers who were called upon by Corwin to check on alleged defects in the plans for the New Orleans building. One of the engineers on the team was Major P. G. T. Beauregard, a member of the Corps of Engineers, who played an important superintendency role in the public building program during the 1850s. Young also was asked to report on the foundations of the federal building at Bangor, Maine, and to prepare duplicate plans for the Charleston custom house.

Young's work on the various federal buildings won the approval of the secretary of the treasury; in March 1852, Corwin wrote to Young in Boston:

> The Department agrees to allow you a salary at the rate of $3,000 per annum, commencing from 1st January for which you are to render your exclusive services to the Government in all matters which it may require of you in connection with the building of any Custom Houses, Marine Hospitals, or other public buildings under the Superintendence of the Department.[3]

In June 1852, Young was referred to as "Architect of the Department"[4] and by December of that year, he was referred to as "Supervising Architect."[5]

By late 1852, Young was not only called upon to handle inspection matters, but he was also already preparing designs for federal buildings. These designs included those for new custom houses at Norfolk, Virginia, and Cincinnati, Ohio. By early 1853, Young had produced drawings of the new custom houses at Bath, Maine, and Astoria, Oregon. Upon completion of the drawings and specifications, advertisements were placed in newspapers soliciting bids for the construction of each building. The local building commissions or the customs collectors received copies of the plans and specifications and made them available to prospective bidders. One of the building commissioners served as the disbursing agent.

Corwin's departure from the Treasury Department in March 1853 portended changes to the public building program newly centralized under Young. During the first weeks of the tenure of Corwin's successor, James Guthrie, several local building superintendents were removed and replaced with new superintendents. For the troublesome and "costly" New Orleans custom house, Guthrie removed Dakin and appointed Beauregard as superintendent, asking him to look into the unequal settlement of the foundations and fractures in the interior walls.[6] Guthrie's regard for the skills of the members of the Corps of Engineers was further exemplified by the appointment of Captain Danville Leadbetter to superintend the construction of the custom house at Mobile, Alabama, which Young had designed. Guthrie's views on qualifications for superintendents was expressed by Assistant Secretary P. G. Washington in 1855:

> While it is not absolutely necessary that a Superintendent be a practical architect and builder, it is proper that he will be acquainted with the principles of construction, that he knows the quality of materials and be conversant with their prices, that he be a good judge of work, and have had experience in the management of laborers and in the construction of public works.[7]

Establishment of the Bureau of Construction

While his predecessor centralized civilian architectural services in Washington, Guthrie took the next step to place an officer of the Corps of Engineers over the operation. In correspondence with iron founders James Bogardus and Hamilton Hoppin of New York in August of 1853, Guthrie made the first mention of Captain Alexander Hamilton Bowman who was to serve as the first chief of the Bureau of Construction. Guthrie asked Bogardus and Hoppin to provide an estimate for an iron building that would house the New York assay office. The building was to be appropriate for the assaying, melting, and refinishing of gold and was to be completed quickly. Guthrie then sent Bowman to examine the site for the iron building and to settle on a plan for the building.[8] Guthrie's rapport with Bowman was evident in his later instructions to him to construct the assay office of brick, adding, "It is possible I may be in New York in a few days and can then speak more freely on the subject."[9] Bowman's responsibilities were subsequently expanded as Guthrie dispatched him to building operations in other locations, which were suspended until a personal visit could be made to inspect the site.

A native of Wilkes-Barre, Pennsylvania, Bowman (1803–1865) had credentials important to Guthrie. He was educated at the United States Military Academy, where he graduated in 1825. After graduation, Bowman taught geography, history, and ethics at West Point. Between 1826 and 1851, Bowman was assigned to the defenses and harbors in the southern states, including Charleston, South Carolina, where he was charged with the construction of Fort Sumter. Just before being assigned to the Treasury Department, Bowman again taught at West Point, this time on the subject of "practical military engineering."[10]

During 1853 and 1854, Guthrie referred to Bowman variously as "General Superintendent of Buildings for the Treasury Department," "Supervising Architect," and "Engineer in Charge of This Department." During the same period Young was referred to as the "U.S. Inspecting Agent" for building materials and "Supervising Architect" as well. By the mid-1850s, Bowman settled on "Engineer in Charge" of the Bureau of Construction (sometimes referred to as the Office of Construction) and Young as "Supervising Architect." In this arrangement, Bowman, clearly Young's superior, saw his role as an administrator and an expert on construction and engineering matters.

These developments in the management of the national building program did not go unnoticed by the Congress. In early 1854, Congressman I. Letcher requested from Guthrie the names and rank of Army officers assigned to public building projects. Guthrie listed Beauregard at New Orleans, Leadbetter at Mobile, Captain G. W. Cullum at the New York assay office, and Bowman, assigned in June 1853 to "assist in the general supervision and management of this description of business under its charge." In listing these Army engineers, Guthrie cited the twenty-nine public buildings then under construction and his claim that in 1853, no coherent system existed to manage the program. Convinced "it was necessary that the Department should have at hand, and under its control, an officer of scientific education and practical experience and judgment, to aid it in the supervision and management of the business," Guthrie applied to Secretary of War Jefferson Davis to assign Bowman to this duty. The use of Army engineers also overcame "objections on the score of improvidence or extravagance in expenditure, or of tardiness in the construction of the works." Army engineers were especially appropriate for the Treasury's building program "by education, character, and experience." The use of Army engineers on civil works was common: General Simon Bernard had performed surveys of the land between Little Falls and Georgetown in the design of the capital city's water supply, and other Army engineers had conducted surveys for roads. Guthrie concluded, "I am satisfied such employment must result in works of improved character and construction and in great savings to the public."[11]

Guthrie's high regard for Bowman and the latter's fidelity to his job made for a highly productive working relationship during the four years of Guthrie's tenure as secretary of the treasury. After Guthrie's departure in March 1857 and replacement by Howell Cobb, Bowman continued contact with Guthrie; on occasion, Bowman sent Guthrie copies of drawings of the Office of Construction's works. On one such occasion, Bowman sent Guthrie a photograph of the Treasury extension, anticipating that it would "revive recollections of your varied and useful public labors where so much of your time has been bestowed (and not in vain) for the benefit of the country and of this community." Bowman assured Guthrie that "the feelings of regret with which we all parted from you are deepened by time and absence while one and all would gladly hail your return to public life."[12]

While Guthrie extolled the technical skills of the Corps of Engineers staff through the selection of Bowman and his associates, their managerial abilities and experience were also valued. In his 1854 annual report to the secretary of the treasury covering his first year as bureau chief, Bowman related his "marching orders" from Guthrie:

> The general regulations, proposed at your suggestion and under your direction, for securing a uniform system of accountability, and in efficient discharge of the duties of those to whom the construction of these buildings is entrusted, have now been in operation for nearly a year, and have produced decidedly favorable results.

These systems included a calendar of reports, disbursement procedures, and accounting oversight.

The consolidation of design responsibilities under the Treasury Department also fit into Bowman's efforts to rationalize the production of buildings. As he noted in his 1854 report:

> [T]he preparation of the plans, specifications, estimates, and contracts in this office, under the immediate direction of the department, where the number of occupants and the precise amount of business to be transacted in each building are known, has many advantages. Errors committed in buildings already in use can be avoided, a proper apportionment of office-room made, and such an arrangement of the different offices as will facilitate the transaction of business effected. This can be better done where the conveniences and inconveniences of similar buildings are subjects of frequent discussion with those who occupy them, than if the buildings were designed by some one less acquainted with the uses

for which they are required, and who would probably be more likely to make a beautiful than a suitable structure.[13]

Justifying and Siting Federal Government Buildings

During the 1850s, the process of producing a federal building began with a consideration of the cost of a building. The Treasury Department supplied Congress with estimates of buildings according to a fairly standardized formula. For example, in 1854, Secretary Guthrie wrote to Hannibal Hamlin of the Senate Committee on Commerce that a fireproof building, two stories high, brick exterior, with a plan similar to that of a "minimum size" custom house, 45 feet by 32 feet, and 32 feet high, plus 10 percent to cover the cost of architectural, superintendency, and advertising services would cost $20,000.[14] The Treasury Department was also called upon to comment on the need for federal buildings at specific locations and on the sufficiency of appropriations for public buildings. The final decision to appropriate funds rested with Congress.

On occasion, members of Congress proposed buildings at locations which the secretary of the treasury judged to be unwarranted. In 1856, Guthrie responded to a memorial from citizens of Galena and the draft bill for a $88,000 building. "I am unable to perceive the necessity for the proposed building at the present time," wrote Guthrie, noting that Galena had become a port of trade only two years earlier and attracted no foreign trade. In addition, only $183.90 in duties had been collected there.[15] However, Guthrie later noted, "Congress thought differently," and a custom house was constructed at Galena.[16] In response to efforts by citizens of St. Joseph, Missouri, to secure a marine hospital, Guthrie wrote, "In my opinion it is not expedient to make provision for the same." In expressing his views, Guthrie pointed out that St. Joseph was not a port of entry or delivery, and it was not likely to get foreign trade. In addition, no federal representative was on site to collect the hospital tax from seamen or to dispense "the temporary relief to which they may be entitled." Marine hospitals ought to be located at points where voyages originated or where they terminated.[17]

Treasury Secretary Howell Cobb, Guthrie's successor, viewed the system of authorizing federal buildings with skepticism. In 1857, he suggested that "no public building should be authorized until an official report had been made to Congress showing the necessity for its erection and its cost."[18] Cobb's view was amplified by Bowman in his accompanying report; Bowman noted the lack of equal distribution of buildings among the states and among the cities and towns of each state "based upon the actual need of such buildings." Reflecting on his experiences of the previous five years, Bowman observed that "expensive custom houses and post offices have been erected by the government, the joint revenue from which does not pay the expense of collection; and marine hospitals maintaining a corps of physicians, stewards, nurses, and other employees outnumbering the patients."[19]

Once the buildings were under construction, the secretary of the treasury made recommendations to Congress regarding the need for supplemental funds to complete buildings and to increase their size. For example, in 1856, Guthrie stated that the new custom house and post office building in Toledo, Ohio, was too small for the functions to be housed. He suggested that another story be added to accommodate these functions and to make the building compatible with "all buildings in the immediate vicinity of the custom house site." The surrounding buildings had not been in existence at the time the plans for the building were prepared. "This fact is an evidence of the rapid growth of the city."[20] For the new custom house in Petersburg, Virginia, Guthrie rejected the request by members and citizens for a portico to be added to the buildings, while agreeing with the request for an additional story to be added.[21] For especially large and troublesome projects, such as the New Orleans custom house, Guthrie was unable to report how much additional funding, beyond the $2,075,258 already spent on the building, would be required to complete the construction and to overcome the problems caused by the settlement of the building's walls.[22]

Once an appropriation was available for a building, no monies could be spent on the purchase of the property or the design of the building until the legislature of the relevant state ceded jurisdiction and the right to tax the property. The U.S. Constitution made this requirement, which was clarified by a Joint Resolution of Congress in 1841. The title to the property was conveyed to the U.S. Attorney General for his review and approval as to its validity.[23] This was a sticking point for many building projects and the process frequently caused delays in commencing construction.

Prospective sites were recommended by the customs commissioners, superintendents, or members of the building commissions, guided by advice from local merchants and citizens. When the site recommendations were assembled, the following considerations governed the site:

> 1st. That the site should be as near the present and prospective centre of population of the city as practicable. 2nd. That it should be near to (but not on) the great thoroughfare of the city. This is necessary to secure the quiet required by the court, and for the convenience of women and children visiting the post office. 3rd. The prices demanded for lots . . . 4th. Other things being equal, the site best calculated to show the building to advantage.[24]

In planning for a federal building, efforts were made to make the building project compatible with local conditions. In October 1854, as Bowman readied himself to embark on an inspection of sites offered for federal buildings, Guthrie suggested that he note the position of the lots offered, the building materials available at several points, and the wages of day laborers. Guthrie recommended that Bowman observe "the material most in use in the best buildings in the place together with such other information as will enable the Department to select a suitable site and adopt a style of building in harmony with other valuable public and private buildings in the place."[25]

The local building commissions that oversaw the construction of the building were composed of local citizens who served in a voluntary capacity. As Assistant Secretary P. G. Washington wrote to Commissioner John T. Hudson of Buffalo, New York, "it has been generally expected that the interest felt by the commissioners in the prosperity of their town, would prompt them to perform the honorary duties of their position gratuitously."[26] After the state's consent had been given to relinquish jurisdiction over the site, the title approved, and the land given over to the possession of the federal government, the design for the building proceeded.

The Design and Construction Process

Although Captain Bowman headed the Bureau of Construction, Ammi B. Young remained the chief designer of all federal buildings that fell within the jurisdiction of the Treasury Department from 1852 to the outbreak of the Civil War, when building projects were halted. By 1856, the design staff of the bureau consisted of J. Goldsborough Bruff, P. Nenning, A. E. Drake, S. B. Dixon, I. Louis Hayes, Adolf

Cluss, and I. R. Barber.[27] Of these designers, the two most notable were Bruff, an important figure in the Washington, D.C., art world, and Cluss, one of the best-known figures in Washington architecture in the second half of the nineteenth century.

J. Goldsborough Bruff (1804–1889) entered the Bureau of Construction in 1853 as a "draftsman and artist" and stayed until his removal in 1869. He returned in 1875. Bruff had already attained celebrity status in Washington, D.C., for leading an expedition to California during the height of the Gold Rush between 1849 and 1851.[28] He was also well known in Washington art and historical circles. In the Bureau of Construction, Bruff produced drawings for ornamental work for the Treasury and other buildings and specialized in exotic designs for light fixtures. Bruff also critiqued the designs for light fixtures prepared by Cornelius & Baker of Philadelphia, which manufactured fixtures for many federal buildings during the 1850s. One of Bruff's creations of this period was the title page for the sets of lithographed drawings (figure 3.1). Here the hierarchy of figures associated with the national building program—Guthrie, Bowman, and Young—was laid out at the base of a set piece that expressed the integration of science, art, and national pride in the design and construction of custom houses, courthouses, post offices, and marine hospitals. Few icons represent the national building program as completely as does this sketch.

A native of Germany, Adolf Cluss (1825–1905) was trained as an architect and an engineer. Embroiled in the political upheaval in his native land in 1848, Cluss emigrated to the United States. He worked as a draftsman at the Washington, D.C. Navy Yard and later at the Bureau of Construction in the 1850s and 1860s; he established a private practice in 1861. His most notable commissions (all in Washington, D.C.) included the Franklin and Sumner schools, the Centre Market building, Calvary Baptist Church, the U. S. National Museum (now the Arts and Industries Building), the Department of Agriculture building on the south side of the Mall, the rebuilding of the Smithsonian building after the fire of 1865, and numerous houses and apartment houses throughout the city.[29] The nature of Cluss's contributions to the design of federal buildings is not evident from the records of the Bureau of Construction during the 1850s. However, his knowledge of the operations of the Office would prove useful in the 1870s when the American Institute of Architects prepared legislation to alter the scope of the Supervising Architect's responsibilities.

Ammi B. Young's trademark for designs produced for the Treasury

Department during the 1850s was the Italian Renaissance palazzo style, adapted to public buildings. The popularization of this style has been credited to Sir Charles Barry of Great Britain whose Travellers' Club and Reform Club buildings in London sparked a rage for buildings that resembled an Italian Renaissance palace. As compared with many picturesque Italianate residences, these public buildings were more in the classical mode, with carefully balanced proportions, heavy rustication at the ground floor, and quoins or pilasters at the corners. Young's designs lent an air of simple official dignity to the federal government's presence in the communities in which they were located. The Italian palazzo model required less building materials per unit of usable space than the temple model and could be built flush with the building lot line, making it a compatible neighbor with the surrounding urban street.[30]

The buildings for Rutland, Vermont (figure 3.2), and Mobile, Alabama (figure 3.3) typify the range of Young's designs. In these multipurpose buildings, postal functions were assigned to the first floor because it was the most accessible to the public. Customs collections normally occupied the second floor. If a third floor was available, it was usually assigned to federal judicial functions because it was the farthest from the street noises. Marine hospitals were designed as large functional structures but ornamented with elaborate porches and balconies for convalescents.

After the design and specifications were complete, the next task at hand was to prepare copies for distribution to prospective contractors by the superintendent of construction. These copies also allowed the staff at the Treasury Department in Washington and the superintendents at the building sites to work and communicate from identical documents. Copies of the written specifications were printed and published as small books. The drawings were duplicated through the lithographic process. Lithography, a method to produce inexpensive printed images, became perfected in the late eighteenth century in Germany. Greasy ink drawings were made on a large stone that had its surface polished with special machinery. When the stone was wetted, the water passed over the ink. A sheet of paper was then pressed on the stone, thereby creating a reversed impression of the drawing. Gum arabic and a weak acid solution kept the inked design from spreading on the stone.[31]

The lithography firms used by the Bureau of Construction included August Köllner of Philadelphia and Bradford & Co. of Boston. Of the two, Köllner was the one most frequently listed on the printed

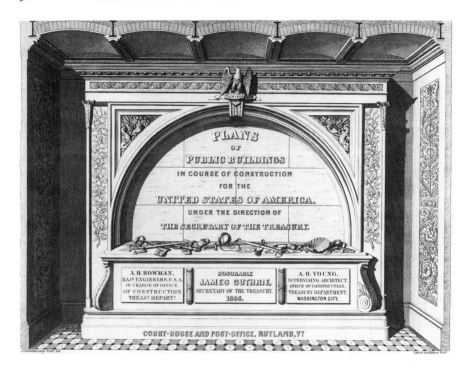

Figure 3.1
Title page of *Plans of Public Buildings in the Course of Construction for the United States of America under the Direction of the Secretary of the Treasury,* 1856. Courtesy National Archives.

drawings. Köllner studied lithography in his native Germany and came to the United States in 1839. He is best known for his *Views of American Cities*.[32] The production of the lithographic copies of federal buildings was described by Secretary Guthrie in a letter to Köllner:

> After printing the above 200 copies for the Burlington Custom House, you will substitute "Toledo, Ohio" for "Burlington, Vt." and print the usual numbers on thick and thin paper for that building. You will then please preserve the drawings on the stone, as it will probably be needed for another building.[33]

A similar exchange of correspondence indicated nearly identical designs at Wheeling, West Virginia (then Virginia) (figure 3.4) and Cleveland, Ohio[34] (figure 3.5). In October 1855, Guthrie advised Köllner to keep the stones illustrating the custom house at Wheeling; Gloucester, Massachusetts; Sandusky, Ohio, and Ellsworth, Maine, available for other buildings.[35] In December 1856, the secretary wrote to Köllner, instructing him to replace the word "Georgetown, D.C." (figure 3.6) with "Galena, Ill."[36] (figure 3.7).

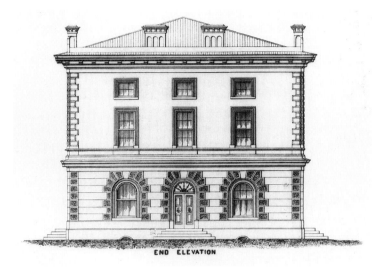

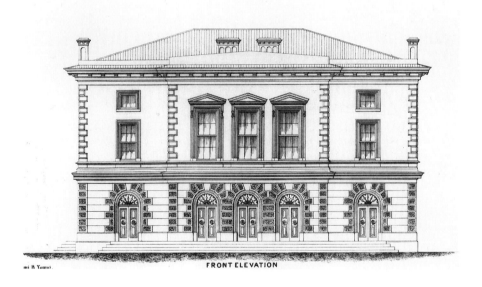

Copies of the lithographed drawings and printed specifications were sent to the local building commission or custom collector who made this information available to prospective bidders for the construction contract. The contract was intended to cover the cost of all materials and necessary labor, limited by the amount appropriated for the building. Additional contracts were let to procure specialized building items, such as iron work, lighting fixtures, vaults, and decorative features. When supplies of plans and specifications had been

Figure 3.2
U.S. courthouse and post office, Rutland, Vermont, constructed 1857–1859, Ammi B. Young. Courtesy National Archives.

Figure 3.3
U.S. custom house,
Mobile, Alabama,
1851–1856, Ammi B.
Young. Courtesy
National Archives.

exhausted, the commissioners or collectors kept one copy for examination by other parties. The contractor who was awarded the project was required to provide a bond for his services.

The appointment of the superintendent of construction was key to the conduct of the building operations at the site. In theory, superintendents were selected from those who had applied to the department for such an appointment. However, in reality, it was politic for the superintendent to be selected from the locality in which the building was located, someone who was well connected with the congressional delegation. In areas where no qualified architect or builder could be located, the department assigned, with the cooperation of the secretary of war, a member of the Corps of Engineers. Or, in the case of the Galena building, Guthrie's successor as secretary, Howell Cobb, appointed Ely S. Parker of Buffalo, New York, as superintendent. No competent builder could be identified in Galena, and Parker was described as a civil engineer of known and tried capacity who was "recommended by sundry practical men known to the Bureau of Construction whose names were not recorded."[37] The

Figure 3.4
U.S. custom house,
Wheeling, West Virginia,
1856–1860, Ammi B.
Young. Courtesy
National Archives.

position of superintendent was an unstable one, because changes in the personnel at the Treasury Department frequently spelled changes in the superintendency at the local level. Disgruntled building suppliers often complained to the secretary of the treasury of mismanagement on the part of the superintendent, charges that were then investigated by the department.

Because of the far-flung construction projects, the Treasury Department depended on the superintendents to have the work performed in a timely fashion. As Secretary Guthrie noted to William H. Pettis, superintendent of the custom house at Buffalo, "It is nearly impossible for the Department to decide upon every minute detail in buildings constructed at a distance (such as the clamps of stone, etc.). It is part of the duty of the Superintendent to see and direct them, as the building progresses."[38] Regulations for superintendents set forth methods for procurement of building materials and labor, for paying bills by the disbursing agent, and for reporting on the progress of the work on a monthly basis. The superintendents also prepared entries for the annual report of the Bureau of Construction. For some su-

END ELEVATION.

FRONT ELEVATION

Figure 3.5
U.S. custom house, Cleveland, Ohio, 1856–1859, Ammi B. Young. Courtesy
National Archives.

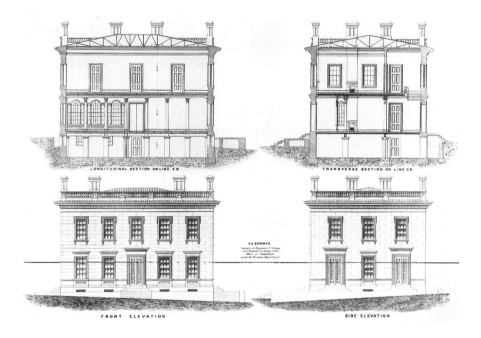

LONGITUDINAL SECTION ON LINE A B   TRANSVERSE SECTION ON LINE C D

A.B. BOWMAN,
Captain of Engineers U.S.Army
and Engineer in charge of the
Office of Construction
under the Treasury Department

FRONT ELEVATION   SIDE ELEVATION

perintendents, work on a federal building did not preclude them from undertaking private work. However, a lack of full-time attention to the project often meant delays in the building's completion.

A requirement for the frequent reporting on the progress of the building project provided the Treasury Department with some confidence that the construction process was going well. The monthly, quarterly, and annual reports were intended to keep any one project from falling too far into arrears. By 1857, for the annual report, Secretary Cobb asked all fifty-two superintendents:

> Instead of illustrating the work by drawings, as required in the be-fore cited paragraph of the Regulations, you will cause to be taken a clear photograph of the several fronts of the building and adja-cent grounds, and forward them with your Report. If photographs cannot be procured in your vicinity, you will substitute the best Daguerreotypes at your command.[39]

Bowman thought that photography was very useful in managing a nationwide public works program. Photographs provided a reliable check on reports written by superintendents, and if the prints were good, he could determine the materials and style of workmanship

Figure 3.6
U.S. custom house and post office, Georgetown, D.C., 1857–1858, Ammi B. Young. Courtesy National Archives.

with an accuracy equal to personal inspection.[40] The superintendents also were asked to submit a financial report showing the amount of the original contract, the amount paid to the contractors, and the amount due the contractors at the completion of the work.

In order to verify the progress of the construction work, the superintendents were often asked to inspect buildings in nearby locations. For example, Cobb wrote to Captain John Kurtz of the Corps of Engineers, who had been assigned to supervise the federal building at Bucksport, Maine:

> The new custom house at Ellsworth, Me. is reported to be completed, and I have to request that you will proceed there, and make a careful and critical inspection of the work and report to this Department in detail, the condition and character of the work, whether or not it is completed according to the contract, and if not, what it is necessary for the contractor to do to put the work in a condition to be accepted by the Government under the contract.[41]

At the center of the national building program was the Bureau of Construction in Washington, D.C. The staff was composed not only of designers, most often called draftsmen, but also of administrative and clerical workers. The position of draftsman was especially precarious, because the position depended on continued appropriations for federal buildings at a consistent, if not increased, level. All staff were paid out of the funds appropriated for buildings and thus were liable to discharge when building appropriations decreased. Personnel records are filled with successive appointments. For example, in late 1856, S. M. Clark was appointed chief clerk in the Bureau at a salary of $2,000 per year.[42] Mr. Clark had already been employed in the office since early 1856.

The Bureau received many inquiries about employment on federal building projects in Washington, D.C., and at the local building sites. Because of such a deluge, the office frequently depended on references from trusted associates. For example, in 1858, during a downturn in public building construction, Bowman wrote to Colonel Alexander Provost asking for a name of a first-rate marble cutter. "The man for the place must be one in a thousand," Bowman wrote, adding, "Please do not name this to anyone, or I should have half the marble cutters in Washington pleading their individual fitness for the place."[43]

In the capital, the only building project under the control of the Bureau of Construction during the 1850s was the southern extension of the Treasury Department building. That Bowman and Young would receive responsibility for the Treasury extension was by no means a certainty. Philadelphia architect Thomas U. Walter (1804–1887) had been hired in 1851 to serve as architect of the Capitol extension and dome. During the next fourteen years, as "Architect of Public Buildings" in Washington, Walter also was assigned to the projects that Robert Mills had superintended, including the Patent Office building and the Post Office, as well as new projects, such as St. Elizabeth's Hospital and the President's House. Walter also prepared designs for the Treasury extension; the State, War, and Navy Building, which was never executed; and numerous other federal building projects. Walter's long tenure in Washington, D.C., and his situation at the Capitol gave him access to information on the bureaucratic intrigue that determined the fate of public building projects. In March 1855, Walter wrote to his friend John Rice of Philadelphia that Captain Montgomery C. Meigs, then superintendent of construction of the Capitol work, had said that "it is not improbable that Captain Bowman may eventually be placed over that work (Treasury extension)."[44] By May of that year, Walter wrote to Rice in a "confidential letter" that rumors had intensified about the Treasury extension going to Bowman and Young, adding, "I have heard some rich things about it, but more when I see you."[45]

During the 1850s, the Treasury Department's Bureau of Construction and Walter's architectural establishment at the U.S. Capitol coexisted in the capital city. The Treasury Department maintained its control over nearly all civilian federal buildings located outside Washington, D.C., and, due to political maneuvering, was delegated responsibility for the Treasury Building extension. In his position as architect of the Capitol extension and dome, Walter was tapped by congressmen and other government officials to prepare designs for other buildings in the capital city and elsewhere. The lines of responsibility between Bowman / Young and Meigs / Walter for buildings in the capital city constituted a gray area of authority.

Despite the possibilities for friction inherent in the presence of two architectural offices, the relations between the two offices were cordial. Part of the good will can be ascribed to the fact that both Bowman and Meigs were members of the Corps of Engineers. Young also contributed to a cooperative spirit by sending Walter

copies of lithographed drawings of federal buildings. In one such instance, Walter acknowledged receiving drawings, commenting "they
make a very valuable addition to my portfolio—they are admirably
got up, considering the purpose for which they are intended, and the
details are particularly good."[46] Later, while sending copies of the
drawings and specifications for the Marine barracks in Brooklyn,
New York, Walter enclosed a note to Young, stating, "You will find
the buildings far less expensive and enduring than the noble structures you are erecting for the Treasury Dept. but their economical
character was made necessary by the limited appropriation, and the
determination of the [War] Department not to exceed it."[47]

Standardization of Federal
Government Buildings

The scope of the national construction program in the 1850s necessi-
tated the rationalization of the design and management of the building projects. This effort to rationalize and standardize also extended
to the procurement of building materials. Studies were done of stone
in the locality of the proposed building and other sites from which
the materials could be sent along major transportation routes. This
period also witnessed studies on the use of iron in the construction
of federal government buildings, in part to achieve as much fire-re-
sistance in a building as possible (see discussion later in this chapter).
Iron beams and columns were used as structural members. Iron was
also used in shutters, doors, roofs, vaults, and on occasion, mantles.

The search for building materials for federal buildings in remote
locations presented a challenge for the Bureau of Construction. In
early 1857, Secretary Cobb requested Ely S. Parker, superintendent of
the new custom house at Galena, Illinois (figure 3.8), to investigate
and report on the stone found in the vicinity. Cobb instructed Parker
to look at the outcrop or any portion exposed to the elements and to
"see if the surface is rounded or smoothed, as if by abrasion, or if it
still retains the original irregular fraction." Cobb felt the limestone in
the area was of a bad color and not of uniform texture. Once he located sites of usable stone, Parker was to inspect the "facility which
owners may have for furnishing stone in quantity."[48]

The greatest technological leap of the decade was the introduction of iron into public building construction. As was noted earlier,
the Treasury Department considered constructing the New York as-

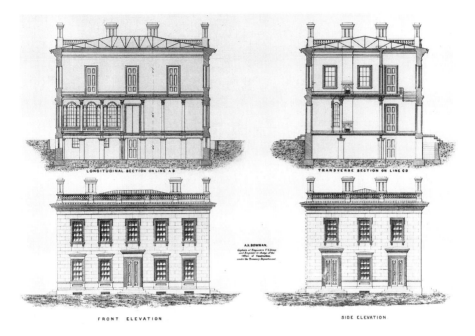

LONGITUDINAL SECTION ON LINE AB

TRANSVERSE SECTION ON LINE CD

FRONT ELEVATION

SIDE ELEVATION

say office of iron. In the end, however, it was built of brick supported with wrought iron beams. In 1853, Congressional legislation that appropriated funds for the erection of several federal buildings required the structures to be fireproof. Consequently, the Bureau of Construction took the initiative in the testing of iron building elements. Secretary Guthrie asked R. M. T. Hunter, chairman of the Committee of Finance, for $3,000 to "meet the expense of a complete series of experiments to test the strength of wrought iron beams and girders."[49] Four years later, Guthrie made a similar request of Hunter to cover a series of experiments and analyses of cast iron to enable the government to make proper selections of iron for public works projects. Guthrie noted that this topic was made urgent by the "increasing consumption of iron in public buildings for permanent use."[50] The section for the Alexandria, Virginia, courthouse illustrates the use of iron in the columns of the longitudinal section (figure 3.9).

The Treasury Department pressed on with its efforts to introduce iron into public buildings already under construction or those still in the planning stages. Secretary Guthrie encouraged Colonel White, superintendent of the Charleston custom house, to contact suppliers of iron frames, shutters, and sashes. Guthrie listed Athouse & Co., George R. Jackson & Co., Bogardus & Hoppin, and James & Beebe

Figure 3.7
U.S. custom house and post office, Galena, Illinois, 1857–1858, Ammi B. Young. Courtesy National Archives.

Figure 3.8
U.S. custom house and
post office, Galena,
Illinois, 1857–1858,
Ammi B. Young.
Courtesy National
Archives.

as "responsible men in the iron business."[51] The list of suppliers was later increased to include other foundries. Changes were made to other public buildings under construction to make them "fireproof," given the danger inherent in the oil lamps and candles used for lighting. Details for the custom house at Wheeling, West Virginia, illustrates the use of iron (figure 3.10).

By 1858, the use of iron elements for federal buildings were standard practice; Secretary Cobb wrote to George R. Jackson & Co. regarding the iron work to be produced for the Indianapolis court house, "The building at Springfield is precisely similar to all its Ironwork (with the Indianapolis building), and a copy of the plans and specifications for that work are this day mailed to your address."[52]

The Treasury Department took great pride in its sponsorship of advances in public building design and construction technology. Secretary Guthrie sent copies of the lithographed plans and drawings and the printed specifications to all major colleges and universities in

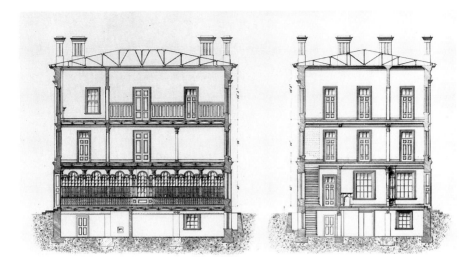

the country, to Joseph Henry at the Smithsonian Institution, to learned societies, and to foreign missions (figure 3.11). In the cover letter, Guthrie wrote:

> The introduction of wrought iron beams and girders in these Edifices, instead of groined arches as formerly used, is, I believe, wholly new, and this improvement, as well as other particulars indicated in these Drawings and Specifications will, it is hoped, prove interesting and useful to you, or to those who, through you, may have the opportunity of inspecting them.[53]

While Guthrie was promoting the Treasury Department's achievements in public building design and construction, Captain Bowman claimed credit for himself and the United States Military Academy at West Point. In a letter written in 1856 to Colonel Sylvanus Thayer, former superintendent of the Academy, Bowman stated, "It is a great satisfaction to me to be able to transmit this evidence of my labors for the past few years in endeavoring to improve our Public Buildings by rendering them strictly fireproof." Bowman related the difficulties in employing wrought iron beams in public buildings, adding:

> That I have succeeded in overcoming them [the difficulties], as well as the many others met on these works I feel that I owe en-

Figure 3.9
Sections, U.S. custom house, Alexandria, Virginia, 1856–1858, Ammi B. Young. Courtesy National Archives.

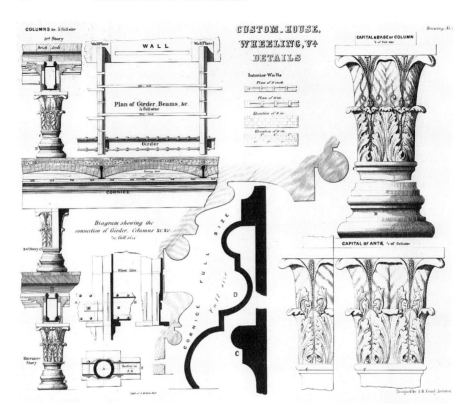

Figure 3.10
Details, U.S. custom
house, Wheeling, West
Virginia, 1856–1860,
Ammi B. Young.
Courtesy National
Archives.

tirely to the training I received at the Institution so much beloved
by all graduates and so honorably and closely interwoven with
your own and our country's heritage.[54]

Bowman's training and experience had been couched in a broad
view of the role of civil and military engineering in the larger world
of science. Before the Civil War, the United States possessed few institutions that offered instruction in architecture and engineering
subjects. The United States Military Academy was an exception. Its
graduates were pioneers in the application of scientific theory to the
design and construction of public works projects. Army engineers regarded themselves as members of the scientific community that included scholars and intellectuals associated with universities and
learned institutions both in the United States and abroad. As
Bowman related to a friend of his, R. Clarkson of Lancaster, Pennsylvania, employment in the Bureau of Construction could not be
valued for its financial renumeration (the pay was low), but for the

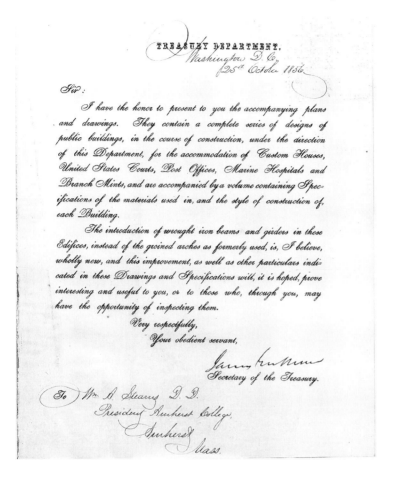

TREASURY DEPARTMENT,
Washington D. C.
25th October 1856.

Sir:

I have the honor to present to you the accompanying plans and drawings. They contain a complete series of designs of public buildings, in the course of construction, under the direction of this Department, for the accommodation of Custom Houses, United States Courts, Post Offices, Marine Hospitals and Branch Mints, and are accompanied by a volume containing Specifications of the materials used in, and the style of construction of, each Building.

The introduction of wrought iron beams and girders in these Edifices, instead of the groined arches as formerly used, is, I believe, wholly new, and this improvement, as well as other particulars indicated in these Drawings and Specifications will, it is hoped, prove interesting and useful to you, or to those who, through you, may have the opportunity of inspecting them.

Very respectfully,
Your obedient servant,

[signature]
Secretary of the Treasury.

To Wm A. Stearns D. D.
President Amherst College.
Amherst
Mass.

wide dissemination of the bureau's works that reached "the *savants* of the old world with whom I am in regular communication."[55]

For himself, Ammi B. Young sent copies of the lithographed drawings to his brother, Ira Young, a professor at Dartmouth College for presentation to the college's Chandler Scientific School. Young thought that students of architectural drawings might find them useful.[56]

Although the existence of the Bureau of Construction gave credibility to its methods of operation, Bowman thought the lack of an enabling law for the bureau or an office of construction limited the authority of the secretary of the treasury to control the entire building process from the authorization to the completion of construction. Bowman recommended:

Figure 3.11
Letter from Secretary of the Treasury James Guthrie to William A. Stearns, President Amherst College, dated October 25, 1856. Courtesy National Archives.

There should be a bureau of construction, authorized by law, and a competent person permanently appointed as its chief, with an assistant, an architect and an assistant, chief clerk, and as many assistants as the proper discharge of the duties may require. There should also be a general disbursing agent, who, in addition to disbursing the works in Washington now under the Treasury Department, and for local payments of distant works, should, under the chief of the bureau, examine and adjust all accounts, claims, and estimates for the various works, and refer them to the proper office for settlement; and a computer, whose duty it shall be to estimate the exact cost of each building offered for contract, so that when the bids for the work are reviewed, there may be in the hands of the department a standard by which to measure the bids offered. Draughtsmen, to copy the plans of the architect, should be employed, so long as their services are required, to complete the drawings of all buildings directed by Congress to be erected.[57]

The Dimming of the Federal Government Building Program

By the end of 1858, the looming conflict between the North and the South and the financial panic that gripped the country caused the U.S. Congress to slow the pace of appropriating funds for federal buildings already under construction. In addition, Congress did not appropriate funds to commence new buildings. In November of that year, Secretary Cobb dismissed Mathius Martin, who was working as a "special agent" for the Bureau of Construction, because "it having been determined to commence the construction of no new Building at present, and many of those in the course of construction at the date of your appointment having been completed and occupied."[58] Several major federal buildings, most notably the Charleston custom house, the New Orleans custom house, and the Treasury Extension, were still under construction. Suggestions that these works be stopped prompted Cobb to state that such a move would, in the long run, cause additional costs and constitute a "serious detriment to the public service."[59] He urged that the works be completed. However, by late 1859, Bowman was calculating the cost of preserving the major unfinished buildings in their current condition.

In early 1860, Bowman took an extended leave of absence in his native Wilkes-Barre because of ill health. In granting Bowman this leave, Cobb expressed his gratitude to Bowman for his:

> long and unremitting attention to the numerous harassing details your position, and of your faithful and arduous discharge of the various complicated duties you have been called upon to perform, as well as by the fact that, in view of the policy indicated by Congressional action in regard to the progress of works constructing under your charge, your absence will be less sensibly felt than during a period of active progress on the Public Works.[60]

Secretary Cobb appointed Chief Clerk S. M. Clark as Acting Engineer in Charge, indicating his view that the position of the head of the Bureau of Construction now was primarily an administrative one. Young was assigned to superintend the construction of the Treasury Extension, in addition to his position of supervising architect. It was evident that Cobb had more confidence in Clark than Young in the latter's description of Clark to Solomon Foot of Rutland, Vermont, "The Acting Engineer in Charge, to whom the Secretary entrusts all matters of construction, etc."[61] By February 1861, however, Captain William B. Franklin of the Topographical Engineers was appointed "engineer in charge" of the Bureau of Construction.

Franklin had distinguished himself at the United States Military Academy, having graduated first in his class. In 1845, at 22 years of age, Franklin joined the expedition of Colonel Stephen W. Kearny to survey the Platte River to the Rocky Mountains and South Pass, considered the "gateway to Oregon." Before his appointment to the Bureau of Construction, Franklin had succeeded Captain Meigs on the construction of the Capitol dome. After the Civil War and his resignation from the Topographical Engineers, Franklin's career took a decidedly architectural turn. While residing in Hartford, Connecticut, to work at the Colt Fire Arms Manufacturing Company, he presided over the Connecticut state capitol commission and served as a consulting engineer on the construction of the building, which had been designed by Richard M. Upjohn. He also chaired the committee of judges for the engineering and architectural exhibits at the Philadelphia Centennial Exhibition.[62]

With the election of Abraham Lincoln as president, Salmon P. Chase became secretary of the treasury on 7 March 1861. The arrival

of Chase and the outbreak of the Civil War the following month signaled a major change in the Bureau of Construction. Franklin was
called away to military duty in July. Clark resumed his position as acting engineer in charge. Young, now 62 years of age, had been passed
over in the several personnel changes at the head of the office. Young,
who ordinarily welcomed the opportunity to discuss employment
prospects at the office with draftsmen, now responded to such requests with, "I have no power to give anyone a situation in the
'Bureau of Construction' if a vacancy existed therein, but which
there does not."[63]

Isaiah Rogers

In June 1862, Secretary Chase took the initiative to place the Bureau
of Construction under new leadership. Chase contacted Isaiah
Rogers (1800–1869), one of the country's distinguished architects.
Rogers had lived in Cincinnati since 1848 and likely knew Chase from
this Ohio connection. From Rogers's response to Chase's letter of 10
June 1862, it is apparent that Chase's first step was to replace Young
as supervising architect. Rogers wrote:

> I have received your kind note of the 10th enquiring if I would ac-
> cept the Office of the Supervising Architect in the Treasury
> Department. The suggestion was so unexpected to me that I did
> not know how to beside [*sic*] at the moment but on reflection be-
> lieve it will be for the best to accept if tendered to me.[64]

Chase's letter to Rogers soon became known to Young when one of
Young's supporters, E. P. Walton of Washington, D.C., wrote to
Chase regarding Young's rumored removal. Walton, who knew
Young from his days on the Vermont State Capitol, urged Young's re-
tention as "I know of no man who more thoroughly minds his own
business, or who is more sensitive when he supposes anybody is
interfering or marring his own. The complaint, I am told, grows out
of this sensitiveness. Should not the virtues outweigh the fault?"[65]
Isaiah Rogers was appointed engineer in charge of the Bureau of
Construction on 23 July 1862. S. M. Clark became disbursing agent for
the Treasury Department. Two days later, Secretary Chase informed
Young that the duties of the supervising architect had "devolved" on
the engineer in charge and that Young's services were terminated.[66]

Young spent the last years of his life in the capital city, dying in 1874 at his house on Fifteenth Street in full view of his southern extension of the Treasury Department building (figure 3.12).

The selection of Rogers as engineer in charge put one of the nation's acclaimed architects at the head of the Treasury Department's architectural operations.[67] Rogers was only a year younger than Young. Nevertheless, he brought a freshness of view to federal government architecture, a view that had been formed by a career devoted to major architectural commissions. Rogers's first major project was the Tremont House in Boston in 1828, the first hotel design of its kind. The Tremont House served him well in subsequent hotel commissions. He also designed the Merchants' Exchange in New York, which is generally regarded as his masterpiece, and the Merchants' Exchange in Boston. In 1848, Rogers left his strongholds of Boston and New York to move to Cincinnati. The credit for Rogers's move to Ohio was claimed by A. B. Coleman. In a letter to Secretary Chase, Coleman stated that he was the "instrument of bringing him [Rogers] to the West for the purpose of constructing the 'Burnet' House. I have known him thoroughly and do not hesitate to say. You will find him intelligent and liberal in his views, and a man of the most strict honesty and integrity."[68]

Figure 3.12
South wing, U.S. Treasury Department building, 1855–1861, Ammi B. Young. Courtesy National Archives.

Rogers's appointment also meant that a practitioner from the mainstream of the architectural profession had been brought to the head architectural position in the federal government. Rogers had been one of the founders, in 1836, of the American Institution of Architects. (This group, however, never evolved further. It was not until more than twenty years later, in 1857, that a group in New York, chaired by Richard Upjohn, formed a different organization, the American Institute of Architects [AIA]. The AIA became the major professional organization to represent the interests of architects, both privately and publicly employed, and it was to play a major part in defining the role of the federal government in public architecture.)

Inherent in Rogers' appointment was the official recognition of the architectural profession and the importance of an architect as head of the federal government's architectural office. This achievement notwithstanding, in 1862 Rogers was sixty-two years of age and his best work lay behind him. In addition, Rogers served as "Engineer in Charge," a title changed to "Supervising Architect" in June of 1863, during a time when the Civil War brought the national building program to a virtual halt. Rogers's major work of the period was the supervision of the west wing of the Treasury Department building. Other works included repairs and alterations to several federal buildings across the country, including some that had been built in the 1850s.

Rogers's staff during his three-year tenure as engineer in chief, and then supervising architect, included computer Bartholomew Oertly from Switzerland; draftsman William G. Steinmetz, a native of Prussia; and J. Goldsborough Bruff, then described as a "draftsman and artist." Oertly had been associated with the Bureau of Construction since 1855 as a draftsman and had risen through the ranks of clerkships to become "Assistant Architect of the Treasury Department" in 1866. He left the Treasury Department in 1868.[69]

Steinmetz was employed by the Bureau of Construction from 1863 to 1877 and was a party in the later New York Post Office controversy (see chapter 4).[70] Bruff stayed with the office from 1853 until his death in 1888. This period of longevity broken only from 1869 to 1875, when he worked in the Treasury Department's Office of the Register, after being removed by Supervising Architect Mullett.[71]

The most crucial person affecting Rogers's eventual fate as supervising architect was Alfred B. Mullett (1834–1890). From outward appearances, Rogers and Mullett would have the makings of a mentor–

protégé relationship. Mullett had entered the Cincinnati architectural firm of Isaiah Rogers, Son & Co. in 1856. In 1859 or 1860, Mullett became a partner in the firm, but in short order he struck out on his own. Why Mullett should have left so abruptly is unclear, but evidently the parting was not under the friendliest of terms. According to some sources, at the outbreak of the Civil War, Mullett helped raise the Dennison, Ohio, regiment and traveled with it to Washington, D.C., in 1861. However, the Ohio quota had been filled and the regiment was disbanded.[72] In June 1861, twenty-seven-year-old Mullett found employment as a clerk in the Office of the Secretary of the Treasury.[73] It has been supposed that Mullett noted a vacuum at the head of the Bureau of Construction and lobbied hard to succeed Clark and Young. He was not successful, but he finally entered the Bureau of Construction in early 1863 as a clerk under Rogers.[74]

The title of "clerk" was one that was applied generally to a wide range of positions throughout the federal bureaucracy, including technical ones. As a "clerk" in the Bureau of Construction, Mullett was assigned by Rogers to examine stonework and investigate a dispute at the Indianapolis courthouse and post office and attend to other architectural duties. Although Mullett was clearly Rogers's subordinate, he maintained direct communication with Secretary Chase. In April 1863, Mullett wrote to Chase asking to be named chief clerk of the Bureau of Construction "in order that I might determine upon my course, as I had concluded to return to the practice of my profession, unless you could give me that position I requested." If he did not receive the position, Mullett told Chase that he would return to Cincinnati. Mullett cited his investigations of the Indianapolis courthouse as representing a reason why he would leave his position.[75] By spring 1863, Mullett assumed the title of chief clerk, and soon after, first assistant superintendent of the Treasury Extension. By this time, Mullett had assumed the second position in the Office and acted in Rogers's stead during the latter's absence from the office. When Rogers's title was changed to supervising architect in June 1863, Mullett took on the title of assistant supervising architect.

As chief clerk and later assistant supervising architect, Mullett continued to inspect federal buildings. In late 1863, one long tour took him to Cincinnati, St. Louis, Dubuque, Chicago, and Indianapolis. Upon his return, he made a report that found the accommodations for the surveyor at Cincinnati to be "totally inefficient to enable him to discharge the duties of his Office;" the custom house at St. Louis to be in a "disgraceful condition;" the temporary roof of the Dubuque custom house to be "entirely inadequate to preserve the Building from serious injury;" and the custom house in Toledo to be in the "most disgraceful condition I ever saw." As an exception to this lot of buildings, Mullett felt the custom house at Chicago to be in good condition, a credit to the customs collector.[76]

In the spring of 1864, Mullett was detailed to supervise alterations to correct the problems he had observed with the Cincinnati building. The alterations needed to the post office portion were substantial, because it was envisioned that the location of the "ladies delivery window" be changed. Rogers objected to the new location, feeling that it would be a "much more convenient and natural place for disreputable women to congregate and make their assignations than if more publically [sic] placed, as contemplated by me."[77]

The Cincinnati alterations presented the occasion for a protracted dispute between Rogers and Mullett. In June 1864, Rogers visited the Cincinnati building and was surprised to find that the "original and approved plans have been very materially changed, and I think made objectionable, inconvenient and even dangerous." These changes included the placement of steps from the sidewalk to the building; the cutting through of the cast iron columns in the basement; the use of day labor to handle the carpentry work, rather than a regular machine shop of which Cincinnati had many; and the omission of the portico that had been included in Rogers's original design. Rogers recommended to Secretary Chase that the building be placed under the supervision of another person "who would pay more attention to economy as well as to safe construction."[78] Mullett responded to Secretary Chase's successor, William Fessenden, characterizing Rogers's letter as containing "misinterpretations or untruths" and calling for an investigation of Mullett's own conduct in order to exonerate himself from the charges.[79]

In July, Mullett informed Rogers that he was resigning as assistant supervising architect. However, Rogers was unsure about the acceptance of the resignation by Treasury Secretary Fessenden because Mullett then left for a "distant part of the country." Given the apparent departure of Mullett, Rogers requested that Bartholomew Oertly be appointed his assistant supervising architect.[80] In actuality, Mullett was reassigned to San Francisco by Secretary Fessenden to inspect sites for a mint and oversee the repairs to the marine hospitals lo-

cated there. Upon Mullett's return to the office in November, he did
not report or speak to Rogers. As Rogers described the situation to
Fessenden:

> Ever since my disapproval of his management of the alterations
> of the Cincinnati Custom House, and his recall from there in con-
> forming to instructions from your predecessor, Mr. Mullett has
> been greatly incensed at me and has been treating me in such a
> manner that both of us cannot be retained in the positions we now
> occupy. If I am to be sustained I must and do most respectfully ask
> that Mr. Mullett be relieved from duty in this Office, and another
> Assistant appointed.[81]

Circumstances conspired to undermine Rogers's authority. Treasury staff members mailed materials to Mullett without Rogers's approval. In late November 1864, Rogers's office in the Treasury Department was moved. In January 1865, Mullett embarked on a second
trip to San Francisco, this time to prepare plans for the mint and oversee repairs to other federal buildings in the city. Mullett did not return to Washington, D.C., until June. In his absence, Hugh McCulloch had become secretary of the treasury in March 1865. However,
this appointment did not serve to clear the air. From Mullett's diaries
that covered most of 1865, it was clear that he was pressing the
Treasury Department to decide between Rogers and himself. In response to Mullett's request to have his conduct with the Cincinnati
custom house investigated, Assistant Secretary William E. Chandler
concluded, "I do not think that there is any occasion for the continued hostility which exists between these two gentlemen." However,
because the hostility continued and appeared to be "insuperable,"
Chandler recommended to McCulloch that Mullett be detailed to
special duty outside the Treasury Building and report directly to the
secretary.[82] On 3 August 1865, Mullett recorded in his diary that he
wrote a letter to the Secretary about Rogers's handling of the
Treasury extension project."[83] The following day, Mullett recorded
that he wrote another letter about Rogers's management, adding
that when he talked with Secretary McCulloch about the matter, the
secretary thought that Mullett was overly critical of Rogers[84]

The final stroke came in September. Mullett reviewed the estimate
for alterations to the custom house in Louisville, Kentucky, prepared
by John Shaw of the Cincinnati custom house and endorsed by

Rogers. Mullett submitted his proposal for the same work, with a total that was more than $20,000 lower than Shaw's estimate.[85] Mullett's recommendations held and the superintendent at Louisville was instructed to carry out Mullett's plan "under his instructions."[86] This was too much for Rogers. On 20 September, Rogers sent a letter to Secretary McCulloch tendering his resignation as supervising architect, citing "circumstances of peculiar embarrassment beyond my control and preventing that usefulness as an architect to which I have always aspired during my long career of professional life, have rendered my further continuance in the Office impossible."[87] Rogers returned to Cincinnati, where he resided until his death in 1869.

The departure of sixty-five-year-old Rogers left the position of supervising architect open. Mullett, thirty-one-years old, stood ready to succeed his former employer. From his performance over the previous three years in the Treasury Department, he had made his ambitions obvious to his superiors and, no doubt, to his political supporters. The Civil War was over and the nation was returning to peacetime concerns, including the construction of federal buildings. The post-Civil War growth in governmental functions presented an unparalleled opportunity for architectural achievement. Mullett seized the moment and increased public visibility of the federal architecture program to a level that would have astonished his predecessors.

4

ALFRED B. MULLETT

1866–1874

Alfred Bult Mullett is the best known of the fifteen men who served as supervising architect of the Treasury Department. Part of his reputation can be ascribed to the survival and growing appreciation of his sprawling State, War, and Navy Building located on the block just west of the White House. He also personified the supervising architect's near total control over public building design in an era when the architectural profession was becoming defined to the public. Thus, his was a monopoly that drew increasing levels of opposition from the community of private architects, now banded together into the American Institute of Architects (AIA). He was like an entrepreneur—although in this case a bureaucratic operator—in that he fought his enemies bitterly to hold onto his power. Long after Mullett left the Supervising Architect's Office, his name continued to be cited by private architects as representing all that was wrong with federal government architecture.

The rise of Mullett to the position of supervising architect coincided with a period of prosperity and political stability. The buildings designed for federal government purposes were on a scale that dwarfed Ammi B. Young's buildings. As one observer noted, "This transition from the plain and cheap utilitarian to costly art betokens a stage in the national progress where a people believe that they are not bound to the necessities of to-day [sic], but may build for posterity."[1] In large cities, such as New York, Philadelphia, Boston, and St. Louis, these buildings assumed levels of magnificence and grandeur that contrasted with the federal buildings that preceded and immediately followed them. The total array of federal buildings designed under Mullett also display a versatility with a variety of architectural styles. The numbers, scale, and public visibility of these buildings, all associated with Mullett's name, were the cause of increasing alarm among private architects, who were left out of this program. Mullett's success was also his undoing.

The nature of the times—prosperity and governmental growth— was Mullett's springboard. But equally important were Mullett's own ambition and the force of his personality. His triumphant climb to the top of the Supervising Architect's Office was one indication of his ability to persuade his superiors and political allies of the wisdom of his vision. He had an attractive personality that drew friends and supporters to his cause, yet his personal magnetism had a dark side as well. His explosive temper was legendary and found its way into his official correspondence. His climb to and fall from power was not tempered by a philosophical outlook. He never fully accepted his fate, and anger over the circumstances of his removal from office haunted him over the remaining sixteen years of his life.

Mullett's Early Life and Career

Mullett was born in 1834 in Taunton, Somerset County, England, the eldest son in a family engaged in farming and the running of a dry-goods store in town. Drawn by the attractive prospects of the United States, the Mullett family left their native country in 1844 and settled in Glendale, a town to the north of Cincinnati. There they farmed while Mullett attended Farmers' College, an institution founded in 1833 as Cary's Academy and later incorporated into the University of Cincinnati. Farmers' College was described as "an institution of learning especially suited to the wants of the agricultural and business community."[2] In 1854, in his sophomore year, Mullett left the school at his own request, having studied mathematics and mechanical drawing.[3] During Mullett's formative years, Cincinnati was a young upstart boom settlement, dubbed the "Queen City of the West." Proud of its achievements in manufacturing and the creative arts, Cincinnati held major exhibitions to display items produced there. The Ohio Mechanics Institute emerged as another center of architectural training in the 1850s. It is not certain that Mullett enrolled in any of the Institute's courses, although evening lectures on architectural topics were open to the general public.[4] The Institute also supported a library and reading room that contained a collection of architectural books.[5]

What Mullett did between leaving school in 1854 and entering Isaiah Rogers's firm in 1856 is unknown. Family lore credits him with designing an Episcopal church before his twentieth year.[6] It is likely that he moved from Glendale to Cincinnati proper during the period 1854 to 1856. From 1856 to 1860, as has been described, he worked as an architect in the firm of Isaiah Rogers, Son & Co., first as an apprentice and later as a partner. By 1860, Mullett had struck out on his own. Clearly, Mullett had made his mark on the city and was not as some later claimed, "an obscure draftsman" from Cincinnati.[7]

In late 1860, Mullett made an extended sojourn through Europe. He visited his English relatives and embarked for the Continent on 13 October. His European diary concludes on 7 December, 1860. During the European trip, Mullett traveled through France, Belgium, and Germany, making special note of the cathedrals and the appearance of cities and towns that he visited. Although the diary contains occasional references to Cincinnati, Mullett made no mention of Rogers. One can assume that his former employer was no longer a factor in his life.[8]

Mullett brought to the Supervising Architect's Office a network of political supporters that stretched from Ohio to Washington, D.C. He had practiced architecture at least since 1856 and had taken at least one grand tour of the Old World. In September 1865, Mullett married Pearl Pacific Myrick, a daughter of a ship captain and ship owner, whom he met several months before on his way from San Francisco back to Washington, D.C. Mullett was also a firm Republican, an essential qualification for government employment during the Civil War and its immediate aftermath.

As for personal qualities, Mullett brought with him a voracious appetite for work and a willingness to devote long hours to the tasks before him. He also possessed a realistic view of the operation of bureaucracies and the influences exerted upon them by highly placed politicians. In short, he knew how to get political supporters to intercede at high levels on his behalf. Privately, however, he suffered from melancholy. During the fateful year of 1865, he felt deeply the loss of two of his brothers, Frank and Augustine, who had died in 1864.[9]

When Rogers departed from the Treasury Department in September 1865, Mullett did not take on the title of supervising architect for another eight months. In the interim, he continued as assistant architect and was assigned to projects outside the Treasury Building. Bartholomew Oertly was appointed acting assistant architect and was charged with the work of the supervising architect except that which was assigned to Mullett. During these months, Mullett's political friends rallied to his cause to be appointed supervising architect. Secretary McCulloch appointed Mullett supervising architect effective 1 June 1866.

Mullett at the Helm of the Supervising Architect's Office

Adept at the operation of bureaucracies, Mullett knew how to enlarge his architectural office. He witnessed the expansion of building operations from the lean years of the Civil War era to its rapid expansion under President Ulysses S. Grant. In his first annual report, in 1866, Mullett described the scope of his office's work as being "principally confined to the repair, remodelling and completion of the different buildings under the control of the department."[10] Plans were being prepared for ten new buildings. By 1874, when Mullett left the position of supervising architect, he had supervised the design and construction of approximately forty new buildings, including the massive federal buildings in New York, St. Louis, Boston, Chicago, Philadelphia, Cincinnati, and San Francisco, as well as the new State, War, and Navy Building in Washington.

Mullett was a party to the increase in the number of buildings under his supervision. He derided the buildings constructed by his predecessors and urged the construction of new edifices in their place. He also was careful to keep under his control projects that might have gone to private architects or other federal agencies. And, as some cities were beneficiaries of new federal buildings, other cities observed the benefits of construction and also lobbied for new buildings. In the end, the workload became overwhelming and far exceeded one man's ability to maintain personal oversight of each construction and repair project.

Mullett dismissed the structures of his predecessors as plain and inefficient. He noted in his first annual report that he endeavored to avoid the "repetition of style and design so common heretofore, that, while exhibiting a poverty of idea, has retarded instead of encouraged the cultivation of correct taste and a love of art, without effecting the slightest saving, except in the labors of the designer."[11] Mullett characterized the buildings constructed since 1853 as failures, most exhibiting "an almost incredible lack of judgement and architectural knowledge."[12] However, he felt that the Savannah custom house, designed by John Norris, while "scarcely in accordance with modern taste," was a "well constructed and durable building." The postal facilities of the Savannah building were located in the basement level, a plan Mullett described as "inconvenient and unfit for the purpose as can well be imagined."[13]

Mullett credited his former employer Isaiah Rogers with calling attention to the buildings' defects but faulted Rogers for adopting a "system of temporary expedients and cheap work that remedied none of them [the defects] permanently, but in effect continued the original errors, [and] under the guise of economy maintained a system of waste and extravagance."[14] According to Mullett, these defects included the use of corrugated iron roofs. Mullett reported that many of these roofs would be removed and replaced with copper ones.

He justified the need for new buildings in citing not only the defects in their design and construction, but also the inadequacy of their accommodations. A case in point was the Chicago custom house and post office. When it was constructed in the 1850s, this building was considered to be on the outskirts of the business center and "entirely too large for the present or prospective wants of the government, and extravagant in cost and construction." Just over a decade later, the building found itself in the heart of the business district and too small for the demands made upon it. When compared with the "ornate buildings" that surrounded it, Mullett considered the building to be "plain and unassuming."[15] In another example, Mullett cited the post office in Philadelphia as being too small for a city of its size and not fireproof."[16] The Pittsburgh courthouse was "perhaps the worst and most unsightly building of any importance under charge of this office," as well as "wretched" and a "disgrace to the government."[17]

Another justification for a new federal building was the construction of new buildings in localities intended to house state or local government functions. For example, when the "new and magnificent" state capitol building was being erected in Albany, New York, Mullett urged that a new federal building be constructed in that city: "It

hardly comports with the dignity of the United States to have its officers provided in such a shabby manner, when the state and local officers have suitable and secure buildings in which to transact their business and deposit their records."[18] Mullett also felt that state capital
cities should receive special and equal attention in decisions about
federal buildings. When discussing the need for a new federal building at Atlanta, Georgia, Treasury Secretary William A. Richardson,
speaking for Mullett, pointed out that not only was Atlanta "one of
the most important and flourishing cities in the South but is the
Capital of the state of Georgia, and it would appear invidious and
unjust to erect a building inferior in architectural importance and
value to the buildings that have been erected in the capitals of other
states."[19]

Population growth was another reason for constructing new federal buildings. Mullett described the situation at Fall River, Massachusetts:

> It is proper to remark that the city of Fall River has suddenly risen
> from a country village of 3,000 or 4,000 inhabitants into the largest
> cotton manufacturing city in the United States, where over
> 1,000,000 spindles will soon be in operation and which will when
> the mills now in progress of erection are completed, number a
> population of at least 50,000.[20]

Mullett's Political Allies

In moving building projects from the stage of recommendations to
appropriations, Mullett made use of his political supporters. Once
requests were handled, these supporters expected that business establishments in their districts would receive contracts for the construction of federal buildings and that their friends would be employed on construction projects. Some of the most important
political figures in the workings of the Supervising Architect's Office
during this period were from Maine, such as Lot M. Morrill, Hannibal
Hamlin, and in particular, James G. Blaine.

Blaine entered Congress in 1863 and became Speaker of the House
in 1869. In 1876, Blaine filled Lot M. Morrill's unexpired term in the
U.S. Senate when the latter became secretary of the treasury. Blaine
was later elected to the Senate on his own and on several occasions
was a leading candidate for the presidency. A charismatic speaker and

powerful political figure, Blaine was a key person in Mullett's success as supervising architect. Both the secretary of the treasury and Mullett looked to Blaine to guide appropriations for new buildings and repairs of existing buildings through the House of Representatives. Mullett also kept Blaine closely informed of the progress of construction on federal buildings in Maine.

In exchange for Blaine's support, Mullett was expected to perform personal favors for him. One of the most enduring favors of the period was Mullett's agreement to hire Rodney L. Fogg, one of Blaine's friends, on federal building projects. These favors were repeated many times for other political supporters. It is clear that the progress of public building construction could be ascribed as much to the abilities and energy of the supervising architect as to the situations imposed upon him by political leaders.

In 1868, Mullett wrote to Blaine, agreeing to employ Fogg as a foreman on the repairs to the custom house at the Suspension Bridge site in New York City.[21] Evidently, Fogg's performance did not meet Mullett's standards, because he sent Blaine a copy of an independent report on Fogg's superintendency of the New York City project. As Mullett related, "I do not doubt his integrity and believe him to be a fair workman but it is absolutely necessary that he should take more interest in the work and drive things with more vigor than he has done or his superintendency will be but a repetition of similar failures." Mullett urged Blaine to "aide me in stirring him up to a proper sense of his responsibilities."[22] Later, Fogg was appointed timekeeper at Dix Island, Maine, where granite was cut for the massive New York post office. Mullett had originally opposed the appointment because, as he explained to Blaine, clerical work was not Fogg's forte.[23] Although he was supplied with clerical assistance, Fogg's performance on the job was less than satisfactory to Mullett, who wrote that work was proceeding too slowly and at too high a cost. Mullett urged Fogg to lower costs, adding, "I have not in any way stinted you of assistance and your contingencies are certainly large enough to suit the most extravagant."[24] When Fogg's cutters began sending cut stone to the site of the New York post office for the second story of the building instead of the stone necessary to complete the first story, Mullett remarked, "I consider such conduct simply disgraceful."[25]

Another of Mullett's political supporters was Alexander R. Shepherd, president of the Board of Public Works and later governor of the short-lived Territory of the District of Columbia. Shepherd operated a successful building supply business, engaged in real estate speculation, and became involved in local politics. From 1870 to the end of Mullett's tenure as supervising architect in 1874, Shepherd represented the Vaux Anti-Freezing Pipe and Roofing Company. This firm was named for Ethan P. Vaux, a former "master machinist" with the Treasury Department and an individual whom Mullett described as a "first class machinist, plumber, and gas fitter" and "in whose judgement I have great confidence."[26] At a more forthright moment, Mullett characterized Vaux as an honest and honorable man, but on the "high road to ruin in company with a whiskey bottle."[27]

The Vaux Company specialized in a patented copper roof design. The Vaux copper roofs replaced the galvanized iron roofs that had been put on federal buildings in the 1850s and which had been so derided by Mullett. Although Shepherd was listed as the treasurer of the Vaux Company, he actually managed the teams of workmen, including Vaux, who were dispatched across the country to replace the iron roofs. While Mullett was procuring building elements through Shepherd, he was also serving with the latter on the Board of Public Works during 1871 and 1872. Mullett rationalized the arrangement between his office and the Vaux Company. As he stated to Treasury Secretary George S. Boutwell, the company was "honest" and provided the cheapest metallic roofs used by the government. Although he preferred slate, copper was used for decks of mansard roofs "in which the span is so great as to preclude the use of slate."[28]

The political pall cast upon nearly all activity in the capital city led Mullett in 1867 to write to George D. Whittle, Deputy Assistant Treasurer in Boston, "Your telegram [arrived] declining to visit this wicked place for which refusal I feel sorry but shall console myself with the reflection that you are spared the perils of the sea."[29]

Mullett's Architectural Associates

While Mullett's governmental career hung in a delicate political balance, it was also marked by increasing tension with the architectural profession. However, he worked successfully with several nationally recognized architects. One of these architects was Gridley J. F. Bryant, who in 1869 was appointed superintendent of the post office and subtreasury building in Boston. Mullett referred to Bryant's appointment as a "credit to the government."[30] By the end of his administration, Mullett might have thought less of Bryant's administrative skills, but he maintained a cordial relationship throughout. Another noted architect of the times, John McArthur Jr., served as superintendent of repairs for federal buildings in Philadelphia and later as superintendent of the new post office there. Samuel Hannaford, a well-known Cincinnati architect, served as superintendent of the new custom house located in his city, and Edmund G. Lind, well-known architect of Baltimore, served as superintendent of repairs to the Mobile, Alabama, custom house.

Mullett also employed recognized architects in his regular staff. In 1869, Mullett hired architect William P. P. Longfellow of Boston as assistant architect. Mullett described Longfellow as an "accomplished architect and gentleman" who enjoyed the "confidence and esteem of Hon. Charles Sumner and other distinguished men of Massachusetts." Mullett characterized Longfellow's job as consisting of supervising the draftsmen and preparing "original sketches under my direction and by this means enable me to obtain that close inspection and supervision of the draftsmen and their drawings so necessary to avoid error and economize labor."[31] After two years, Longfellow resigned his position, causing Mullett to respond, "While I regret that your business makes it necessary for you to sever your connection with the Office, I of course cannot ask you to sacrifice your personal interests to remain."[32] After Longfellow's departure, Mullett hired F. W. Chandler, also of Boston, as assistant architect. Chandler stayed with the job until shortly before Mullett's own removal at the end of 1874. Later, Chandler became head of the architecture school at the Massachusetts Institute of Technology. In the waning days of his administration, Mullett appointed James G. Hill as assistant architect, in appreciation of the latter's many years of service. Hill had worked in the Office since 1867, at which time Mullett referred to him as a "very able and efficient young man."[33]

Mullett also maintained a cordial relationship with Thomas U. Walter, former architect of the Capitol dome and extension and a leading figure in AIA. Because of Walter's professional stature, however, he was viewed as a competitor—a potential architect of a federal building that Mullett preferred to keep under his control. The prime project to which Walter laid claim was the design for the new State, War, and Navy Building to be located to the west of the Executive Mansion, later called the White House. At President Millard Fillmore's request, Walter had prepared designs for the building in 1852 and revised them in 1854. Walter also prepared updated designs in 1870 because of what he referred to as "added culture, and increased experience in architecture"[34] since his designs of the 1850s.

There is some question as to whether or not Mullett wanted to add the State, War, and Navy Building to his already heavy workload. However, Mullett wrote to Walter in the fall of 1869 that there was "no prospect for the erection of a new War Department at present." He instead offered Walter the job of examining "that miserable abortion called the New Orleans Custom House" and preparing plans for its completion.[35] Walter declined the assignment. While Mullett was discouraging Walter's interest in the new State, War, and Navy Building, he was also writing to Senator Joshua Mix regarding the location of the building and his expectation that he would be consulted on architectural questions.[36] Later in 1871, when Congress made the first appropriation for the building, Walter wrote to Mullett, stating "If it would not interfere either with you or Mr. Clark [architect of the Capitol], I would like to be the architect of that work."[37] Walter's vehicle for returning to the capital city did not materialize because, as he noted, Mullett had the "inside track."[38]

Mullett's constellation of professional associates included former Civil War battlefield artist Henri Lovie, who prepared presentation drawings of many Mullett-designed federal buildings, and William J. McPherson, an interior decorator from Boston, who prepared designs for rooms at the White House and other federal buildings and whom Mullett described as possessing "exquisite taste"[39] and as "the most accomplished architectural decorator in the United States."[40] Also among Mullett's Washington, D.C., associates was Adolf Cluss, who served as superintendent of the District of Columbia jail for which Mullett prepared designs. John L. Smithmeyer, a superintendent of repairs under Mullett, had a falling out with his supervisor and left the Office to enter the private sector. Smithmeyer later formed an architectural partnership with Paul Pelz and initiated lobbying efforts to persuade the U. S. Congress to break the architectural monopoly held by the supervising architect. Mullett's subordinates included Bartholomew Oertly, who left the office in 1869 and whom Mullett referred to as a "scoundrel"[41] over accounting and measurement errors. James C. Rankin entered the office in 1868 and rose to the position of assistant supervising architect, a job that put him in charge of the preparation of estimates and the examination of monthly reports. Rankin later became superintendent of the new custom house in Chicago—the work which, above all others, led to Mullett's downfall. Mullett also hired Count Richard Von Ezdorf as a draftsman, whose interiors for the State, War, and Navy building won him considerable acclaim, and William G. Steinmetz, the assis-

tant superintendent of the New York post office and later a partner
with Mullett in an architectural firm in New York in the 1880s.

Mullett clearly relished his position as supervising architect, but
he also saw its limitations. As he related to Smithmeyer when the latter was superintendent of repairs to the Toledo federal building, "In
my opinion the only value of a position such as yours or mine to a
competent and honest man is a chance to display his qualifications
and to ultimately obtain private employment at renumerative
prices."[42] He did not view his office as appropriate for training apprentice architects, as he required only "first class draftsmen." The
Office of the Supervising Architect was "one of the poorest schools
for anyone desiring to learn anything of architecture and drawing. I
have no time to show anyone myself and the time of all my draftsmen is so fully engaged in keeping up with the work that they cannot act as instructors."[43]

Mullett's hard-driving work habits and standards of work predis-
posed him to relate best to subordinates possessed of similar drives,
many of whom were of German origin. As Edward W. Donn Jr. later
related:

> A. B. Mullett when supervising architect of the Treasury Depart-
> ment had his office filled with german [sic] draftsmen and they are
> [sic] responsible for the State, War and Navy Building. Some of
> these old german draftsmen were still in the Supervising
> Architect's Office when I became a draftsman in that office under
> James Knox Taylor and Edward A. Crane. This was in 1901.[44]

Mullet was also viewed by critics as an authoritarian administrator.
"Mullett was not one of those persons who are diffident about skip-
ping in where angels fear to tread. He ruled his office with a rod of
iron. His finger was in every pie."[45]

While Mullett made his home in Washington, D.C., he maintained strong ties with his former associates in Ohio. Chief among
them was Colonel John F. Morse of Painesville, Ohio, who served as
superintendent of several of the more troublesome building projects.
From one such project, the Ogdensburg, New York, custom house,
Morse threatened to resign. Mullett urged him to stick with the project as he was "compelled to draw upon your friendship to me which
I have never doubted and wish you would never doubt mine."[46]
Mullett also employed Garrett Barry of Cincinnati, another Ohio
friend. Barry had worked as a designer and modeler for Mullett in

Cincinnati. Once in Washington, D.C., however, Barry proved a poor worker, left the office "very unceremoniously," and forced Mullett to locate a replacement.[47]

Mullett's most important Ohio connection was John M. Mueller, who provided Buena Vista sandstone for several federal buildings. This connection was also Mullett's greatest headache, because Mueller provided stone for the disastrous Chicago custom house. According to Mullett in a letter to Jonas Gies, superintendent of the custom house and post office in Omaha, Nebraska, Buena Vista stone was used for buildings in several major U.S. cities. Mueller furnished the best quality of the stone.[48] When bids for furnishing the stone for the Chicago custom house were reviewed, Mullett persuaded Secretary George S. Boutwell of the superior quality of Mueller's stone and the extensive use of the stone in Cincinnati.[49] The Secretary agreed and Mueller's proposal was accepted.

Of all the working relationships that Mullett found problematic, the most troublesome was with the superintendents of construction. Part of Mullett's difficulty lay with the dispersed nature of the building projects and the inability to keep a constant eye on the progress of the works from afar. The frequent replacements of superintendents due to personnel changes at the Treasury Department or to poor performance left the Supervising Architect's Office as the sole anchor of continuity in constructing a building. As Mullett noted in 1866, he had difficulty in locating competent and experienced superintendents. To remedy the situation, Mullett recommended:

> dividing the country into districts and appointing competent professional men as resident architects in each, whose duty it will be to make the necessary examinations and reports and to superintend the execution of the work within their districts. I feel confident that as a matter of economy in salaries alone such an arrangement would prove more beneficial than the present system and must ultimately be adopted.[50]

Failing the creation of such a system, Mullett urged that the superintendent positions be made permanent so that upon the completion of one building, the superintendents could be transferred to another project.[51] Mullett's idea of regional architects did not take root until many years later, in the form of a regional office system of the General Services Administration, which also decentralized the Public Buildings Service.

Mullett's public views on the qualifications for superintendents may have antagonized the architectural profession. Because he felt that the duties of the superintendents were "onerous and exacting," he thought they should not be allowed to work on private business at the same time:

> It is true that the appointment of gentlemen of high social standing, who have a large and lucrative private business, may nominally secure the services of trustworthy and talented persons; but as the duties of superintendents require . . . the entire time of just such talent as is necessary to overcome and supervise the execution of the plans of an architect, it is but proper that gentlemen accepting the superintendence of public buildings should understand that their entire time will be demanded by the work under their charge.[52]

Mullett also felt that he should be permitted to appoint superintendents according to his own judgment rather than according to the endorsements of the congressional delegation.

Major Public Building Projects

The best-known Mullett buildings were the large Second Empire piles located in large cities, such as the post office in New York City, the custom house in Chicago, the custom house and post office in St. Louis, and the State, War, and Navy Building in Washington. In smaller cities, Mullett's work demonstrated variations on the French theme and an ability to execute designs in other styles.

One of the first considerations in the design of federal buildings was its location within a community. Based upon experience with several major urban fires in the 1850s and 1860s, Mullett thought that stone and iron construction had proven unsuccessful in resisting such conflagrations. He recommended that "all government buildings should be isolated by wide streets or open spaces." Viewing the location of buildings in the 1850s, he thought that site selections were not "made with regard to the architectural necessities, but has been directed by local preferences, or the views of persons incompetent to decide such questions."[53] Mullett also stressed the importance of securing "good light on all sides of the building" and convenience of location to a "large majority of the inhabitants of the various places."[54]

Mullett's design philosophy, as publicly stated, was guided by the "wants of the public service" and the "peculiarities of locality, climate, materials, and to the importance of the structures." He endeavored to vary the style of architecture in order to "avoid monotony and repetition." In regard to the special demands of public buildings, he sought to make each building convenient, durable, and creditable to the government.[55] As he stated:

> Experience having demonstrated that cheaply constructed buildings, though costing less at first, are the most costly in the end, I have endeavored to secure the best, most substantial, and permanent structures, and have not attempted to exhibit economy by the use of inferior materials, or at the expense of the quality of the work.[56]

To make his architectural designs more tangible, Mullett commissioned renderings of his buildings, such as those made by Henri Lovie. As Mullett wrote to Lovie, the objectives of having these renderings were to satisfy himself that the building would be a success in mass and details; to satisfy the Treasury officials, the congressional delegation, and others that the building would look well; and to produce a drawing that could be reproduced widely in order to satisfy individuals who did not have access to the original drawings. These renderings were published in Mullett's annual reports to the secretary of the treasury.[57]

Mullett's earliest designs for a new federal building were for the mint in San Francisco (figure 4.1). They were developed during Mullett's 1865 trip to the West Coast, although construction was not started until 1869. The mint was designed in the classical revival style with a Roman Doric portico. The building is reminiscent of Robert Mills's public buildings in Washington, D.C., of the 1830s, such as the Patent Office and the Treasury building. The only other classical revival building designed by Mullett was the courthouse and post office at Portland, Maine, built 1867 to 1873 (figure 4.2). In light of the prevailing architectural trends of the 1870s, the classical San Francisco mint was an exception and is credited as the "last major example of classical revival architecture" in America.[58]

The evolution of Mullett's association with the Second Empire style followed a circuitous path. The project that may have had the greatest influence on his "adoption" of this style was the New York post office and court house. As an exception to the established prac-

Figure 4.1
U.S. Branch Mint, San
Francisco, California,
1869–1874, Alfred B.
Mullett. Courtesy
National Archives.

tice regarding the design of federal buildings, John T. Hoffman, the mayor of New York City, headed a commission appointed to acquire a design for this new building through competition. This procedure may have occurred due to the influence exerted on the Congress by the AIA, which by 1867 was a ten-year-old organization located in New York City and was composed primarily of architects who resided in that city. The holding of a competition may also have been influenced by the competition held for the New York state capitol at Albany, which resulted in a Second Empire design by Thomas Fuller and subsequent alterations by the architects Leopold Eidlitz and Henry Hobson Richardson. The size of the contemplated building in New York City may also have been a factor; the Supervising Architect's Office had not handled a building of that scale since the design of the Treasury Building extensions.

The announcement of the New York post office competition drew criticism from the AIA, which objected to the site—a portion of the park adjacent to New York city hall, an area judged to be of value as "open breathing space" and on "artistic grounds." The site also suffered from being located astride "two most thronged thoroughfares of the city."[59] The AIA also made suggestions regarding the amount of information available on the requirements of the building, the length of time necessary to prepare plans, the need for a public exhibition of the drawings, the ultimate ownership of the plans,

Figure 4.2
U.S. courthouse,
Portland, Maine, 1866–
1873, Alfred B. Mullett.
Courtesy National
Archives.

and the size of the fees to be paid to the winning architect. These suggestions went unheeded. Because of what the AIA judged to be unfavorable conditions, many prominent architects did not submit designs for the building. Eventually fifty-two designs were submitted. However, none of them was considered to be satisfactory and no award was made. As the *New York Evening Post* reported:

> There is not one design among those shown for the Post office [*sic*] which has the artistic expression of the purpose for which the building is erected. . . . All of the incongruities of the Renaissance from the Louvre down to the country meeting-house are, as it were, carted together in piles of either the most erratic irregularity, without meaning and repose, or the most distressing monotony, without expression or character.[60]

After the competition debacle, the commission employed five architectural firms to produce a single design. These firms included Renwick & Sands, Napoleon LeBrun, Schulze & Schoen, Richard M. Hunt, and John Perret. The collaborative design was in the French Second Empire style (figure 4.3), a style that James Renwick Jr. had used successfully with the Corcoran Gallery of Art in Washington in the late 1850s. The Second Empire style had also been used in the

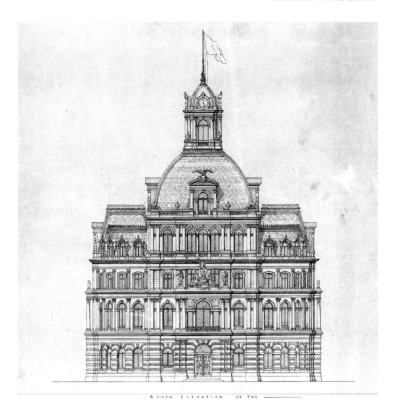

SOUTH ELEVATION OF THE

early 1860s by Gridley J. F. Bryant and Arthur Gilman for the Boston
city hall. John McArthur Jr. adopted the style for the Philadelphia city
hall, as would other architects from the 1860s to the 1880s. The collaborative design appears to have served as the basis for Mullett's own
design for the building, published in May 1868. He wrested control
over the building by persuading the interested parties that all of the
plans submitted were for buildings that exceeded the appropriation.[61] This maneuver infuriated the private architects who con-
demned Mullett's building as a "blot on the landscape," "dark and dis-
mal," and "an ugly backdrop for the beautiful simplicity of City Hall
park."[62] Other reviewers, however, judged the New York $8.5 million
post office to be one of Mullett's best buildings in a collection of
"masterpieces of mediocrity"[63] (figures 4.4 and 4.5).

  With the "success" of the Second Empire style, Mullett applied it
to large federal buildings in other cities, such as the post office and
subtreasury in Boston designed in 1869, the custom house and post
office in Chicago in 1871 (figure 4.6), the custom house and post office

Figure 4.3
New post office and
United States courts,
New York, New York,
Renwick & Sands,
Napoleon LeBrun,
Schulze & Schoen,
Richard M. Hunt, and
John Perret, ca. 1867.
Courtesy National
Archives.

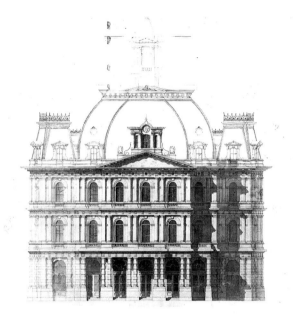

Figure 4.4
U.S. post office and
courthouse, New York,
New York, 1869–1880,
Alfred B. Mullett.
Courtesy National
Archives.

in St. Louis in 1871, the post office in Philadelphia in 1872 (figure 4.7), and the courthouse and post office in Cincinnati in 1874. Although private architects expressed loathing for these buildings, local press and guidebooks exuded enthusiasm for the imposing buildings and pride in their contributions to the architectural development of their communities.

While plans were being produced for these large buildings, Mullett and his staff designed a large number of modest buildings for smaller communities. In established communities, he designed variations on the French and Italian styles. Some designs, such as those for the courthouse and post office building in Madison, Wisconsin, and Raleigh, North Carolina, were somewhat reminiscent of the Italian Renaissance federal buildings of the 1850s, although on a grander scale and with French motifs, such as mansard roofs. Other buildings, such as the courthouse and post office in Hartford, Connecticut, resembled scaled-down versions of the larger Second Empire buildings (figure 4.8). Still other buildings, such as the custom house and post office in Port Huron, Michigan, maintained a heavy classical flavor despite the French-styled dome.

In less-established areas, such as Nevada and Idaho, buildings took on a rough-hewn "territorial" character. The stone-walled mint in

Carson City, Nevada, designed in 1865, resembles an academic build-ing on a major land-grant college (figure 4.9). It served as the model for the Nevada state capitol building. The assay office in Boise, Idaho, was also a modest stone building. The appearance of these buildings may have been due to the local supply of building materials and to the expectations of these young communities as much as to their lo-cation. The modest assay office in Boise inspired pride on the part of the inhabitants for "this important Government building in their midst."[64] The granite custom house and post office in Rockland, Maine, may have been a function of its small size as well as the mod-est scale of the surrounding buildings.

Figure 4.5
U.S. post office and courthouse, New York, New York, 1869–1880, Alfred B. Mullett. Courtesy National Archives.

Figure 4.6
U.S. custom house and
post office, Chicago,
Illinois, designed 1871,
Alfred B. Mullett, with
alterations by William
Appleton Potter.
Courtesy Chicago
Historical Society.

The range of architectural expression was common among many architects of the day, despite the strong "typecasting" of architects with a particular style. In fact, in 1871, while Thomas U. Walter was still expressing hope of being appointed architect of the new State, War, and Navy Building and soliciting Mullett's aide in obtaining the position, he stated that he was "inclined to favor a classic building, in general harmony with its companion, the Treasury, simply because its relationship to that structure seems to call for it." However, noting the prevailing taste in favor of the French style, Walter was prepared to make designs in this style as well that would "balance the Treasury in general outline."[65]

Mullett's Public Buildings in Washington, D.C.

Unlike many supervising architects, Mullett left an indelible imprint on the architecture of Washington, D.C. This legacy is due to his de-

Figure 4.7
U.S. courthouse and post office, Philadelphia, Pennsylvania, 1874–1884, Alfred B. Mullett. Courtesy National Archives.

sign for the State, War, and Navy Building, a project that initially was not under his jurisdiction. The discussions revolving around the State, War, and Navy Building during the late 1860s and early 1870s presented an ambiguous picture as to who would design the building. In late 1866, the War Office invited architects to submit designs for the new building. Architects from across the nation responded in a joint petition, saying that few architects "who have attained a high standing in the profession" would be submitting drawings. The reasons for this position included the question of responsibility for superintending the building's construction, the payment for services, and the ownership of the drawings. The architects concluded their petition, urging

the proposed new War Office . . . to be a work of National Importance, and one in which, it is needless to say, every citizen is interested. Therefore we appeal to you as citizens, as well as professional men deeply interested in all that pertains to artistic progress, to do all in your power to secure for the important building that you have in view, a design that will best express the character and intelligence of the age in which we live.[66]

Figure 4.8
U.S. courthouse and post office, Hartford, Connecticut, 1873–1882, Alfred B. Mullett. Courtesy National Archives.

A commission composed of representatives from the three departments to be housed in the building initiated discussions, advised by Edward Clark, architect of the Capitol, and Mullett. Plans for the new building had been long postponed, due first to the Civil War and then in the late 1860s to prospects that the seat of the federal government might be moved from its Potomac River site to a new location closer to the center of the country. Given the latter possibility, Thomas U. Walter judged in November 1869, "It seems altogether probable that Congress will appropriate as little as possible for public works in Washington."[67] By March 1870, however, interested parties, including Senator Justin S. Morrill, chairman of the Commitee on Public Buildings and Grounds, reviewed a "sketch of

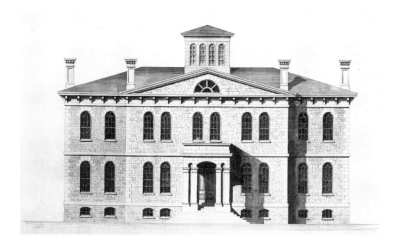

the new State Department."[68] This sketch may have been the one produced by Walter or a new one by Mullett. Later that month, Treasury Secretary George S. Boutwell instructed Mullett to prepare sketches for the new building and to confer with Secretary of State Hamilton Fish on the project. Mullett then wrote to Secretary Fish, asking him for his "views in regard to the material of which it is to be erected or the style of the same."[69]

By March 1871, Walter, unaware that Mullett had been asked to design the new State, War, and Navy Building, was still maintaining correspondence on the subject with the supervising architect as well as with his former subordinate, Edward Clark. Clark professed no desire to be connected with the project in any way.[70] Later, when it appeared that Mullett would be the designer of the building, Walter decided that the only way for him to wrest control of the project from Mullett was to persuade Secretary Fish to take the project out of Mullett's hands "on the ground that he has entirely too much to do without, and to appoint me the Architect thereof, as the execution of that building rightly belongs to me, and with my whole attention devoted to it, exclusively, it would be worth far more to the government."[71] Mullett turned aside Walter's pleas on the basis that the latter was not as proficient with the Renaissance styles as the more classic methods of Greece and Rome.[72] Mullett had effected this "typecasting" of Walter in his 1868 annual report when he praised the design of the Treasury building and Walter, "whose knowledge of classic architecture is probably unsurpassed by any living architect."[73]

Figure 4.9
U.S. Branch Mint, Carson City, Nevada, 1865–1870, Alfred B. Mullett. Courtesy National Archives.

The construction of the State, War, and Navy Building began in 1871 and continued to its completion in 1888 (figure 4.10). To some critics, the building was "in fact a pleasing structure, by far the most satisfactory that emanated from the office under [Mullett]." There was speculation that the building was actually the work of William P. P. Longfellow, who served as assistant architect when the plans were being formulated. In regards to Mullett's suit in the U. S. Court of Claims in the 1880s to receive compensation for his work on the State, War, and Navy Building (which he considered to be a responsibility above and beyond his duties as supervising architect), Longfellow noted that he had "worked at the drafting board on the preliminary drawings under 'Mullett's explicit instructions and criticism'."[74]

Mullett described the new State, War, and Navy Building as being in the "French style" in the treatment of the masses "with central and corner pavilions joined by curtains" and the mansard roof. The details, however, are "everywhere treated with the simplicity of the Classical Italian," as superfluous ornamentation was "avoided." The

Figure 4.10
State, War, and Navy
Building, Washington,
D.C., 1871–1888, Alfred B.
Mullett. Courtesy
National Archives.

design depended more on harmonious proportions and carefully studied masses and on the workmanship of the building materials. Only the Roman Doric order was used in the belief that "enough variety is attained in the different stories by the necessary modifications in regard to their height from the ground." The pavilions received special treatment; their upper stories are "surmounted by sculptured pediments, above which rises a Mansard roof with heavily moulded copper pieces and curb, with a rich cresting above." The granite in the basement was from Maine and presented a dark surface, contrasting with the granite from Richmond, Virginia, for the upper stories, which was of a lighter color.[75]

Mullett's other major works in the capital city included the completion of the Treasury Building's north wing and the design and construction of the D.C. jail. Mullett credited Walter with the designs for the extension of the Treasury Building beyond the original east wing designed by Robert Mills. In his 1867 annual report, Mullett noted that, "It has been my effort to carry out the architectural features of the building as nearly as possible in accordance with the original design."[76] Mullett's major deviation from the original plan was the Cash Room in the north wing, intended for the U.S. Treasurer's cashier and assistants. It was the only room in the Treasury Building that would be visited by the general public. In consultation with Treasury officials, "It was considered that this room should in the purity of its design, and by the avoidance of all shams and imitations of materials, be emblematic of the dignity of the nation and the stability of its credit."[77] (figure 4.11).

In 1872, Mullett designed the D.C. jail in accordance with instructions from Columbus Delano, secretary of the interior, because there was no regular design procurement process for such buildings. Its progress was overseen by a commission, on which Alexander R. Shepherd served in his capacity as governor of the District of Columbia. In order to carry out his plan, Mullett hired Adolf Cluss, a former employee of the old Bureau of Construction in the 1850s, as superintendent of construction. In October 1873, Mullett described the jail designs as guided by the strictest economy of construction, absolute security, and proper sanitary arrangements. In all, Mullett thought the jail to be "unsurpassed in quality."[78] Mullett noted:

> It also appeared to be desirable that the exterior appearance of the building should show its use. I have endeavored to embody this idea in the design, and believe that the building will indicate the

Figure 4.11
Cash room, U.S. Treasury
Department,
Washington, D.C., 1869,
Alfred B. Mullett.
Courtesy National
Archives.

purpose for which its is intended, and be a model jail, both as regards its exterior appearance and its internal arrangements.[79]

True to form, Shepherd submitted a proposal to furnish the plumbing work for the new jail.[80]

Mullett offered suggestions for other federal buildings that might
be built in Washington, D.C. They included a brick building for the
printing functions of the Treasury Department and a new building
for the Justice Department and the U.S. Courts as an alternative to accommodating the courts in the Capitol building. He also envisioned
that by the end of the century, "public sentiment will demand the
erection of a new Executive Mansion, though the erection of such a
building would not be considered a necessity in any other point of
view, the present one being a substantial and durable structure,
though undoubtedly rather small." He also predicted the Post Office
would need more space, which could be accommodated by adding
an attic story to the post office building at 7th and F Streets.[81]

The Mounting Workload

An increasing workload resulted from the eagerness of Congress to appropriate funds for new buildings in their districts and from Mullett's desire to protect his authority over design and construction projects. Mullett considered work on the new State, War, and Navy Building to be a responsibility separate and distinct from his job as supervising architect and thus devoted his evenings to this work. Mullett also took on a small number of private architectural commissions on the side, including private design work for former Secretary of the Treasury Salmon P. Chase in 1868.[82]

Mullett made himself accessible to all members of Congress in order to discuss the location, design, and construction of new buildings in their districts. As Mullett related to George Bliss, district attorney from New York City, "My morning hours are under control of members of Congress. . . . Saturday is always my busiest day."[83] At times, he tried to keep members of Congress at bay, claiming in late 1869, "I have never been so terribly overworked in my life as now. . . . it taxes my energies and time to the utmost to keep the post offices in New York and Boston going in a proper measure."[84] In another instance, Mullett remarked upon his return from a strenuous trip to San Francisco, "I was driven to death and detained a week longer than I expected."[85] A delay in sending sketches to the printer prompted Mullett to apologize, adding "you can have little idea of how I have been overworked and tormented of late."[86] Mullett cited his workload when responding to a request for a meeting in Chicago: "I have to say that I have not the slightest idea when I shall be in Chicago, neither can I promise to notify you when I am there as my mind is so much occupied with business that if I made such a promise I should in all probability forget it."[87] Toward the end of his tenure as supervising architect, Mullett described the situation in his office, "The pressure of business in this office is so great that I am barely able to keep the various works in progress."[88]

Mullett proved thin-skinned when the popular press critiqued his buildings. As his edifices sprouted up in many U.S. cities, they attracted the attention of the press. One article in the *North American* on the new appraisers store in Philadelphia, built of pressed brick, caused Mullett to respond:

> I am astonished at the ignorance that exists on questions relating
> to architecture, and am surprised that a journal of so much influ-

ence and ability as the North American [*sic*] should be guilty of publishing such an article. Fitness in architecture is the first qualification that an architect has to consider. In this case, a marble or granite building would lack the most *essential* qualification for a building of the nature designed, viz. absolutely secure against fire.

He also offered to "submit the building to comparisons with any in the country. It will be the finest and most convenient structure of the kind in the country—I believe in the world—and if people will only wait with patience I can convince them that the superstructure will be worthy of the foundations and of the city of Philadelphia."[89]

The AIA Lobbies against Mullett

Mullett's near total monopoly over major federal building projects raised concern among private architects. Between 1857 and 1867, the AIA had persisted as "practically a local society" in New York City. In 1867, however, the organization was reconstituted into a national association with local chapters and began holding annual conventions.[90] For its mission, AIA President Richard M. Upjohn viewed the organization as founded for the "pursuit and communication of such knowledge as is conducive to the development of architecture." Upjohn saw the AIA as a source of public improvement and reform in matters related to architecture and "a helper of civilization."[91] In short order, the AIA turned its attention to the federal architecture program.

Members of the AIA were already suspicious of Mullett after the New York post office and the State, War, and Navy building projects, which were initially to be designed through competition, were added to his growing inventory of undertakings. Walter, who was active in both the earlier American Institution of Architects and the later AIA, thought Mullett should join the AIA. In June of 1869, he wrote to Mullett, "shall McArthur and I propose you?"[92] Mullett did not take Walter up on his offer and increasing criticism from the architectural professional precluded any possibility that he would ever do so.

In March 1869 a curious publication, produced in New York City, emerged; it was signed by "Civis" and was titled "The Office of the Supervising Architect: What It Was, What It Is, and What It Ought to Be." Its contents reflected the attitudes of the AIA, at that time cen-

tered on practitioners in New York. The author was likely Adolf
Cluss; his name was written in one of the copies, and its discussion
of the origins of the Office reflects an insider's knowledge of the
Bureau of Construction during the 1850s and the working of
Mullett's office. The publication pointed out "the existing disorgani-
zation of that important branch of the Treasury Department" and
made suggestions on "its redemption from chaos." The author went
on to criticize the lack of complete sets of drawings and specifications
that had been made available to contractors in the 1850s and the absence of the kinds of tests and experiments on building materials that
had been sponsored during that earlier period. The building designs
of the 1850s, while "recognized as multiples of one and the same architectural motive . . . at least, did not sin against good taste, and followed the precepts of recognized masters of the art." The writer denounced the "one-man system," defects in the management of the
building projects, the lack of standard works on the strength of materials in the Office's library, the high cost of projects, and the inability of the current system to take advantage of the "great amount of
vigor and talent in the profession all through the land." The essential
question was, "Shall this creative genius and learning be shaped and
fettered in Napoleonic fashion, and must our public architecture
needs be bobtailed by a 'mullettizing' process?"[93]

Mullett's Resignation

The arrival of Benjamin H. Bristow as secretary of the treasury in
June 1874 portended the beginning of the end of Mullett's hold on the
position of supervising architect. Bristow was not a member of
President Grant's inner circle, but as solicitor general he had been a
strong supporter of the president. Bristow had a reputation for honesty and integrity, and his appointment promised to bring a cleaner
image to an administration beset by political irregularities and scandals. Soon after Bristow's appointment, Mullett submitted a routine
document for signature. "Bristow, too good a lawyer ever to sign a
document without understanding it, summoned Mullett and questioned him lengthily before approving the order. Mullett was impressed and a trifle shaken by the Secretary's interest in what was going on among his subordinates."[94] One of Bristow's first actions was
to review the design for the office of the assistant treasurer in the new
San Francisco Mint prepared by William J. McPherson. As Mullett in-

formed McPherson, while the secretary liked the design and was willing to pay for it, he felt that the designs should be executed by mechanics in San Francisco.[95] As Bristow reviewed more of Mullett's financial records, he observed practices that favored particular suppliers of building elements, such as Alexander R. Shepherd.

The major issue that led to Mullett's departure from his position was the Chicago custom house. Mullett had sent his former deputy, James C. Rankin, to superintend its construction. However, Mullet was unable to get Rankin to adhere to the regulations in regard to building elements and labor procurement. In addition, the stone supplied by John M. Mueller was of an inferior quality because it was of the wrong color, speckled, and some of it cracked by frost.[96] As Mullett said to Rankin after berating him for being unable to discipline his staff and accepting poor stocks of stone, "You have been led in these irregularities by degrees."[97]

By 1874, press coverage of the work of the Board of Public Works of the Territory of the District of Columbia was extensive. Mullett's brief membership on the board and the ongoing relationship between the Supervising Architect's Office and Alexander R. Shepherd brought Mullett into the spotlight. As one newspaper report stated, "He [Mullett] was undoubtedly the most mischievous member of the Board of Public Works. He encouraged its extravagance and approved its excesses" such as the grading of streets.[98]

By the autumn of that year, public scrutiny of Mullett's work reached a peak with a flood of newspaper articles on his alleged imperious demeanor. No doubt these outpourings were encouraged by the private architects who were still smarting from the loss of the New York post office and the State, War, and Navy Building projects. Mullett's close association with President Grant's administration made him vulnerable to public criticism. The press also found fault with his being of English descent and thus "possessing no sincere respect for the Government of the United States." The press examined the size of the budget administered by Mullett and concluded: "The idea of turning the Treasury Department into a bureau of architects, and giving one man—an utterly incompetent man at that—power to plan and construct all public buildings in the United States, and to disburse $10,000,000 a year, with scarcely a check on him, is simply monstrous."[99]

The growing public storm over Mullett gave the private architects the signal that an auspicious time had arrived for them to make their move. John L. Smithmeyer, who had maintained a poor working re-

lationship with Mullett during his tenure as an employee of the
Supervising Architect's Office, took the first step (figure 4.12). In 1874,
Smithmeyer, together with his business partner, Paul J. Pelz, were enjoying great public recognition for having won the national competition for the new Library of Congress building the previous year. In
October 1874, Smithmeyer submitted a draft plan for the creation of
a "Bureau of Architecture." In submitting his plan, Smithmeyer
stated, "I need not say anything concerning the objectionable features and the detrimental results emanating from the existing architectural monopoly of our government; detrimental to the interest of
the people at large as well as to our profession in particular."[100]

Smithmeyer's plan called for the consolidation of all architectural
activities of the federal government under an Office of the Government Architect, except those that fell under the jurisdiction of the
Army and Navy. To be included in this new office was responsibility
for the Capitol and its related buildings as well as other public buildings and grounds in the capital city. The government architect's func-

Figure 4.12
John L. Smithmeyer.
Courtesy National
Archives.

tions were to be supervisory, with architectural designs to be obtained through open competition according to rules and regulations developed by him. The successful architect would superintend the construction of the building. The AIA printed Smithmeyer's plan and distributed it freely for comment, but further action on this plan did not occur until the following year.

By late 1874, it became apparent that Bristow and Mullett would be unable to work together. While a disagreement over the control of furniture purchases for the Treasury Department was the immediate cause of the break, Mullett's resignation was a reflection of a deeper disagreement between the two men. As a newspaper article reported, "The Secretary says he has no reason to doubt the integrity or ability of Mr. Mullett, but he did not like his manner of doing things, and he thought him extravagant and insubordinate."[101] In his resignation letter dated 21 November 1874, Mullett described some of the circumstances surrounding the difficulties of the recent past. As Mullett wrote to Bristow, "My health is, as you know, broken down. I am consequently nervous, and perhaps more irritable than I am aware of." Mullett also cited the inadequacy of the salary for a position that could be valued only for the "opportunity for making a reputation." In submitting his resignation, Mullett said that he felt a "sense of relief that I have not felt for many years."[102] Secretary Bristow accepted Mullett's resignation, praising the latter's integrity and faithfulness to his official duties. The secretary concluded his letter with the hope that Mullett's return to private life would restore his health.[103]

As Mullett's departure date approached, he assured Asa Snyder, supplier of iron for the State, War, and Navy Building, "I have made arrangements to enter into a much more profitable business."[104] Despite Mullett's efforts to leave on a high note, his letter to a long-time associate, General William L. Burt, custodian of the new Boston post office and subtreasury, related:

> I must confess that your tribulations in regard to the ventilation of the post office are rather amusing, and can assure you that you have my entire sympathy, and I would be with you if I were physically able, which is not, however, the case. I spent yesterday in bed, and am barely able to sit at my desk and answer these letters.[105]

Mullett's resignation was greeted heartily by the press which associated him with the "rings" of corruption that swirled around

President Grant. The *Baltimore Sun* called the resignation of Mullett "the neatest trophy of Secretary Bristow."[106] Another article underscored the "rivalry" between Bristow and Mullett. It reported that "the good looking Kentuckian [Bristow] . . . has labored for months under the delusion which Mr. Mullett endeavored to dispel, to wit: that he was Secretary of the Treasury." When Mullett attempted to apologize and withdraw his resignation, Bristow stuck to his acceptance of it. The effect of the resignation on President Grant's associates was predicted to be great. "Boss Shepherd, whose fat contracts with Mullett are taking bodily shape in newly-constructed edifices all over Washington, made two visits to Grant today to have the matter [the resignation] squelched and let Mullett stay in, but it was too late. . . . This affair is regarded as a very serious blow to the city Ring."[107]

Mullett's Postgovernment Career

The "profitable business" that Mullett entered after his departure from the Treasury Department was as vice president of the Chrome Steel Company, in its Washington, D.C., office. This choice was not out of keeping with Mullett's previous work, as he once described himself as an "architect and engineer."[108] The new position proved short-lived and did not prevent him from becoming entangled in the affairs of his successor.

Within a few weeks, he was engaged in a dispute with his successor, William Appleton Potter, over the ownership of photographs of federal buildings. Later, Mullett claimed that he had given advice and assistance to Potter without charge to the government, but the latter refused all offers of assistance. Mullett characterized Potter as an architect inexperienced in fulfilling the demands of public service. He also decried Potter's attempts to destroy Mullett's legacy and reputation, particularly Potter's efforts to alter his designs and Potter's depiction of the Chicago custom house as so defective that it should be demolished and rebuilt in a different manner.[109]

After Potter's departure in 1876, Mullett applied for reappointment as supervising architect. By that time, he was no longer associated with Chrome Steel. His application was endorsed by thirty-six members of Congress. However, when James G. Hill was appointed, Mullett related that if he "did not know the influence granite companies exert in the state of Maine, the reason for my rejection would remain a mystery to this day."[110] In the heat of speculation as to Potter's successor, Thomas U. Walter wrote to Edward Clark, architect of the Capitol, "I don't see how the President could think for a moment of directing the appointment of Mullett, and I don't see how the Secretary could hesitate for a moment to appoint me."[111] Even after Hill's appointment, Mullett urged Secretary of the Treasury John Sherman that he be returned to his job in "recognition of the principles of civil service."[112] For a short time in 1877, Mullett was appointed superintending architect of several of the major buildings designed under his administration, a position created specially for him (figure 4.13).

In the years that followed, Mullett developed a private practice centered in Washington, D.C. His work also took him to many parts of the country. For a short time in 1882, he was listed in the New York

Figure 4.13
Alfred B. Mullett.
Courtesy the Historical
Society of Washington,
D.C.

City directories as in partnership with architects Hugh Kafka and his former associate, William G. Steinmetz. Also in that year, he was in correspondence with Walter regarding the eastern and western extensions of the Capitol.[113] For several years, he served as a civil commissioner for the U.S. Navy and prepared a report on the management of shipyards.[114] Mullett also designed a great number of commercial, institutional, and residential structures in the capital city. In 1889, when his sons Thomas A. and Frederick W. were of an age to enter professional life, he formed the firm of A. B. Mullett & Co., a firm that endured for nearly fifty years.

Although Mullett remained active in the architectural profession, he never gained much financial stability. His precarious finances were cited by his friends who testified to Mullett's integrity and honesty. Mullett's fortunes were aggravated over the long legal battle to gain compensation of $158,450.91 for his work on the State, War, and Navy Building. On the evening of 20 October 1890, Mullett fatally shot himself at his home. An obituary ascribed his suicide to financial difficulties associated with the construction of three residences on his Washington, D.C., property at 25th and Pennsylvania Avenue, N.W., a severe case of grippe the previous winter, and despondency.[115]

Mullett's death occurred two days before the opening of the twenty-fourth annual meeting of the AIA in Washington, D.C. Mullett's relationship with the AIA had been stormy and the bitter feelings persisted for years after he left the position of supervising architect. Even in 1887, as the Washington Chapter of the AIA was being formed, Mullett was included in the list of architects who should be invited to join the chapter.[116] However, Mullett never joined either the national organization or the local chapter. The discussion of Mullett's death and possible AIA representation at the funeral testified to his alienation from the professional body. Glenn Brown, by then a well-known architect in Washington, D.C., claimed that he was not acquainted with Mullett at all and passed on the question of representation. William M. Poindexter, who was a former employee of the Supervising Architect's Office under Mullett, moved that the entire convention attend the funeral "as a mark of the respect to him and the high office that he formerly held." Others argued that since Mullett was not a member of the AIA, only a committee should be appointed to attend. In the end, only Alfred J. Bloor of New York City, and Samuel Hannaford of Cincinnati, a loyal associate from Ohio, attended the funeral.[117]

On closer examination, however, it is clear that Mullett's work was regarded with greater appreciation. In an obituary that appeared in the *Cincinnati Tribune*, Mullett was credited as the "author of the best feature of the plan of public improvements which were adopted under the Shepherd regime and in various ways has done much for the development of the National Capital."[118] Even the cream of the architectural profession gave his architecture belated praise. For example, during the 1887 meeting of the Western Association of Architects in Cincinnati, Chicago architect John Wellborn Root and several other members rode past Mullett's Cincinnati post office. Root "spoke in terms of high praise of the structure, and declared that it was the finest thing that Mullett ever did, and possibly the finest public building architecturally in the U.S." (figure 4.14). Root's companions agreed with his statement.[119]

Mullett's death signaled the passing of one of the first architects whose name was recognized from coast to coast. His achievements

Figure 4.14
U.S. post office,
Cincinnati, Ohio, 1874–
1885, Alfred B. Mullett.
Courtesy Cincinnati
Historical Society.

as supervising architect can be measured in the large architectural output over the decade in which he served as head of the Supervising Architect's Office, a level of productivity that exceeded any record posted by the federal architecture program up to that time.

Chicago architect Peter B. Wight, an active AIA member but a more moderate observer of the political realities of Mullett's position, captured Mullett's achievements as an administrator. He placed Mullett's era within its historical context as succeeding the "military role" of the Bowman/Young era and the brief Rogers era. As Congress ordered the construction of new buildings:

> a governmental architectural office was in actual operation in the Treasury Building, [and] it became a matter of great convenience to have all the architectural work done in this office. The admirable executive ability of Mr. Mullett enabled him to organize the machinery of the office in a comprehensive and systematic manner.

As the federal architecture program grew:

> the patronage bestowed upon it was enormous, and became the greed of aspiring politicians. The eyes of the whole country were directed upon its transactions. It was the battlefield of many a hot dispute, and the interests of contending sections were centered in its operations.

Mullett did not flinch from the rising workload and executed it with "remarkable speed, precision, and economy."[120]

Mullett's achievements, however, were overshadowed by the essential role he was forced to play with members of President Grant's administration and politically influential suppliers of building materials and building elements. The architectural profession resented his many major buildings, viewing the projects as a threat to the public's appreciation of their profession. For the private architects, Mullett was an easy target for their lobbying efforts to change the structure of the federal architecture program. Mullett's downfall was as much a product of his own personal failings as it was a result of the architectural profession's hunger for some of the acclaim that accompanied the design of major public buildings. Although Mullett played an important role in the development of Washington architecture after 1874, he never again reached a comparable level of public visibility to that he had been accorded as supervising architect. His death underscored his own sense of failure and it removed the private architects' most prominent symbol in their cause to open federal architecture projects to competition.

5

THE SUPERVISING ARCHITECT'S
OFFICE IN THE GILDED AGE

1875–1894

The financial panic of 1873 and the subsequent depression lasted for nearly a decade and influenced the course of the federal architecture program. Mullett's Second Empire building designs seemed incompatible with the economic times. The national mood and taste swung to a more spartan style that bespoke economy and efficiency. Coincidentally, the federal buildings designed during this period, for the most part, were located in smaller cities, as the large urban centers had already been provided with structures from Mullett's administration. Economic considerations as well as locational factors called for federal buildings that differed dramatically from those that had preceded them.

The federal architecture program, as well as state and local public architecture, fell under the spell of the national architectural trend that favored first the Gothic and then the Romanesque styles. Dissemination of John Ruskin's writings and information on the architectural works of Viollet-le-Duc popularized the Gothic style in the United States. Later, the works of Henry Hobson Richardson were to exert a strong influence in shaping public architecture around adaptations of his Romanesque style. These styles allowed for flexible floor plans and an external appearance that better expressed the internal arrangements. For an expanding federal bureaucracy, these approaches provided federal buildings that were more adaptable to later additions and alterations. They also allowed federal architects to vary the arrangements or masses and architectural details in order to achieve a greater variety of buildings from one location to another. Indeed, the styles were so well adapted to the need to provide a large number of architectural designs, while providing each locality with its own unique building, that the picturesque forms took on the robes of an "official style" in federal building design.

During the twenty-year period starting in 1875, there were seven supervising architects. The longest tenure was that of James G. Hill, from 1876 to 1883. The remaining served for brief periods, ranging from eighteen months to four years. While several were nationally recognized private practitioners before they took the position, none achieved a stature as supervising architect comparable to Mullett's. In fact, the rapid turnover of supervising architects underscored the position's ties to the perils of politics rather than to professional ability. The political nature of the position added fuel to the argument of private architects that the federal government's architecture program needed to be restructured to open building projects to private practitioners.

William Appleton Potter

In the wake of Mullett's departure, several architects were considered as his replacement. Among those listed in the press were Peter B. Wight and John C. Cochrane, both of Chicago; Thomas U. Walter and John McArthur Jr., both of Philadelphia; and Thomas Walsh of St. Louis. All the names discussed were important figures in the archtiectural profession, although most had local practices. Wight had been a prolific architect in New England, until the Great Chicago fire of 1871 and the city's rebuilding lured him to the Midwest. Cochrane was architect of both the Iowa and the Illinois state capitol buildings. McArthur was architect of the new city hall in Philadelphia and numerous other important buildings in his city. Walter's work in Philadelphia and on the Capitol dome and extensions in Washington, D.C., made him a perennial favorite each time the supervising architect's position was open. Walsh, superintendent of the St. Louis custom house, was a successful practitioner in his city.

Of the five candidates, it appears that only McArthur was actually offered the position. According to Walter, McArthur "did not seek the appointment, but has all along been anxious for me to have the position—he has done all he could with the Secretary in that direction. Should he decline, I fear they will not give Philadelphia a second chance. From a conversation I had with Mr. McA today, I am inclined to think he will accept."[1] McArthur turned down the position in mid-December and urged his political supporters to back Walter. Walter was to be disappointed; Secretary Bristow selected William Appleton Potter, a thirty-three-year-old architect who was a member of the AIA.

Potter had established himself as a rising young architect with his design of the Chancellor Green Library at Princeton University. He had previously served as an apprentice in the architectural office of his half-brother Edward Tuckerman Potter. Well-connected socially, the Potter brothers were practitioners of the High Victorian Gothic, which combined elements of the Gothic styles from English and French architecture. Edward T. Potter's affection for the Gothic style brought him many commissions for churches, as well as academic and residential buildings. William A. Potter's major works prior to 1875 included the South Congregational Church in Springfield, Massachusetts, and the Berkshire Athenaeum in Pittsfield, Massachusetts. Potter's appeal for Secretary Bristow stemmed from the former's accomplishments to date as well as to the secretary's partiality to blue blood, gentlemanly manners, and prominent connections.[2]

Quite naturally, Mullett took a dim view of his successor. In an interview published just six months after Potter's arrival in Washington, Mullett characterized Potter as an unknown in the architectural profession and inexperienced in the construction of large buildings. He also questioned Potter's work habits that allowed him to "go into the office in a morning dress, stay a little while, leave for lunch, return in an afternoon dress, and says that he finds it easy to transact the whole business in three hours a day." Mullett also noted that:

> Mr. Potter belongs to a little clique in New York who believe that nothing is architecture that is not Gothic, and who utterly deny that classic, or renaissance, architects are anything better than mere carpenters and masons, and who believe that they are the sole repositories of knowledge and sole judges of art.[3]

It is unclear how long Potter intended to stay in the position of supervising architect. Just as he was assuming his new position, he entered into partnership with Robert Henderson Robertson to form the firm of Potter & Robertson, located at 54 William Street in New York City. During the year and a half he was supervising architect, he spent several weeks at a time at his New York office and the partnership produced designs for several buildings at Princeton University. His attention to his private work gave him an air of detachment in dealing with government matters.

While Potter's enthusiasm for the administrative requirements of the job was likely subdued, he possessed vigorous opinions regarding an ideal architectural style for public buildings. He regarded the "eclectic gothic style" as entirely appropriate for public buildings. As he stated:

> Its great superiority consists in its pliability. It is the best adapted to the varied requirements of our times. It is suited to any and all purposes and shades of purposes. There is nothing cumbersome, and little that is invariable about it. It does not require, like the classic styles, perfect symmetry. It can be absolutely symmetrical, too, but with almost any irregularities, it still remains picturesque.

Although a fully decorated Gothic building might be costly, Potter felt that buildings designed in the Gothic style could be executed with less ornament:

> Considerable open wall spaces are not only permissible but desirable, to give proper value to the ornamentation where it is to be used. The classic style requires interminable columns, pilasters, panels and architraves; extensive vacant spaces are out of keeping. It is hemmed in by a thousand conventional requirements in the way of diameters, modules, and intercoluminations.[4]

Potter's buildings were also characterized by rich polychromatic effects, achieved through the combination of brick and stone of different colors, such as granite, limestone, marble, and sandstone.

One of Potter's first designs was for the courthouse and post office at Atlanta, Georgia (figure 5.1). By the time the Atlanta building was being designed, Potter must have made his preferences known to the draftsmen on his staff, leaving the execution of a building's details to them. In early May 1875, when he was at his New York office, his chief clerk, Horace C. Jacobs wrote, "[Paul C.] Lautrup asks if towers on Atlanta perspective will be open, or with windows."[5] The Atlanta building, with its round arches, appeared more Romanesque than

Gothic and was described as copied after an ancient Italian villa but revised into the Italian Gothic style.[6] One critic described its windows as "Romanesque Gothic."[7] Its massing was broken into a central block fronted with a two-storied open porch. Projecting wings with towers rose out of the center of the wings. Unlike many picturesque buildings of the period, the Atlanta building, as with nearly all of Potter's designs for federal buildings, was characterized by carefully balanced masses and details. Because of the use of the Romanesque style and the classical massing, one viewer thought that the building "will look more at home in [the Southern town] . . . than would gothic." He admired its simple and grave character.[8]

In the following month, June 1875, plans were prepared for the custom house at Fall River, Massachusetts (figure 5.2). Potter's attention to the details of federal buildings was evident in his letter to Edward T. Avery, a native of New London, Connecticut, and later superintendent of construction of the Fall River building. As Potter wrote, "I desire you to prepare plans for the Fall River building here. Please report in person to this Office."[9] The Fall River custom house presented the usual arrangement of massing, but the wings were rounded. The window and door openings were more obviously Gothic. The entire building was crowned with a high French roof.

Potter's other federal buildings offered great variety, considering the sameness of the functions to be contained in the buildings from

Figure 5.1
U.S. courthouse and post office, Atlanta, Georgia, 1876–1880, William Appleton Potter. *American Architect and Building News,* 1 (May 20, 1876), n.p.

Figure 5.2
U.S. custom house, Fall
River, Massachusetts,
1876–1882, William
Appleton Potter.
Courtesy National
Archives.

one location to another. The much admired custom house and post office in Evansville, Indiana, was arranged with the massing broken into a central block and wings, but the window openings and details provided for a facade of great complexity and richness (figure 5.3). The *American Architect and Building News* critic found the building "picturesque, dignified, and elegant, a kind of design which should be very attractive with successful carrying out."[10] The Nashville post office and courthouse announced its prominence with a 190-foot clock tower rising out of the central block, reminding one critic of "one of the beautiful town halls of Belgium"[11] (figure 5.4). However, another critic found the tower inadequate for the corner masses and "the group of pinnacles and balconies which belts it round is not yet quite satisfactorily harmonized."[12] The Covington, Kentucky, courthouse and post office had a central block that was more prominent than its wings, which were themselves balanced by a pair of towers (figure 5.5). The courthouse and post office in Grand Rapids, Michigan, was Potter's only other federal building besides the Atlanta building that was more Romanesque than Gothic and appeared to

forecast the style of federal buildings for the next two decades. Potter also produced designs for federal buildings in Albany, New York; Memphis, Tennessee; Auburn, New York; and Little Rock, Arkansas, none of which were executed until the appointment of James G. Hill as supervising architect.

In addition to new buildings, Potter was responsible for the completion of federal buildings already under construction. Rather than complete them according to Mullett's designs, he attempted to modify them to bring them into closer conformity with his own design philosophy. The top of the ill-fated Chicago custom house was relieved of its towers and domes and was completed with a wedge-shaped roof and dormer windows. In addition, the Boston post office and subtreasury was redesigned with details that represented Potter's own interpretation of the Second Empire style. As a critic described Potter's addition:

> His renaissance is scholarly; he has his materials perfectly in hand and understands the logic of their connections. There is an imposing entrance archway to this Boston building two stories in height in the French manner. The roofs are stately and finished

Figure 5.3
U.S. custom house and post office, Evansville, Indiana, 1876–1879, William Appleton Potter. Courtesy National Archives.

Figure 5.4
U.S. post office and
courthouse, Nashville,
Tennessee, 1876–1882,
William Appleton Potter.
Courtesy National
Archives.

with an abundance of detail. The design is pervaded by feeling, that subtle quality which is the essence of all true art.[13]

The press greeted Potter's buildings as "poems in stone, which represented an extraordinary revolution" in government architecture. His adoption of the Gothic style was lauded because it was the "prevailing style in England, and also among the foremost members of the profession among ourselves." Critics waxed rhapsodic over the "variety, picturesqueness, sentiment—color, carving, polished granite and a reminiscence of the great achievements of former ages." Potter was praised as a "man of fine sensibilities and artistic tastes, thoroughly cultivated."[14] Another viewer suggested that the general public, more familiar with the classical style for government buildings, would regard the use of the Gothic style as inappropriate. However, the reviewer thought that expression and treatment were independent of style and "Mr. Potter's use of Gothic is for the most

part bold, broad, massive, and dignified; as becomes the design of the buildings of the State." On occasion, however, Potter yielded "to what is naturally the besetting temptation of the style he chooses— the sacrifice of dignity and simplicity of expression to picturesque- ness." This criticism was especially true of the ultimately unexecuted design for the post office at Auburn, New York, judged to be "too pic- turesque; a group of apses, gables, and turrets, too complex and un- quiet to seem appropriate to the uses of a government building."[15]

Chicago architect Peter B. Wight admired Potter for bringing a "fine artistic instinct to bear upon the important duties of his office" and felt reassured that "insofar as one man can labor, the artistic de- velopment of our government architecture in the present status is in good hands." However, Wight questioned whether the federal gov- ernment should assign all of its architectural functions to one man, no matter how talented. In light of what Wight considered to be poor public architecture at all levels of government:

Figure 5.5
U.S. courthouse and post office, Covington, Kentucky, 1875–1879, William Appleton Potter. Courtesy National Archives.

it behooves the government of a great country to set an example in this respect. It not only has all past experience before it, but has its own painful experience to look to. The time has come when the nation must assert its manhood, and meet these questions which now arise with an intelligence becoming an enlightened age and country. Let us hope that our centennial year will not pass without a solution of the problem before us, and the establishment of a national architecture on a sound and enduring basis. If this is done, we may congratulate ourselves that in this respect at least the Republic is not a failure.[16]

Federal government policy toward its architecture program was the subject of intense debate in the architectural profession. In his October 1874 draft of a bill to create a Bureau of Architecture, John L. Smithmeyer fired the first salvo in this enduring discussion. Alfred J. Bloor, secretary of the American Institute of Architects (AIA), sent a summary of Smithmeyer's plan to Secretary Bristow. The members of the AIA then held their collective breath until they could see what Potter would do. He did not disappoint them. In his first (and only) annual report to Secretary of the Treasury Benjamin H. Bristow, dated 1 October 1875, Potter recommended that the supervising architect be restricted to duties solely of a supervisory nature. Because the nature of the office opened it to various political influences, Potter thought that political friends would be liable to fill the position of supervising architect and would be inclined to produce buildings "utterly lacking in those architectural qualities which should be found in the works of a great nation." Even if a qualified architect held the position, the immense amount of routine administrative duties would leave him insufficient time to devote to the study of his architectural designs. "Architecture is an art, and, like all arts, he who practices it successfully must give himself up to it without restraint. No good work has ever been done without severe study, and the artist must be able to throw himself into the contemplation of the problem." Potter urged that some other system be devised to obtain "more artistic and worthy work."[17] Clearly, Potter sided with his AIA compatriots as he realized that his private practice was the mainstay of his career.

The AIA enthusiastically embraced Potter's report during its annual meeting held in Baltimore in November 1875. The board of the AIA, headed by its president, Richard M. Upjohn, complimented Potter for sacrificing his own personal interest to the good of the profession and considered the report to be sufficient justification for:

seeking a practical method for lifting the architectural service of
one of the great powers of the world, with a probably much
longer future and wider opportunities for the practice of art than
any other, to that appropriate atmosphere of serenity and dignity
in which alone the great architectural monuments of the Old
World have been created.[18]

At the conclusion of the meeting, the AIA agreed to appoint a committee to confer with Potter on a bill that might be presented to
Congress to create a Bureau of Architecture.

During the following months, members of the AIA met and cor-
responded on the form that the envisioned bureau would take.
However, few could look beyond the immediate situation or their
own personal interests. Peter B. Wight urged that the bureau remain
in the Treasury Department rather than become an independent
agency because it would be less liable to political influences. A case
in point was the situation Wight observed in late 1875: "The President
now in office is known to be a friend of A. B. Mullett, who would be
very glad to regain his position independent of the Secretary of the
Treasury, and would thereby gain a triumph over Mr. Bristow."[19]
Thomas U. Walter thought that the responsibilities of the architect
of the Capitol should not be included in the proposed bureau, because the Capitol "is an unfinished building, and I expect to finish it,
under the same regimen that I executed the portions of the building
already completed." In any case, Walter thought a bill with the in-
corporation of the Capitol into the bureau would not get through
Congress.[20] The AIA decided, however, to ignore Walter's suggestion
and pursue the version of the bill that incorporated the Capitol.
Walter then attempted to disassociate himself from the AIA's efforts
on behalf of the bureau.

As far as tactics were concerned, John L. Smithmeyer became concerned over Potter's preparation of his own bill, described as "less
ambitious," and the appearance of Potter as the prime mover on the
matter of the bureau, with the members of the AIA as mere follow-
ers. The House of Representatives, controlled by the Democratic
party, likely would not view with favor a recommendation offered by
a representative of the Grant administration. In late 1875, Smithmeyer recommended an action independent of Potter so that the bureau idea "would seem to come directly from us, the people."[21]

Representative Abram S. Hewitt of New York, a Democrat, introduced the AIA's bill to establish a Bureau of Architecture. Hewitt
was the son-in-law of Peter Cooper, founder of the Cooper Union,

and was knowledgeable about architectural matters. In the interest of "securing artistic merit as well as intrinsic value in the public edifices to be erected by the Government of the United States," the bill called for the creation of a Bureau of Architecture in the Treasury Department to be headed by the government architect, to be selected from the members of the AIA, to supervise all buildings exclusive of those attached to the military. All designs for new buildings were to be obtained through competition with winners selected by a board of four experts. The winning architect also would superintend the construction of the building. In addition, the government architect would sponsor the scientific testing of building materials and make the results available to the public.[22]

The AIA's proposals were not greeted with unanimous acclaim, not even from fellow architects. J. Jardine, an architect from New York City but not an AIA member, thought that if approved, the bill might "have the effect of creating a ring through the American Institute. . . . The American Institute was rather given to dictation."[23] Architect Stephen D. Hatch, also of New York City, thought that there were as many good architects outside the AIA as in it. He recommended that architects of long standing be appointed government architect, adding, "this would do away with the chance of having any more Mulletts to supervise our public buildings."[24] Other journalists questioned the need to expand the business of government and place architecture under the "patronage of government."[25] The editors of the New York *Evening Post* recommended that the government "keep out of the building business as far as possible, just as thus far as it has kept out of the shoemaking business."[26]

Paul Schulze, who was then in partnership with Mullett's former associate, William G. Steinmetz, protested the exclusivity of the AIA and its membership that the bill embraced. Schulze testified to instances of past "unprofessional conduct" and "discourteous behavior" on the part of AIA members; he also pointed to the present arrogance of the AIA in claiming the "right and sole privilege of doing all public work, and erecting those monuments of art which should and which do, in every civilized country, redound to the credit of the members of the architectural profession."[27] The adverse criticism prompted Congressman Hewitt to claim that while he sponsored the Bureau bill, he did not recommend or endorse all of its provisions. Hewitt also referred to Potter's own version of the bill, which was making its way through the Congress.[28]

As 1876 wore on, prospects for the bureau bill dimmed. As early as

March of that year, W. H. Bishop, editor of the *Daily Commercial Times* of Milwaukee, wrote to Bloor of the AIA regarding the personalities on the relevant committee. Bishop doubted that the bill would ever emerge from the committee, because "the necessity of any improvement in the government buildings is not generally appreciated . . . and it will take a good deal of activity to make the Committee on Public Buildings and Grounds feel the importance of taking action." Some members of the committee were not knowledgeable about the subject, while others were convinced that Mullett was "the greatest architect that ever lived."[29] Even Potter proved evasive; he always claimed to be too preoccupied to meet with the AIA's committee and did not share copies of his version of the bureau bill with them. In March, Thomas U. Walter reported to Bloor that the AIA's bill did not have the slightest chance of passage, although Potter's did.[30] By June, John L. Smithmeyer wrote to Bloor that "our Bill for a competitive system will not pass this session."[31]

The continuing adverse publicity regarding the condition of the Chicago custom house placed Potter in an unwanted spotlight. Added to Potter's worries was the departure of Benjamin H. Bristow as secretary of the treasury in June 1876 and his replacement by Lot M. Morrill of Maine. Bristow had been attacked in late 1875 for his alleged associations with the illicit "whiskey ring" in Cincinnati and Louisville that sold the product without paying taxes. These attacks on Bristow followed the secretary's own investigations of the collusion between distillers and government officials, including President Grant's own private secretary, General Orville E. Babcock, a former patron of Mullett. Increasingly, President Grant regarded Bristow's zeal for reform and investigations as a personal affront. This was especially the case where Bristow's attacks centered on those close to the President. Grant was suspicious of Bristow's ambitions and thought that they were aimed at higher office, even the Presidency itself. Where Bristow once enjoyed the support of Grant, by the time the Secretary left government service in 1976, he was anathema to the President.[32]

By mid-1876, Potter took on the appearance of a besieged public official. Rumors swarmed over the city that Potter's tenure was shaky and that Mullett would soon be brought back to reassume his position as supervising architect. These rumors reached Philadelphia and Thomas U. Walter. In a letter to Capitol Architect Edward Clark, Walter asked, "We have all sorts of rumors here to the effect that Mr. Mullett is going into the supervisorship etc. without opposition. Can that be possible, after all the promises and assurances I have had?"[33] About Potter's troubles, Walter remarked that had Potter insisted on his own resignation a few months back, "it would have saved him a world of trouble, and it would have given me the place, he will never be sorry for it but once, and that will be always."[34]

With Bristow gone and the Chicago custom house problems appearing insuperable, Potter too decided to resign. In his departing letter of 13 July 1876, Potter stated that "the sacrifice of my private professional practice is greater than I expected or can afford."[35] Potter left at the end of July, expressing weariness with the:

> great mass of miscellaneous duties, which have no proper place in such a bureau,—the renting of government buildings, and making of leases for them; claims of all sorts, many of them dating back many years, are brought up, and a vast amount of research is necessary. . . . The office is no sinecure by any means; and I doubt whether you could get a capable architect, in good practice, to give up his office for the post. It needs to be made more distinctively artistic, and many of the more routine duties lopped from it.[36]

James G. Hill

The appointment of James G. Hill (1841–1913) as Potter's successor in August 1876 evidenced Potter's residual influence (figure 5.6). An interview with Potter following his resignation revealed that he had recommended Hill for the post of supervising architect, citing the latter's nine years in the Office that gave him "an extensive acquaintance with all the details of management. He is thoroughly honest and capable, and a better choice could not be made."[37] The *American Architect and Building News* praised Hill's appointment as a "welcome example of promotion won by capable service, and not by political influence."[38] Hill's tenure began on shaky grounds; with the election of Rutherford B. Hayes and the appointment of John Sherman as secretary of the treasury, the return of Mullett again appeared imminent. Sherman had endorsed Mullett to succeed Potter the previous year. However, adverse publicity on Mullett's possible return doubtless contributed to an environment in which he could not be reappointed.

James G. Hill, a native of Malden, Massachusetts, received his ar-

chitectural training in the Boston office of Gridley J. F. Bryant and
Arthur Gilman from 1857 to 1862. He arrived in Washington, D.C., in
1862 and applied to Secretary of the Treasury Salmon P. Chase for a
position in the Bureau of Construction. Two years later, in 1864, he
succeeded in obtaining a clerkship in the Treasury Department.
Later, he worked as a clerk in the Quartermaster General's Office and
in the Loan Branch of the Treasury Department. In 1865, Hill went

Figure 5.6
Secretary of the Treasury
John Sherman and his
staff, including James G.
Hill in upper left-hand
corner. Courtesy
National Archives.

to New York; in 1866, he returned to Malden to be married. In 1867, Mullett employed him in the Office of the Supervising Architect. Because of Mullett's high regard for Bryant at that time, Hill may have received his appointment through the recommendation of his former employer.[39]

One of Hill's first actions as supervising architect was the preparation of his first annual report dated less than two months from the commencement of his administration. In it, he called attention to Potter's remarks on the method for procuring designs for federal buildings. He further sought the AIA's support by recommending passage of legislation to limit the responsibilities of the supervising architect to supervisory work and to obtain designs through competition.[40] The *American Architect* hailed Hill's report and hoped that "successive recommendations will in time bring the thing to pass."[41] A curious episode occurred the following year when the *American Architect* reported that Hill's job was to be divided into two, leaving Hill with supervisory responsibilities. The design work would be offered to James K. Wilson of Cincinnati, an "artist and designer." (Coincidentally, Wilson was the architect of the monument to be located in Spring Grove Cemetery for John M. Mueller, owner of the famous Buena Vista freestone quarry.) As the periodical commented, "If the duties of the office are to be assigned in a way we have mentioned, they will be glad that the Government secures so capable a man for the new position." However, it was also felt that such a setup was not as advantageous to "national architecture" and the government as a "well-administered system of competitions" would be.[42] Nothing came of this report.

Despite the shelving of the bureau bills, members of the AIA continued to urge converts to their cause. In December 1879, John L. Smithmeyer addressed an audience on the "difficulties and dangers of the Supervising Architect's position." Smithmeyer argued that "our government architecture is on the whole not creditable; that the architectural chief is likely to be, and has too often been, a mere political appointee; that he has too much power, too much work to do, and too much money to spend; and that he is not responsible for his administration." The standard AIA solution was to distribute the work to private architects by competition. The *American Architect* thought that Smithmeyer's remarks were overstated, because neither Mullett, Potter, nor Hill were political appointees.

The publication questioned whether or not competitions would improve public architecture on the average. "The existing habits of competition among us do not induce one to look upon a great increase of it as an unmixed benefit, yet a habit of government competition might be of a source in fixing a liberal and honorable standard." However, the periodical acknowledged the heavy administrative duties attendant upon the supervising architect's position that made it "almost impossible for him to put his best strength into his designs" and praised Potter and Hill for possessing "the manliness to set this before the Secretary in their reports, and to propose to surrender to others of their profession what is the most attractive part of their work."[43]

The architecture of the Hill administration emerged out of an era of great austerity in government spending. Parsimonious appropriations were made for major federal buildings, causing interruptions in the construction of buildings and later resumptions. The national atmosphere of austerity also affected the appearance of buildings. Hill's buildings were described as a "quasi-Italian style, but treated with a good deal of freedom, and generally with breadth and massiveness that give them a dignity becoming their office."[44] Several of Hill's buildings, such as the post offices at Harrisburg, Kansas City, and Topeka had a more "semi-classical character" in their massing. The *American Architect* received them with enthusiasm and credited them with:

> [a] solidity and a dignity of design that well becomes public buildings, an air of reserve and simplicity in detail that will be an agreeable contrast to the exuberance and ostentation that we are apt to find in our private architecture, especially in that of our newer cities.[45]

The publication also cited the federal building in Pittsburgh as "architecture of a very high class" (figure 5.7). In general, Hill's buildings presented a welcome change from the "costly classicism of former years." The picturesque style, such as in the courthouses in Charleston, West Virginia (figure 5.8), and Baltimore (figure 5.9), was "much more troublesome to the architect than the other, but more interesting and satisfactory to the rest of the world."[46]

With a retrospective of twenty years, Hill's designs held up well, according to the *American Architect*. In 1895, the publication described them as:

Figure 5.7
U.S. post office,
Pittsburgh, Pennsylvania,
1881–1891, James G. Hill.
Courtesy National
Archives.

simple, straightforward, mercantile buildings, wherein the public business might be conducted: they were not architecturally pretentious, no one would buy photographs of them as works of art, but almost all of them had a certain sturdy common sense about them; they showed that the design had been studied and sometimes suggested that, under happier conditions, architecturally better work might have been done; at any rate, there are no "aberrations" amongst them.[47]

Hill's tenure as supervising architect was a particularly tumultuous one. It was characterized by bad luck, numerous charges of

Figure 5.8
U.S. federal building,
Charleston, West
Virginia, 1881–1883,
James G. Hill. Courtesy
National Archives.

mismanagement and improprieties, at least one indictment, and a departmental investigation into the handling of his job. That he survived in his position for as long as he did—seven years—and that he entered into a successful private practice following his departure from the government, is testimony to both the depth of his political support and that of his comrades in the AIA.

The appointment of Alfred B. Mullett in the fall of 1876 as superintending architect of his major French-style buildings still under construction was likely Secretary Lot Morrill's way of aiding Mullett without incurring the wrath of the architectural profession or of the press. Mullett's roving superintendency was tenuous; Hill informed the superintendents of the buildings that Mullett had no authority over their work whatsoever. After a few months on the job, Lot Morrill's successor (and Mullett's old friend) John Sherman asked Mullett to give him his impression as to the operation of the Supervising Architect's Office over the two years since his departure.

Figure 5.9
U.S. courthouse and post office, Baltimore, Maryland, 1881–1890, James G. Hill. Courtesy National Archives.

Mullett used the opportunity to present Sherman with a twenty-nine-page letter, outlining a list of errors and improper expenditures that had been incurred in that time. He also pointed to the endorsements Hill obtained from the state of Maine, which were "procured through the influence of the contractors" of granite being used in federal buildings. For example, Jonas French of the Cape Ann Granite Company, which supplied granite for the Boston post office, strongly supported Hill's appointment. At the end of the letter, Mullett urged that he be reappointed supervising architect, but Sherman declined.[48] However, rumors spread throughout the city and the architectural profession in the spring of 1877 that Hill's departure was imminent.

In May 1877, a portion of the roof of the New York post office collapsed and killed four workmen. A few months earlier, the press had noted the departure of William G. Steinmetz as superintendent of the building and his replacement by Thomas A. Oakshott. Mullett seized the opportunity to ascribe the accident to the dismissal of Steinmetz. A grand jury investigation into the accident revealed that the roof truss had not been properly bolted to the framing. Oakshott, neither an architect nor an engineer, was apparently uninformed as to the construction or placement of the roof truss. Hill was relieved of any major responsibility for the accident; the *American Architect* concluded that "an instance of negligence is not proof of incompetence, and no one who is familiar with the organization of the Office of the Supervising Architect can doubt that more is laid on him than one man can properly accomplish."[49] Oakshott was dismissed and replaced by Thomas J. Jackson, described as "an old architect of this city" and "somewhat of an iron man."[50] Mullett later charged the death of the four workmen "either to murder or manslaughter."[51] In the midst of Hill's troubles, Thomas U. Walter wrote to William Stickney of Washington that, "if Mr. Hill is to be removed, I would be glad to accept the position, but under no circumstances would I do anything adverse to his interests."[52]

The troublesome Chicago custom house, which had loomed over the Mullett and Potter administrations, threatened to overtake Hill's as well. Press coverage of the building's construction focused on the various contracts by which John M. Mueller's stone was procured and the manner in which it was cut. The 15 percent labor contract between Mueller and the federal government set a premium on stretching out the job, increasing the cost of the project, and thereby increasing the commission. Mueller's stone was determined to be irregular in color and quality. The situation was complicated by the various locations in Chicago where the stone was being cut and the efforts of Mullett as superintending architect to alter Potter's designs for the fourth story of the building, which had themselves been alterations of Mullett's original designs.

In the autumn of 1878, a grand jury in Chicago indicted Hill, along with Potter and six other persons, for fraudulent dealings associated with the Chicago building. Other names were mentioned in the charge, such as Mullett, Rankin, and the respective treasury secretaries, but the statute of limitations prevented their inclusion in the indictment. The charge was conspiracy to defraud the government of $850,000 and other acts of specific fraud. The indictment revived rumors about Hill's imminent removal and the appointment of a Chicago architect as his replacement.[53] Instead, Hill was suspended from his position and John Fraser, superintendent of the new building for the Bureau of Engraving and Printing in Washington, was appointed acting supervising architect. Fraser, an architect who had made a name in Philadelphia, served in this capacity from December 1878 to May 1879. During this time, Hill's future as supervising architect again appeared clouded. Elijah E. Myers, the architect of the Michigan State Capitol, wrote to Thomas U. Walter, asking him to serve as a reference in obtaining Hill's position. Walter declined the request, because "in the event of the removal you anticipate, I shall be a candidate for the place." In any case, Walter did not feel that the charges would be substantiated and believed that Hill would be retained.[54]

During the trial, the prosecution failed to prove conspiracy and the court discharged Potter and Hill from the case. "The court went so far as to disclose, in view of the case submitted by the prosecution, that [they] . . . should never have been indicted."[55] In the end, all the trial proved was that the stonework for the custom house and the contracting methods were unsatisfactory and that the grand jury was guilty of "extreme folly" in being "moved by blind wrath to lay its charges, without weighing the personal bearing of the evidence before it, in the idea that if it indicted all of the principal persons who were concerned in the work, it might find among them some one who was responsible."[56] Potter's defense lawyer, Leonard Swett from Chicago, wrote to Secretary Sherman, "as a looker on at this trial for another party nothing has occurred reflecting upon Mr. Hill in any manner whatsoever."[57] Upon the decision of the court, Thomas U. Walter wrote a letter to Hill, attesting to his confidence in Hill all along, adding, "Your triumph is so signal that I cannot refrain from tendering you my hearty congratulations."[58]

Hill's acquittal still left seeds of doubt in Secretary Sherman's mind as to who was responsible for the mismanagement of the Chicago building: the supervising architect or the superintendent. In referring to his doubts, in December 1879 Mullett characterized Hill to Sherman as "incompetent, untruthful, and corrupt" and that "if he is not himself corrupt, he is but the creature and tool of those who are." For these reasons, Mullett claimed that he declined the positions of superintendent of the St. Louis, Cincinnati, and Chicago buildings because the situation would render him "unable to correct the existing evils, or protect the interests of the Government, or my own reputation."[59] Hill survived these accusations and spent the next two years in relative tranquillity.

The elevation of Chester A. Arthur as president in September 1881, following the assassination of President James Garfield, brought into play a new cast of characters in the Treasury Department. When Charles J. Folger was appointed secretary of the treasury in November 1881, Washington was again flooded with rumors regarding Hill's possible dismissal. This time, it appeared that William G. Steinmetz, then a partner of Mullett in New York City, might gain the appointment. Mullett denied the story "in a letter published throughout the country."[60] The *American Architect* feared dissatisfied contractors inspired the efforts to remove Hill:

During the five years of Mr. Hill's administration the vast and difficult business of the office has been managed with so much ability, faithfulness, and success that we should view with grave apprehension any movement to displace him, particularly if such movement, as appears at present to be the case, were founded on nothing better than a fancied political expediency.[61]

The rumors that circulated in late 1881 and early 1882 signaled Hill's last successful effort to rise above personal attack. In early 1882, he answered charges that his office performed personal design services for Secretary Sherman and for Hill's own house. Hill claimed that while he and draftsmen in the office worked on the designs, this work was not performed on government time.[62] Again, the AIA rallied to his cause with letters attesting to Hill's fitness for his position.

In the spring of 1883, a new investigation of Hill's conduct of the Supervising Architect's Office was underway. This time, a special investigating committee of the Treasury Department conducted the inquiry, following the lead of Senator Henry Murch of Maine. The *American Architect* reported that the investigation was being made into charges that government contracts were not being awarded to the lowest bidders and that machinery and materials were being sold and bought back so as to defraud the public treasury. The publication also observed that a "former Government architect" (that is, Mullett) was prominent in the present investigation. As the investigation wore on, the *American Architect* observed that:

> One of the most active promoters of the inquiry has been obliged to demand access to all the records of the Architect's office, in order, as it seems, to search for some evidence to substantiate his own assertions. The other reforming enthusiast appears to have found his ardor a little damped on learning that the archives of the office over which he once himself ruled were to be overhauled in the pursuit of scandals and has discreetly withdrawn himself from obvious participation in the proceedings. Meanwhile, the public business suffers, while the officials designated for service on the investigating committee wait for the presentation of the first item of that overwhelming mass of evidence [that] was said months ago to be ready for them.[63]

Coverage of the investigation in the *American Architect* presented Hill in a favorable light and in a likely position to come out of the turmoil with his reputation intact. The publication speculated that one of the objectives of the investigation was the restoration of the 15 percent system in order to benefit certain suppliers of stone for federal buildings. On the other hand, the published report, *The Investigation of James G. Hill*, was hardly complimentary of Hill and concluded that the "Treasury Department, in spite of all the honor, honesty and integrity of the Secretary is being run by or run in the interest of a few men."[64] The report stated:

> while evidence sufficient to effect Mr. Hill's removal was obtained, no evidence that could reach higher and strike at those whom the prosecution believed to be far more guilty was admitted. One member of the ring, and that one believed to be the least guilty, was alone made to stand the brunt of the charge, not originally designed against him personally.

In the end, the investigating body "denounced the methods in vogue in the Architect's Office."[65] The contents of the report were quite at variance with the conclusions of the *American Architect*, which thought that Hill was "vindicated."[66] On the matter of the reorganization of the Supervising Architect's Office, Hill reported to Secretary Folger that he had "given the matter considerable reflection, [but] I am still unable to submit any scheme of reorganization which has not in it serious defects. It may be that a long experience in the office has lead me to entertain an undue appreciation of the difficulties of the problem."[67]

For the instigators of the investigation, the turmoil had its desired effect on Hill. His work fell into arrears, causing him to complain that "at present my whole time is occupied in a defense against the malicious attacks of enemies which interferes very seriously with the transaction of the public business."[68] Hill repeated this complaint in his annual report for 1883, calling attention to the lateness in issuing plans for and commencing the construction of new buildings."[69] On 18 September 1883, Hill submitted his resignation to Secretary Folger.

Hill's postgovernment career was decidedly successful and apparently devoid of the regrets that characterized Mullett's. He designed many residences, office buildings, apartment houses, and bank buildings throughout Washington, D.C. One of his largest commissions was the red brick Government Printing Office building on North Capitol Street in Washington, designed in 1899 and supervised by the Office of the Commissioners of Public Buildings. In 1900, he prepared designs that accompanied a report on housing for the working classes.[70] Unlike Mullett, Hill was active in the American Institute of Architects, having been elected a fellow in 1888. He also participated in the passage of the Tarsney Act in 1893 (see chapter 6) and served as president of the Washington Chapter of the AIA in the early twentieth century. He died in 1913 in Washington at the age of 72.[71]

Hill's departure served as the occasion for Thomas U. Walter to express gratitude for the "kindness and courtesy I have received from you."[72] This time, Walter's hoped-for return to official life was aided by his former nemesis, General Montgomery C. Meigs. Meigs promised Walter that he would see Secretary Folger and "use his best endeavors to promote my appointment." However, at the age of seventy-nine, Walter admitted that he was "not very sanguine" about his chances.[73]

Mifflin E. Bell

In November 1883, the *American Architect and Building News* warmly greeted the appointment of Mifflin E. Bell (1846–1904), a native of Iowa. Bell had been associated with the construction of the Illinois and Iowa state capitols, which John C. Cochrane of Chicago had designed. This work had given Bell "an extensive experience of building operations of the large scale."[74] Bell took on the position with some misgivings because he was familiar with the many criticisms heaped upon it. In addition, the actions of Congress, authorizing many new buildings, made the heavy workload even more overwhelming. At the same time, the size of the budget for the technical force was reduced. The building boom that grew out of a prosperous national economy of the mid-1880s and the higher salaries offered architects in private practice whittled away the corps of draftsmen. As Bell wrote in his first annual report, "It was with the gravest apprehension that the task of conducting its business was assumed."[75]

Bell had the misfortune to head the Supervising Architect's Office during a time of great inconsistency on the part of Congress. Appropriations for federal buildings were frequently altered after designs had been approved and the construction commenced. These changes allowed for more expensive building materials to be used or provided for a building of larger dimension. The appropriations for the technical staff wavered greatly, causing a rapid turnover in the staff. Bell appeared to be constantly reducing, and later raising, the hourly rates of his staff or reducing his force to stay within the limits

of the appropriations. He also devoted much energy to scouring the
nation for new staff to fill vacancies. The erratic funding and staffing
of the Office also resulted in delays in the completion of buildings,
which drew criticism and accusations of mismanagement from citizens and disappointed suppliers of building materials and labor.

Bell's workload was also daunting. The *American Architect* noted
that federal buildings were "multiplying at a rate of about three a
month." The publication warned:

> Even if all Government buildings could, by enlisting the emulation
> of all the architects in the country, be made models of artistic
> beauty and interest, the advantage of this would not be counter-
> balanced by the delays and interferences with a well-organized sys-
> tem which would often be the consequence.[76]

Bell's design philosophy appeared to be fairly straightforward. As
he stated in his first annual report, "In the preparation of the designs
for the various buildings, I have endeavored to avoid monotony; a
difficult task to accomplish, in view of the fact that the uses to which
the buildings are applied are so similar." Bell also felt that buildings
should be provided with ample enough accommodations to allow for
future as well as present requirements.[77] In fact, he thought buildings
should be designed so they could be enlarged, "as the growth of the
city and the increase of business required."[78] Because Congress
placed limits of appropriations which frequently were at variance
with Bell's own estimate as to the requirements of the site, he prepared two designs. In the case of the Brooklyn, New York, post office,
the first design was for the building which should be built, the second
for the building which could be constructed with the present limit on
appropriations.[79] Other buildings were designed and built to accommodate later additions.

It appears that Bell devolved much of the responsibility for design
upon the draftsmen in the office. As he mentioned in a letter regarding his search for draftsmen, he provided "general supervision," but
expected his draftsmen to "be competent to prepare drawings for a
stone building of considerable size from foundation to turret."[80] To
an applicant for a job as draftsman, Bell wrote:

> The position I am able to offer you would give you general charge
> of preparation of drawings of one or more buildings form sketch
> plans furnished, from foundation to completion, including inte-

rior finish and decoration, perhaps making a specialty of interior
and decorative work, subject of course to my own approval and
under the immediate direction of the Head Draughtsman and
Engineer of the Office.[81]

The buildings for Fort Wayne, Indiana (figure 5.10) and San Antonio,
Texas (figure 5.11) illustrate variations on the picturesque theme under Bell's administration.

Because Bell delegated design responsibilities, the buildings produced under his tenure varied in treatment and style. The *American
Architect* praised the design for the Galveston, Texas, court house,
which it felt showed that the Office had at least one designer capable
of "turning out really creditable work" (figure 5.12). But, the publication protested the "preposterous design for the Detroit post office"
which was likely designed by a draftsman playing "a huge practical
joke on his superior" (figure 5.13). The publication felt that if "this
thing of incongruous parts, no scale and less style" represented the
country, the results would be "absolutely discouraging." Because Bell
signed his name to both the Galveston and Detroit buildings, the publication expressed the opinion that a few years as a government

Figure 5.10
U.S. courthouse and post
office, Fort Wayne,
Indiana, 1885–1889,
Mifflin E. Bell. Courtesy
National Archives.

ELEVATION ON AVENUE 'E'

Figure 5.11
U.S. courthouse and post
office, San Antonio,
Texas, 1887–1890, Mifflin
E. Bell. Courtesy
National Archives.

official had nullified his former architectural instincts. The publication concluded, "It seems to us that after such an exhibition as this even the most obtuse legislator must see that the present method of obtaining designs for public buildings is a matter which calls for prompt action and total reconstruction."[82]

Predictably, the Supervising Architect's Office did not appreciate the *American Architect*'s comments on the Detroit post office. John Moser, a German-born architect and a refugee of the 1848 upheavals, wrote a letter to the journal identifying himself as the designer of the building. Moser defended his design from the "cussing out" of the publication and claimed positive responses on this design from prominent American architects. Moser viewed Bell's signing-off on the project as testimony to the supervising architect's qualities as being "liberally-educated, liberal minded—not at all 'hide bound'." Moser also claimed that while the aim of the design was to:

> go away from all beaten tracks—no known or established law in form or construction has been violated. It is one organic whole, practical and convenient for its work, and probably the best lighted large Government building in this country. There are a number of novel features in form and manipulation, overcoming serious

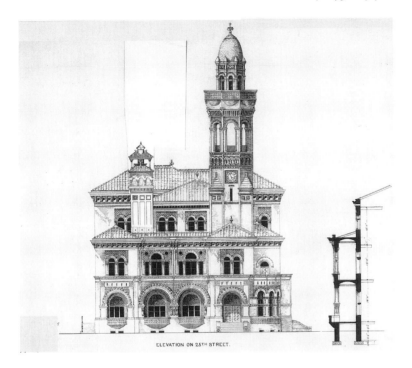

ELEVATION ON 25TH STREET.

difficulties in former methods, that have probably escaped your notice.

The *American Architect* responded to Moser's letters by noting his "great ingenuity" and pointing to his design for a building to house the American Institute of Architects in New York, published in 1884. Moser's AIA building was designed as a historic facade "where every epoch in architectural history shall be represented by details from the best examples now obtainable, following each other in a regular and orderly sequence." The *American Architect* directed attention to Moser's AIA building design as an indication of Moser's "earnestness, sincerity and lavish expenditure of time and thought" but the results for the Detroit building could not be accorded similar respect.[83]

As for Bell, the *American Architect*'s remarks caused him to state that the design had "not yet been 'passed' by me" and that he possessed neither the time nor disposition to enter into a newspaper discussion as to its merits or demerits."[84] Bell's claim that he had not approved of the design when it was held up to ridicule was a response that he made on other occasions. For example, when dissatisfaction was expressed regarding the new government building at Concord,

Figure 5.12
U.S. custom house and post office, Galveston, Texas, 1888–1891, Mifflin E. Bell. Courtesy National Archives.

Figure 5.13
U.S. courthouse and post
office, Detroit, Michigan,
1887, Mifflin E. Bell.
*American Architect and
Building News,* 21 (May 7,
1887), No. 593.

New Hampshire, Bell claimed, "I wish to say that the plans have not been made further than mere sketches and it is my earnest desire to satisfy the citizens of Concord in the plan and appearance of the new edifice." Bell promised to have another design prepared.[85]

Legislative activities surrounding the responsibilities of the Supervising Architect's Office reached a new peak under Bell's tenure. In late 1884, Representative Strother Madison Stockslager of Indiana, chairman of the House Committee on Public Buildings and Grounds, introduced a bill providing for competitions open to private architects for buildings costing more than $50,000. Winning architects would be paid a percentage of the estimated cost of the building, a figure that would be lessened as the cost of the building increased. Selection of the winning designer would be made by a board composed of public officials and architectural experts. The supervising architect would serve no longer than a term of four years. The bill was reprinted widely in the presses to elicit comments from the profession and the public. The *American Architect* urged approval of the bill, describing it as a "law that shall place this nation abreast of other and older nations in their wise provisions for the erection of public buildings."[86] However, there was disagreement over aspects of the supervising architect's tenure, the compensation paid to winning competitors, and the composition of the board. The AIA responded by introducing its own version of the legislation.

As a contribution to these discussions, Bell and Rufus H. Thayer, law and contract clerk in the Supervising Architect's Office, prepared the first published account of the office, *History, Organization, and Functions of the Office of the Supervising Architect of the Treasury Department with Copies of Reports, Recommendations, etc.*, issued in 1886. Among other items, the Thayer publication noted that numerous plans had surfaced in recent years concerning the system for procuring designs for federal buildings. All of them, however:

> failed to give proper consideration to essential elements peculiar to public works as distinct from private works. . . . It is not, therefore, safe to assume that the experience of private architects has given them as a body, or individually, the expert knowledge which fits them entirely for the disposition of this important matter as a whole.[87]

These "peculiarities," beyond the control of the supervising architect, included methods of appropriating funds for building projects, the need to make a permanent record of the Office's work, the need to follow government regulations, the temporary status of superintendents and draftsmen, and the effects of partial appropriations on the cost of construction.

A simultaneous study of the Supervising Architect's Office, conducted by three Treasury Department officials, reinforced the notion that competitions would be too cumbersome and expensive to administer. The examining committee recommended instead that the office employ:

> a suitable number of architects of the highest standing at whatever salaries may be necessary to secure their services. . . . The Government needs, and will need for years to come, the continuous services of competent architects to prepare plans and designs for the numerous costly buildings to be erected. The simple business-like course seems to be to employ by the year the best men that can be obtained for the purpose.[88]

Bell's enthusiasm for his job waned as the full scope of the demands upon the office became clear. He also was sensitive about the criticism leveled upon his office by the press. He complained about the shabby treatment doled out by the Treasury Department, which provided him with poor accommodations and perfunctory treatment. Most important, Bell recognized the rising influence of the architectural profession and the eventual need of the government to take the profession's interests into account. For this reason, Bell approached Thomas U. Walter regarding admission to the AIA as a fellow. As Walter stated, Bell wished to have his nomination "railroaded through. He thinks it would help him in retaining his position in the Department, in the accomplishment of which I would like to help him, as he is well up in our art, well educated, and withal, a high toned gentleman."[89]

Unfortunately for Bell, the AIA rejected his nomination; this somewhat harsh response may have reflected the effects of press attacks on his office. But, as Walter wrote to A. J. Bloor at the AIA, the newspapers that "have so grossly vilified him [Bell] are beneath contempt, and are obviously political." Walter was determined to stand by him.[90]

Bell survived well into the administration of President Grover Cleveland. However, by mid-1887, when he could hang on no longer, he submitted his resignation; when it was accepted, he moved to Chicago. After the election of Benjamin Harrison in 1888 and the return of the Republican party to power, Bell applied for and received the appointment of superintendent of repairs for federal buildings in Chicago. In 1892, Bell became superintendent of repairs for federal government buildings at the World's Columbian Exposition.[91] In early 1893, he ran into trouble with a contract to produce models for the building and resigned shortly thereafter. He remained active in the Midwest, producing designs for buildings for the West Chicago Park Commission and in surrounding communities. He died in Chicago in 1904.

Will. A. Freret

Bell was succeeded by William Alfred Freret, better known as Will; described as a "reliable Democrat" (figure 5.14). Born in 1833 and son of former New Orleans mayor William Freret, Freret had worked as superintendent of the reconstruction of James Dakin's old Gothic

capitol building at Baton Rouge, which had been burned by Union troops in 1862 and rebuilt in the early 1880s. He had also superintended university buildings in Louisiana and had served as state engineer in charge of levees.[92] Freret's cousin, James Freret, was a well-known architect in New Orleans. Upon his appointment, the *American Architect and Building News* praised Freret as "an experienced architect, in the prime of life, and with a reputation for enthusiasm quite exceptional in the South. Mr. Freret's training was one of the best that his time and State afforded. . . . he has since practiced his profession with much credit and success." The publication felt that while the salary for the position was low, Freret could seek consolation in the assurance that "even a few years' administration of it [Supervising Architect's Office] will give him a permanent place in architectural history."[93]

Freret's term as supervising architect was brief and hardly substantial enough to secure the predicted niche. He served from July 1887 to March 1889, leaving just as the administration of President Grover Cleveland gave way to that of President Benjamin Harrison. Of all the supervising architects, Freret appeared to be one of the most politically minded. During his tenure, the Office was investigated for alleged favoritism toward Democratic draftsmen. It was alleged that the Office made the competitive examinations for posi-

Figure 5.14
Will. A. Freret and associates. Courtesy National Archives.

tions there so difficult so as to preclude anyone from passing them. In the absence of any successful examinees, Freret was permitted to appoint the draftsmen himself. Toward the end of his administration, he also was charged with attempting to place as many public buildings as possible under contract to Democratic contractors, before the departure of the Cleveland administration. He attempted to speed up the work of the office by employing office draftsmen after hours to make the required drawings.[94] Part of the motivation for speeding up the design process may also be due to his desire to have the buildings placed into the record of his administration.[95]

Freret's administration was marked by pride in his architectural creations. His annual report, covering the work performed up to the end of 1888, was printed in a large, legal-size publication. In the report, obviously intended for broad circulation, Freret outlined a number of cost-cutting measures. These methods included the "use of standard sheets for the interior finish, plumbing, stairs, etc., thus avoiding considerable labor and incident expense." A single contract for the entire work was now applied to the erection of entire buildings. Selection of sites was now based on reports made by officials from the Supervising Architect's Office, rather than by local commissions.[96]

Freret also cited the congressional request made during 1888 for thirty new buildings. This scope exceeded both the size of the current drafting force and the ability of the civil service system to process new draftsmen. Faced with this situation, Freret decided to contract with "competent architects in the city of Washington" who performed their work under his supervision. Freret claimed that there were "precedents" for this arrangement. He offered further evidence of his desire to involve the services of private architects in the work of the office by stating:

> It has been urged that an artistic gain might be effected, and that a higher architectural standard might be raised by inviting members of the architectural profession to submit designs for buildings authorized, the best to secure graduated awards, the adoption of a design to be subject to the approval of three cabinet officers provided for by an act approved March 3, 1875, viz: the Secretary of the Treasury, the Secretary of the Interior and the Postmaster General.

Freret concluded: "There seems to be many reasons why this plan should secure consideration, and I would suggest that the trial be made in the case of some of the buildings now under contemplation by Congress."[97]

The style of buildings provided under Freret's administration, such as the structures in El Paso, Texas (figure 5.15), Vicksburg, Mississippi (figure 5.16), and Bridgeport, Connecticut (figure 5.17), was similar to that of the Bell period. Most were of the Romanesque style, although a few could be better described as Gothic. All were arranged with a picturesque floor plan and with towers, windows, and massing arrangements that differentiated one building from another. In an analytical article on the work of the Supervising Architect's Office written by Percy Clark for *Harper's Weekly*, Freret was credited with possessing unquestionable ability and with maintaining "the high standard" of his predecessors. During Freret's period, approximately fifty draftsmen were employed. Judging from the prodigious output of the Office, one can surmise that while Freret may have provided the guiding spirit to the architectural designs, actual detailed plans were made by the draftsmen. As Clark noted:

Figure 5.15
U.S. post office and custom house, El Paso, Texas, 1889–1893, Will. A. Freret. Courtesy National Archives.

It often happens that even men of recognized ability who enter this office find it necessary to study long and carefully in order to

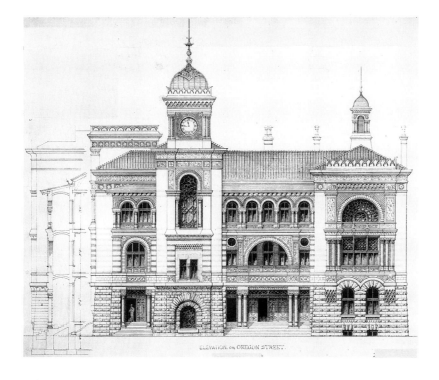

ELEVATION on OREGON STREET.

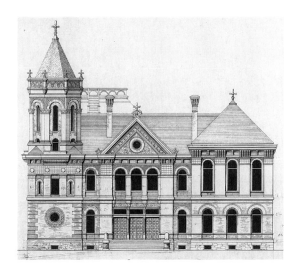

Figure 5.16
U.S. custom house and
post office, Vicksburg,
Mississippi, 1890–1891,
Will. A. Freret. Courtesy
National Archives.

Figure 5.17
U.S. post office,
Bridgeport, Connecticut,
1889–1892, Will. A.
Freret. Courtesy National
Archives.

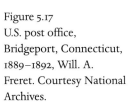

ELEVATION ON CANNON STREET.

make themselves competent for the discharge of the practical duties required in such work. The highest architectural talent is required to create the designs for the splendid structures very often
erected for the government uses. Here it is that the genius of the
artist creates upon paper these monuments to themselves, although, like those built in the Dark Ages, the architect's name is
lost to the public or disassociated from his own creation.[98]

James H. Windrim

Freret's departure with the Cleveland administration in 1889 left the
position of supervising architect open again. John McArthur Jr.
turned the job down. Then, at the recommendation of John Wana-
maker, James H. Windrim (1840–1919) of Philadelphia was appointed
to the position. Windrim had started his career as a stonemason and
a carpenter and subsequently had served as superintendent of buildings designed by John Notman and Samuel Sloan. He made his mark
on Philadelphia at the age of twenty-seven by winning the competition for the acclaimed Philadelphia Masonic Temple in 1867.
Windrim's later career included the design of many public and private buildings in Philadelphia as well as several in Washington, D.C.[99]
Windrim was pictured in the *American Architect and Building News* as
an architect who "has been long and favorably known in the profession, and the appointment will meet with general commendation
among architects." However, the publication doubted that Windrim
should be congratulated because of the pittance of a salary paid for
his services.[100] The *American Architect*'s views were prophetic; Windrim stayed on the job for only two years, serving from March 1889
to April 1891. He left the federal government position only three
months after the departure of Secretary of the Treasury William
Windom. Windrim then took up the position of commissioner of
public works in Philadelphia, which earned him a salary of more than
twice that of his previous position.[101]

Windrim's administration did not differ markedly from that of the
Bell or Freret periods, except that he managed to rise above controversy and served out his term "without the adjunct of a scandal attached to his name."[102] The designs for federal buildings were generally of the Romanesque style, with variations achieved "in the
adaptation of the building to site, which invites variety in form and
exterior design of the structure." His designs were also reminiscent

Figure 5.18
U.S. federal building,
Detroit, Michigan, 1890–
1897, James H. Windrim.
Courtesy National
Archives.

of his work in Philadelphia, which was characterized by "originality and rigid adherence to the principles of the school from which he draws his design. He avoids excessive ornamentation and aims at strength and harmony, with a proper consideration of the use to which the building is to be applied."[103] Under Windrim's tenure, one hundred new buildings were under construction, alterations, or major repairs; another 250 were maintained under the control of the Treasury Department. Windrim's buildings, such as those in Detroit (figure 5.18) and Scranton (figure 5.19), were also the first to adopt electricity on a universal basis.

Of all the recent men who served as supervising architect, Windrim was the first since William A. Potter to be as direct in urg-

WASHINGTON AVE. ELEVATION
SCALE ⅛IN=1 FOOT.

ing the desirability of competitions, an expression of his solidarity with the private practitioners. The AIA embraced Windrim's recommendations to this effect, which he included in his 1889 and 1890 annual reports. The AIA felt that Bell and Freret had not been as supportive on this matter. Even so, there was "opposition from the many hangers-on of that office [under Windrim's administration] and these backdoor influences are very strong in Washington."[104] Windrim found support for the change in the supervising architect's responsibilities from Secretary William Windom, whose own son worked as a draftsman in the office. In fact, the secretary's son, William L. Windom, was suggested as a possible replacement for Windrim in April 1891.

Figure 5.19
U.S. post office, Scranton, Pennsylvania, 1890–1894, James H. Windrim. Courtesy National Archives.

Willoughby J. Edbrooke

After Windrim's exit, candidates for the position of supervising architect included Lindley Johnson of Philadelphia, Joseph C. Hornblower of Washington, D.C., Elijah E. Myers of Detroit, T. Roney Williamson of Philadelphia, Willoughby J. Edbrooke of Chicago, and

Figure 5.20
Willoughby J. Edbrooke.
Courtesy National
Archives.

Frank Furness of Philadelphia. Of the architects considered, Edbrooke (1843–1896) elicited the greatest number of testimonials and was appointed in April 1891[105] (figure 5.20). A native of Massachusetts, Edbrooke had begun his architectural practice in Chicago in association with architect Franklin P. Burnham. The firm of Edbrooke & Burnham was responsible for a large number of public buildings throughout the country, including the Georgia state capitol in Atlanta, residences and commercial buildings in Denver, and a church in Kansas City, Missouri. In the late 1880s, Edbrooke designed the Main Building at the University of Notre Dame, a Gothic building with an impressive gold leaf dome. The Main Building was thought to possess the "dimensions of a state capitol."[106] Edbrooke's Notre Dame work served him well; the university's president, T. E. Walsh, testified to Edbrooke's competency to fill the position of supervising architect, citing his work in drawing all plans for the principal university buildings.[107] Between 1887 and 1891, Edbrooke also had served as the commissioner of buildings for the city of Chicago, a position that put him in charge of building regulations as well as the construction of municipal buildings. He was credited with the design of a dozen school buildings in the city.

Edbrooke's appointment elicited positive reactions from the *Inland Architect*, which pronounced him "as well qualified as his predecessor." He was also described as intelligent, energetic, and possessing relevant experience through his work as "administrator of architectural affairs of the second city in the United States."[108] The *American Architect* was lukewarm about the appointment; the publication was more enthusiastic about Hornblower, "whose selection would have been highly approved by the profession," but his residency in Washington, D.C., deprived him of the necessary political backing from congressmen and state officials. The publication also regretted that T. Roney Williamson was not selected, because he had been recommended by James Windrim and "would have made a brilliant official."[109]

During the two years of Edbrooke's administration, the architectural world was sowing seeds of a dramatic transformation in architectural styles and in the status of the architect. Plans for the World's Columbian Exposition in Chicago were well underway. The exposition would revolutionize the public's perception of an acceptable "official" style for public architecture. However, the design "machinery" already in place in the Supervising Architect's Office appeared to outside observers to be oblivious to this change and continued to produce federal buildings in the Romanesque and picturesque styles

Figure 5.21
U.S. post office, Washington, D.C., 1892–1899, Willoughby J. Edbrooke. Courtesy National Archives.

as it had since the mid-1870s. The length of time required to purchase a site and complete a building's construction resulted in the erection of picturesque federal buildings up to the end of the nineteenth century, including buildings in Washington, D.C. (figure 5.21), Sacramento (figure 5.22), and Worcester, Massachusetts (figure 5.23). By that time, such buildings were viewed as anachronisms and symptomatic of the uninspiring nature of the federal architecture program.

As the designs for federal buildings were now discharged according to a fairly routine method, Edbrooke saw his position as primarily administrative and dependent "upon the executive and executory capacities and abilities of the Chiefs of the several Divisions, and the technical and clerical force of the office, perfection of organization, practicability of method and system, proper discipline, and efficient service." Given his view of the supervising architect as an executive rather than a designer, he set about studying the operation of the Office in order to decide what improvements should be made. The influence of scientific management theories pervaded Edbrooke's view of the Office, because he believed that there was such a thing as a "perfect system of organization and discipline." He described himself as eminently qualified for his position because he possessed a

Figure 5.22
U.S. post office,
Sacramento, California,
1890–1894, Willoughby J.
Edbrooke. Courtesy
National Archives.

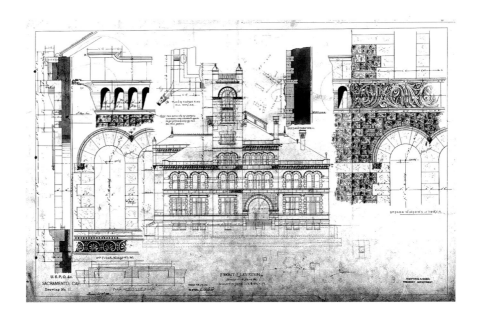

"reputation in a profession that has been the fruit of years of scientific architectural study and work." After a careful analysis of the agency, a task that consumed the first six months of his tenure, Edbrooke pronounced the organization "as perfect as possible," save for some changes in details. These changes included appointing a "Consulting Engineer" to assist the supervising architect with technical matters, filling of the position of "Assistant and Chief Clerk" with an architect, and increasing the salaries for various positions.[110] Edbrooke's distance from the design process was made clear in his description of the qualifications for draftsmen in the office as limited to "those possessing experience and ability to take entire charge of a public build-

Figure 5.23
U.S. federal building, Worcester, Massachusetts, 1892–1897, Willoughby J. Edbrooke. Courtesy National Archives.

ing and make all the drawings and computations necessary for the same."[111]

The system of authorizing and appropriating funds for federal buildings was a subject of great concern to Edbrooke and a problem that he felt could be addressed through scientific study. He thought that a number of recently constructed buildings had been too small when initially completed. Consequently, they required extensions and additions "which necessarily marred the architectural appearance and symmetry of the structures." Planning for the accommodation of federal activities required that the "most careful study should be given not only to the present needs of the various branches of the public service to be accommodated in the building, but to the facts and causes which influence and affect the commercial growth of the cities wherein the buildings are to be erected."[112]

While Edbrooke's study of the operations of the Supervising Architect's Office satisfied him that it was efficiently fulfilling its mission, he also felt the influence of the lobbying efforts of the AIA, which was reaching a fever pitch. As Edbrooke noted in his first annual report, upon learning of the Office's operations, he discovered that criticisms of the Office were "unjust and undeserved."[113] His second annual report was decidedly more defensive in tone. The AIA argued that federal buildings designed under the Supervising Architect's Office were more costly than those erected for state, municipal, and private clients and were inferior in architectural design

Figure 5.24
U.S. post office and courthouse, Fargo, North Dakota, 1893–1897, Willoughby J. Edbrooke. Courtesy National Archives.

and treatment. In response, Edbrooke argued that one could not compare dissimilar buildings. Private clients often were more liberal in the amounts of money they invested in their buildings. Edbrooke agreed to compromise with the demands of the AIA by suggesting that only a limited number of members of the architectural profession submit sketch plans for some of the larger buildings, leaving the balance of the work to the Supervising Architect's Office.[114]

The return to the presidency of Grover Cleveland in 1893 cleared out the top levels of the Treasury Department and Edbrooke was forced to leave as well. Upon his departure in April 1893, he wrote a nine-page letter to the new Secretary of the Treasury John G. Carlisle, outlining his achievements as supervising architect. He cited the designs prepared for eighty-six buildings—including one in Fargo, North Dakota (figure 5.24), and one at the World's Columbian Exposition (figure 5.25)—as well as his sponsorship of the preparation of a series of blank administrative forms which secured "uniformity of action."[115] Edbrooke returned to Chicago to resume his private practice and died there in 1896.

Figure 5.25
U.S. Government building, World's Columbian Exposition, 1891, Willoughby J. Edbrooke. Courtesy National Archives.

Jeremiah O'Rourke

Jeremiah O'Rourke (1833–1915), a well-known architect from Newark, New Jersey, who specialized in ecclesiastical architecture, succeeded Edbrooke (figure 5.26). A native of Ireland, O'Rourke was educated at the Government School of Design in Dublin. He emigrated to the United States shortly after graduating in 1850. Settling in Newark, he

Figure 5.26
Jeremiah O'Rourke.
Courtesy National
Archives.

designed a great number of Catholic churches throughout the state as well as academic buildings for Seton Hall College and parochial schools. His greatest work, Sacred Heart Cathedral in Newark, was designed after the conclusion of his government career. At the time of its completion, the cathedral was described as one of the greatest Gothic structures in the Western Hemisphere. His only previous connection with public architecture was his tenure as superintendent of the new custom house and post office in Newark during the late 1880s.[116] The *American Architect and Building News* regarded O'Rourke's appointment as "more than usually satisfactory," since the publication went on to say that he was "of more than average capacity and information, who during the last twenty years has enjoyed a larger practice than has fallen to most of his fellows."[117] O'Rourke was also a Fellow of the AIA, a credential that, from outward appearances, would have placed him in the organization's good graces.

Unfortunately for O'Rourke, his tenure as supervising architect was one of the shortest on record, from April 1893 to September 1894. The brevity of his administration can be ascribed to a series of actions and public statements that infuriated members of the AIA. O'Rourke also assumed office two months after the passage of the Tarsney Act on February 20, 1893, which, it will be seen, gave the secretary of the treasury discretion to obtain designs for federal buildings by competition (see chapter 6). The passage of this act placed the matter of implementation in the hands of the secretary and his supervising architect. Although O'Rourke was a member of the AIA, he aggressively opposed implementing the measure. Clearly O'Rourke underestimated the political clout of the AIA and the support of the popular press for the measure. A forced exit was the price for his stubbornness.

O'Rourke's first action was the dismissal of Henry C. McLean, who had worked in the Supervising Architect's Office since 1866, rose through the ranks, and in 1893, held the position of assistant and chief clerk. The *Inland Architect* called O'Rourke's action an "inexcusable blunder by the Government":

> [T]he supervising architect under the present system never designs; he can barely sign the papers that come before him, and his ability or his removal does not affect the credit of the office; but with the removal of one who has filled each successive position to the highest, and through the most important years of its existence, it is different.[118]

The AIA glimpsed O'Rourke's attitude toward the Tarsney Act during its annual meeting in the summer of 1893 when it gathered in Chicago, the site of the World's Columbian Exposition. Here, O'Rourke prepared a presentation "On Architectural Practice of the United States Government." In this paper, he defended the standard method of procedure for designing federal buildings:

> It may be stated . . . that while it may be admitted that the work turned out by this office might, and doubtless will, be improved, still a just comparison and analysis would seem to indicate that, all things considered, it will compare favorably, in design, arrangement, construction and cost, with similar works erected by either states, municipalities or private enterprises.

O'Rourke also calculated that the professional costs incurred by the federal government were lower than professional fees charged in private practice. Part of the lower costs could be measured by O'Rourke's yearly income in private practice which would "easily net $100,000 a year," as compared with his current *"munificent* salary of $4,500 with strictly limited traveling expenses."[119]

Publicly, O'Rourke ascribed the Treasury Department's failure to take up the Tarsney Act provisions to "extreme pressure of business, which did not permit delay."[120] In actuality, O'Rourke had already requested of his chief of the Law and Contract Division, St. Julian B.

Dapray, to analyze legal objections to the Tarsney Act. Dapray's response reflected O'Rourke's opinion that competitions should be limited to sketch plans or designs. Dapray prepared a draft bill that would authorize the secretary of the treasury to obtain such plans and designs, while preventing "serious interference with the methods and procedures of the present system."[121]

O'Rourke's foot-dragging came to a head in early 1894 when the AIA protested about plans for the federal building in Buffalo, New York, that the Supervising Architect's Office was preparing. The secretary of the AIA, Alfred Stone, argued that Treasury Secretary Carlisle promised the AIA that the design for the Buffalo building would be put out to competition. In a letter that received wide circulation, O'Rourke responded by describing Stone's letter as at variance with professional courtesy and good breeding.[122] One month later, O'Rourke withdrew the letter, explaining to Daniel Burnham that his actions were caused by the AIA's "superficial and hasty condemnatory criticism, based on entirely insufficient data."[123] Burnham countered with a letter to Secretary Carlisle threatening to introduce a clause to the Tarsney Act ordering the secretary to carry out the intent of the law.[124] Carlisle characterized Burnham's letter as "very offensive and ungentlemanly," and vowed to have no further correspondence with him.[125]

Figure 5.27
U.S. post office, Taunton, Massachusetts, 1895–1897, Jeremiah O'Rourke. Courtesy National Archives.

ELEVATION ON CHURCH AVE.

In the midst of the war of letters between the Treasury Department and the AIA, O'Rourke's office produced designs for a number of federal buildings. As compared with the consistent Romanesque style that emanated from the Windrim and Edbrooke periods, the design staff under O'Rourke returned to the architectural themes of Bell and Freret that provided for greater variations in the adaption of historical styles. For example, the design for the Buffalo post office roughly reflected the major outlines of the standard Romanesque building of the Windrim and Edbrooke eras, but it was finished with Gothic details. In his annual report of 1893, O'Rourke stated that he endeavored to keep the buildings within "the correct canons of art, favoring and expressing as they should a just and proper development of our national architecture."[126] (For examples, see figures 5.27 and 5.28.)

Despite the design advances made under O'Rourke, forces conspired to unravel his authority. The uproar between the Treasury Department and the AIA hardened O'Rourke in his position against the AIA's characterization of the Supervising Architect's Office. His situation proved untenable and he departed in September 1894, leaving the position to Charles E. Kemper, the chief clerk. Kemper served as acting supervising architect from September 1894 to April 1895, when William Martin Aiken assumed the job. O'Rourke resumed his lucrative private architectural practice. At his death in 1915, he was referred to as the dean of the architectural profession in Newark.[127]

Figure 5.28
U.S. post office, Roanoke, Virginia, 1894–1897, Jeremiah O'Rourke. Courtesy National Archives.

The Supervising Architect
As Administrator

By 1894, twenty years had passed since the conclusion of Mullett's highly personal involvement in the design of the federal buildings that bore his name. By this time, the Supervising Architect's involvement in the minutiae of the operations of his office was reduced. For example, much of the correspondence that emanated from the Office during Mullett's period carried the distinct stamp of his personality. In comparison, the correspondence the Office generated during the subsequent twenty years was much more formal, standardized, predictable, and likely written by staff members. By Freret's period, clerks initialed letters before they were presented to the supervising architect for his signature. This detachment from the details of the office was in part a result of the large number of buildings being designed, constructed, and maintained by the office, as well as the increased size of the staff required to handle the workload.

The transformation of the supervising architect from a designer to an administrator was an evolutionary process in the operation of the federal architecture program that was initiated and completed during the late nineteenth century. Although it can be discerned through the buildings and written statements that each supervising architect possessed a well-developed philosophy that guided the design staff, the connection between each supervising architect and the design of each building became more distant with the passage of time. This detachment was reflected in the qualifications asked by the supervising architect of prospective draftsmen, which appeared to entail autonomy and authority in matters of the overall design as well as details. The large number of buildings produced annually and the similar nature of the buildings' functions quite naturally led to a high level of standardization. However, adherence to standard designs was greater under some supervising architects than others. As was noted with the administration of Mifflin E. Bell, designs were produced by his draftsmen, signed by the supervising architect, and issued for public review, only to have Bell disassociate himself from those that received adverse criticism.

The affixing of the supervising architect's name to staff-produced drawings left an abundant historical record of buildings that have been ascribed solely to the head of the Office. Given the actual remoteness of the supervising architect from the design process, it would be more accurate to describe buildings as being produced under the general supervision of the Office head. During the period 1875 to 1894, the office employed a great number of draftsmen, many of whom served for a period of a few years and then left the office to undertake private architectural work in Washington, D.C., and elsewhere. These draftsmen included John Rush Marshall, who later formed the successful Washington firm of Hornblower & Marshall; Henry Hubbard Kendall of Boston, who later returned to his home city to form the firm of Kendall, Taylor & Stevens; Louis F. Stutz, a Washington, D.C., architect who formed a partnership with Frank W. Pease; and George Von Nerta, another well-known name in Washington, D.C., architecture.[128]

It was less common for the Office to attract architects who had already achieved recognition as private practitioners. One such architect was Stanton M. Howard, who had designed the West Virginia state capitol building and a large number of other buildings in West Virginia, Ohio, and Pennsylvania. Howard moved to Washington, D.C., in 1885 and entered the Supervising Architect's Office two years later under Bell. After Freret removed him, he returned to his Washington practice, and applied unsuccessfully for the position of assistant and chief clerk under Windrim in 1889. A few draftsmen entered the Supervising Architect's Office toward the end of their careers when maintaining a private practice became too onerous. One was Henry Searle, who had practiced architecture for many years in Rochester, New York. When he was removed from the Office in 1890, Searle claimed that he was an architect of fifty years standing. The Office also attracted the talents of artists such as Daniel Chester French, who prepared the sculptural details for several of Mullett's Second Empire buildings.

Since the 1870s, the office had employed a growing cadre of women, most of whom were employed as clerks or draftsmen at the lower end of the pay scale. These women included Alice V. Bogert, Annie P. Adams, Emma G. Nelson, Anna A. Elder, and Kate P. Dungan, all listed in 1882 as draftsmen earning $3.00 per day. (Most male draftsmen were earning between $4.00 and $6.50 per day.) Nearly all the women were "never married" or widowed. By 1888, many of the women "draftsmen" were reclassified as "tracers." This position was devoted to making copies of drawings and specifications for examination by contractors in the location where the building was to be erected.

The twenty-year period in the history of the Supervising Architect's Office from 1875 to 1894 witnessed the arrival and departure of seven "permanent" heads of the Office: Potter, Hill, Bell, Freret, Windrim, Edbrooke, and O'Rourke, as well as the appointment of two men who served for extended periods as acting supervising architect, Fraser and Kemper. The federal architecture program also endured alternating periods of austerity and economic prosperity. The congressional system of annually appropriating portions of a building's cost, and of sudden increases or decreases in the overall budget for a building, presented special challenges to the staff at the Supervising Architect's Office. Such a situation was unlike anything most architects faced in private work. In addition, the program was placed under the intense scrutiny of the press and by the architectural profession. The failure of the AIA to persuade the Congress of the wisdom of its plan for restructuring the office's responsibility did not for a minute discourage the organization's dedication to this cause. Every published attack in the professional journals and the general press signaled battle victories, although not the winning of the war (not yet). The Supervising Architect's Office survived numerous real and imagined scandals, some of which were products of political forces beyond the control of the supervising architect and his staff. The sizeable amount of funds the federal government invested in public buildings proved tempting to politicians and contractors alike.

Despite the turmoil that marked the federal architecture program during this period, the designs for the buildings produced were of a remarkable consistency. Variations on the picturesque theme and a recalling of past historical styles constituted the tenor of the era. As a group, these buildings did not differ markedly in style and treatment from many country courthouses or city halls of the period. Rather than pioneering ventures in architectural design, federal buildings were cautiously in step with national taste and practice in public buildings design. However, the characteristics of economy and efficiency that these buildings represented were not received warmly by the leaders of the AIA. As the nation emerged as a world leader, the profession demanded more. The rising chorus of the private architects called for a transformation in the character of federal architecture more befitting the nation's new status.

THE TARSNEY ACT, ITS PASSAGE AND POSTPONEMENT IN IMPLEMENTATION

1893–1896

By the last decade of the nineteenth century, the federal government's architecture program seemed unlikely to pioneer new directions in architectural design. The congressional funding process and the Treasury Department's implementation of congressional wishes kept the noses of government architects to the drafting boards. Responsibility for designing large building, however, put the Supervising Architect's Office in the forefront of building construction and materials technologies. The Office also was charged with designing buildings for now predictable and standard governmental functions. Thus, the apparent sameness of federal government buildings, even with the picturesque style, was largely an outcome of their common purposes.

Private sector architects, rather than the architecturally conservative Supervising Architect's Office, were more likely to blaze new avenues in architectural design. Private architects tended to design a wide range of building types for a greater variety of clients, and for a larger number of functions, with these buildings located in a variety of settings. The disparity between the federal government and the private sectors of architectural practice never seemed greater than during the years 1893 to 1896, even though the seeds of this fracture were sown many years earlier.

Resurgence of American Classicism

The picturesque style had gripped the imagination of the American architect for nearly half a century, and the earlier interest in classicism had been virtually eclipsed. Classical styles had not died out entirely, however, as witnessed by Alfred B. Mullett's heavily classical San Francisco Mint. Interest in classicism was also evident in the 1881 design for the custom house and post office at Jackson, Mississippi, produced under the administration of James G. Hill. By the 1880s, however, picturesqueness had produced such an cacophony of towers, turrets, polychromatic images, and irregular massing that the urban streets looked untidy. Progressive architects looked elsewhere for an appropriate architectural style for the nation's industrial cities.

Feeding this search for an alternative design spirit was the emergence of the United States as a world leader with an enlarged sense of national destiny. After a century, the nation stood ready to reap the benefits of its industrial might. This consciousness of national unity spurred business leaders, as well as architects and artists, to look to Europe as the source for artistic traditions that might benefit America's own search for a cultural legitimacy.

The Old World provided the artistic prototypes and offered the most desirable educational institutions for aspiring architects and artists. A grand tour through Europe had been *de rigeur* for U.S. architects since the early nineteenth century. Now the École des Beaux Arts and, to a lesser extent, other European schools beckoned to American architects. Richard Morris Hunt is generally recognized as one of the first U.S. architects to study at the École. A steady stream of Americans followed in his footsteps. An education at the École provided an aspiring architect with a mastery of architectural history and the architectural elements that were essential to each historical style. In these studies, the "classicism of the Roman, French, or Italian variety dominated." Classicism possessed not only the required cultural connections, but it also had an academic heritage—it was "codified in books."[1] A European architectural education provided American architects with new sources of design inspiration. Attendance at these European schools served as a common bond and provided a sense of unity in outlook among the leaders in the profession.

One of the earliest buildings executed according to this new architectural spirit was the Villard House complex in New York City, designed by the New York firm of McKim, Mead & White and commenced in 1882. Following up on this project, the firm produced an Italian Renaissance design for the Boston Public Library, begun in 1887. The Boston Public Library is generally considered to be the "symbol of the resurgence of American classicism."[2] It also "established a standard of excellence and restrained elegance in public buildings."[3] After the success of this project, the firm adopted Italian Renaissance classicism as its favored style. The later proliferation of the style in the work of the firm and other architects promised a more coherent urban form than that offered by practitioners of the picturesque.

Some architectural innovations took years to penetrate the architectural profession nationwide. The success of classicism came much faster. Its virtues were made abundantly visible with the 1893 World's Columbian Exposition in Chicago. In fact, the exposition's lessons were so powerful that they transformed public architecture for the next five decades. When the 1893 fair was being conceived, only a handful of recently constructed classical buildings could be identified. Even the architects who designed major buildings for the fair had not previously produced many buildings in the style—not even Daniel Burnham, the fair's chief of construction.

The selection of the classical style for the fair was a product of several considerations. Although being inclined toward "conservative traditionalism" in matters of architectural taste, Burnham thought that the Romanesque style had run its course.[4] Another consideration was the common training at the École possessed by many of the architects selected to design the fair's major buildings. The tight construction schedule, from 1891 to 1893, meant that Burnham had to select a guiding theme with which all architects could identify. Classicism became that dominant theme, because "it seemed important to work with an easily understood architectural vocabulary."[5] The specifications had called for formal monumentality, similar styles, and a uniform cornice line.[6] The interest in classicism was also a product of America's rediscovery of its colonial and Revolutionary past, as well as the cultural artifacts associated with these traditions. With so few buildings molded in this style in the nation, classicism seemed novel.

Through the design and construction process, Burnham received the benefit of professional participation from allied artists, for example, landscape architects, sculptors, and artists. Burnham viewed the cooperative spirit among these professionals as a model to be replicated in other large architectural ventures.

The success of the fair exceeded most expectations. Its capture of the American imagination was also a matter of good timing. It opened in the wake of the 1893 depression, and its spirit served as a tonic to the nation gripped by an adverse economy. The lessons of the fair also exceeded the expectations of its planners. Rather than a simple educational exercise in the planning and execution of a major exhibition, the fair was received as a "model for reforming urban America."[7] Its architectural lessons were pervasive among members of the general public. As Burnham noted, the American population was "no longer ignorant regarding architectural matters. They have been awakened through the display of the World's Columbian Exposition of 1893."[8]

Even before the construction process on the fair had been completed, the full scope of the project was apparent to the many political leaders who stopped by to view the work. This creation of the architectural profession raised public recognition of the architect to unprecedented heights. The profession now spoke with stronger authority and with new political clout. The fair project served the profession well, for it allied the architects not only with political figures, but also with business leaders. One of these was Lyman J. Gage, chairman of the Chicago corporation that oversaw local support for the fair. Gage was later to become a kingpin in the implementation of the Tarsney Act. After the closing of the fair, Burnham's reputation was greatly enhanced. He emerged as the leader in the architectural profession and was regarded as a master organizer and promoter. Burnham's status among architects was underscored in 1893 when he was elected president of the American Institute of Architects (AIA), a position he held for two years.

Passage of the Tarsney Act

The legislative battle the AIA waged against the federal architecture program, initiated in the mid-1870s, continued throughout the following decade. By the early 1890s, the AIA began to sense that their long struggle was about to pay off. In the administration of Supervising Architect James Windrim, the AIA found its most fervent "in-house" supporter of opening federal building projects to competition since William A. Potter. Windrim had gained the support of Treasury Secretary William Windom, who endorsed the Windrim's recommendation that "the system of competitive designs for public buildings be tried."[9] Windrim's breakthrough was that, rather than recommending a complete revamping of the federal architecture program, he suggested the insertion of a simple statement as an amendment to regular legislation appropriating funds for federal buildings. In February 1891, for example, in a bill authorizing a new post office and subtreasury building in Chicago, Windrim suggested the addition of a section to the legislation "providing that, at the discretion of the Secretary of the Treasury, the plans for the same be obtained by competition of architects." In another bill, Windrim planted a provision of broader scope. He proposed the addition of an amendment, authorizing the secretary "at his discretion to obtain plans, drawings, and specifications for the erection of public buildings through competition, by architects."[10] No action was taken on either suggestion, but a faster route to the AIA objectives had been mapped out for its membership.

After Windrim left his position as supervising architect in April 1891, he worked with the AIA in drafting a bill that would give the secretary of the treasury discretionary powers in the matter of competitions.[11] By January 1892, Congressman John C. Tarsney from Missouri introduced a bill patterned after Windrim's draft legislation. It was referred to the House Committee on Public Buildings and Grounds, which held hearings on it in March 1892. A large contingent of architects testified on the desirability of the legislation, including a group of architects from Washington, D.C., such as Glenn Brown and James G. Hill. By the summer of 1892, the bill passed the House, but the lateness of the legislative schedule precluded Senate passage in 1892.

When Congress reconvened in 1893, the AIA realized that it had until March 4 to pass the Tarsney Bill because the Congress was scheduled to expire on that date. The AIA launched an intensive lobbying effort to ensure that the Senate would act before this date. Copies of the Tarsney Bill and accompanying materials were mailed to AIA members across the nation. AIA members were requested to lobby their Senators. Those members who resided in states represented in the Senate Committee on Buildings and Grounds were asked to "bring influence to bear upon them . . . [and] communicate with them at once, urging favorable consideration on their part, to the end that the bill may not be lost in committee. The influence of prominent men not members of the architectural profession would be of value in this connection."[12]

The AIA's lobbying prowess paid off. The Senate passed the bill, with only minor amendments. The *American Architect and Building News* concluded:

> The passage of the bill, in nearly the same form, by both houses, shows conclusively that the temper of Congress is favorable to the excellent measure proposed. . . . [The present Congress will] earn for itself the lasting gratitude of every one interested in the artistic advancement of the United States by being the first to take the public architecture out of the Government plan-factory and submit it to the best professional men in the country.[13]

The *Inland Architect* voiced hearty support for the bill, stating:

> There is no class of individuals that will not be benefitted by the change. . . . and the unsightly and needlessly expensive structure which now indicate that the government business is carried on within their walls, will give place to those of pleasing character, so that the stranger in looking for the government building will not be directed to look for the worst architectural monstrosity in the vicinity, but one to which the citizen may well point with pride.[14]

As one of his last official acts, President Harrison signed the Tarsney Act on 20 February 1893. Press reaction to the Tarsney Act was rapturous. The New York *Commercial Advertiser* stated that "by assigning one structure to one architect, it is thought that the grandeur of European public buildings may be approached."[15] The *American Architect* thought that the high standard of American architecture in private buildings testified to the "presence of genius and merit." Designers of private architecture in the United States demonstrated that in "originality, artistic feeling and skill in handling the masses which form the principal source of architectural effect . . . are not to be surpassed, or, as we believe, equalled by any architects in the world."[16]

Although the AIA found Congress receptive to its objectives in regards to federal architecture, the Treasury Department was less enthusiastic. Before the passage of the Tarsney Act, Treasury Secretary Charles Foster expressed the view to the Senate Committee on Public Buildings and Grounds that any measure contemplating a change in the operation of the Supervising Architect's Office should be "most carefully studied, in order to prevent the serious or disastrous effects which would result from any radical change in said system."[17] As the

Tarsney Bill neared passage, Supervising Architect Willoughby J. Edbrooke expressed "grave objections" to the bill; he felt, however, that with the discretionary powers left to the Secretary of the Treasury, it was possible to meet the "wishes of the members of the architectural profession who are so deeply interested in the matter."[18] Alfred Stone, secretary of the AIA, reported to the membership that Edbrooke had advised President Harrison to sign the bill.[19]

Postponement in Implementation of the Tarsney Act

With the passage of the Tarsney Act, the AIA set about the task of advising the new Treasury Secretary John G. Carlisle on the implementation of the act. The AIA recommended limiting competitions to no more than five entrants, "so that the chance of success for the individual may not be too small" and that the successful architect be employed to prepare all necessary drawings and superintend the building's construction. The AIA also proposed to Carlisle that the Tarsney Act be amended to provide expenses to the architects for the cost of preparing competitive plans and in working with the Treasury Department in advising on the competition program. Carlisle received the AIA's views, but by the summer of 1893 he had not acted on any of the suggestions.[20]

By early 1894, it became clear that the Cleveland administration and the Treasury Department had no desire to implement the Tarsney Act. Secretary Carlisle protested that according to a clause in the enactment of 1875, "no government building shall be commenced until after the design for it shall have been previously made by the Secretary of the Treasury."[21] Supervising Architect Jeremiah O'Rourke wrote to G. G. Vest, Chairman of the Senate Committee on Public Buildings and Grounds that the Tarsney Act did not *require* the secretary to procure designs by competition. Formulating a practical method to implement the act "raised many perplexing questions and involved radical changes in the existing organization." O'Rourke claimed that implementation of the act "demands a deliberate consideration which other pressing duties have compelled the Secretary hither to defer."[22]

The *Inland Architect* reflected on the disappointment of the architectural profession that the "secretary of the treasury and the supervising architect are hostile to the law . . . as it is with these gentlemen that the operation of the law rests and . . . it has been dead as a door nail for the year since its passage."[23] Subsequently, the *Inland Architect*, in reviewing the heated correspondence between Burnham and Carlisle / O'Rourke in the early months of 1894, concluded that the course pursued by the latter gentlemen reflected the desire of Carlisle to "give places to political friends, particularly if they are friends to or members of the Secretary's family." O'Rourke's actions could be interpreted as an effort, with his "good, though local reputation . . . [to] leave a national building as a monument to his architectural ability."[24]

Glenn Brown, Washington correspondent for the *American Architect* and an AIA partisan, viewed the continued obstinacy of the Treasury Department as delaying the dawning of a new era of:

> monumental, cultured and artistic Government architecture. . . .
> The work at the World's Fair has shown the architects of this country to be capable of producing effects in every respect equal to the best artistic work done in Europe, a fact which I think few people had before realized. Most people were willing to grant that we were equal to European architects in construction, planning and devices for comfort and convenience, but we were thought too utilitarian for proper artistic productions. When the proper men are selected, this has been proved untrue.[25]

In the 7 April 1894 issue of the *American Architect,* Brown launched his most comprehensive propaganda attack on the Supervising Architect's Office. Brown's article, "Government Buildings Compared with Private Buildings." was the main feature in this issue. Brown reviewed the struggle on the part of the AIA to revamp the federal architecture program since William A. Potter's first annual report. Brown then proceeded to compare the cost per square foot between government and private buildings, the time of construction, the cost of architectural services as a percentage of the total cost of a building, the methods by which the Office conducted its business, and the design of the buildings. The latter discussion compared the likes of Adler and Sullivan's Auditorium Building in Chicago with Mullett's Chicago custom house; it depicted the treatment of the Kansas City federal building as "suggestive of a public school;" and it described the State, War, and Navy Building as "distressing in its small masses, apparently jumbled together, small columns, small windows, awkward mansard roof, and coarse, meaningless details." On the other hand, Brown praised the Mills Treasury Department and Post Office buildings because they were, according to Brown, "designed by a private architect by special act of Congress." Brown concluded his lengthy essay with, "I think the facts show . . . the need of a thorough reorganization of the system."[26]

In the following issue, the *American Architect* urged its readers to "bring our last issue to . . . the attention [of a friend in the daily press] and urge him to aid in stimulating the aroused public opinion and in applying the lash to those at Washington who are wilfully blind."[27] The deadlock between the Treasury Department and the AIA also provoked the *American Architect* to note the importance of having the AIA represented in Washington, D.C., "the seat of the disease" of government public buildings.[28]

Following up on Brown's article, the AIA mailed a form letter to its membership, stating, "We have failed to win our cause through personal, private means and must now go to the Country with the facts." The letter outlined the AIA's arguments regarding what it described as needless costs of public buildings and architectural services. The letter also stated:

> The government buildings obtrude themselves upon us; are inferior not only to the *best* contemporary private structures, but to the *average* ones; few, if any, are well-planned, and all are more or less offensive in appearance. We wish to stop this great waste of the people's money, and to prevent the erection of any more structures which shall debase public taste.

In order to help the AIA with this cause, members were directed to read Brown's article and have at least ten (fifty, if possible) letters from influential men mailed to their respective congressmen and Senators. AIA members were also requested to urge "each and every newspaper and periodical within your reach" to publish articles favoring the passage of legislation opening all buildings projects over $25,000 to competition. As the letter reminded AIA members, "faithful, persistent, urgent effort on the part of all will be necessary in this reformation."[29]

Another "press release" that was printed but not distributed presented a synoptic history of the Office, "Buildings for the U.S. Government," from the AIA's point of view. It ascribed the beginning of the "system which in part still curses the country with its mediocre designs and excessive expenditure" with the "unfortunate day when

A. B. Mullett was appointed, by the Secretary of the Treasury, the Supervising Architect of the Treasury Department." The historical sketch went on to quote Adolf Cluss's 1869 tract on the history of the Supervising Architect's Office, which discussed the higher costs of architectural services for government buildings than those for private buildings. All of Mullett's successors, with the exception of Freret, Edbrooke, and O'Rourke, made recommendations regarding the defects of the system and the need to obtain plans by competition. The press release concluded with a summary of Glenn Brown's article that appeared in the *American Architect*, in which he demonstrated the "inferiority of design, the excessive cost and the enormous cost for architectural services of work done for the Government under the charge of the Supervising Architect's office, compared with private and corporate work under the charge of private architects."[30]

The McKaig and Aldrich Bills

The AIA's new legislative maneuver was to amend the Tarsney Act by spelling out how the act should be carried out administratively. Communications opened once more between the Treasury Department and the AIA at a dinner given by architect Bruce Price at the Union Club in New York City in May 1894. Assistant Secretary of the Treasury W. E. Curtis and a number of prominent architects were present. When pressed, Curtis made suggestions on how an amendment to the Tarsney Act might be worded. After the dinner, George B. Post prepared a draft of this amendment, which was subsequently reviewed by both Carlisle and the AIA.[31] Its provisions were included in a bill Congressman William M. McKaig of Maryland introduced in June 1894 and in an accompanying report.

Among other things, the McKaig Bill report contended that in European countries, central government buildings surpassed those built by municipal authorities and private enterprise in both artistic design and economy of construction. The situation in the United States was the opposite. "In fact, the buildings constructed recently by the United States as compared with those constructed a quarter of a century ago show a marked deterioration in artistic quality." The report also contended that because the supervising architect did not have the time to design buildings, the work of skilled architects was being carried out by "clerks and copyists." The reports also criticized the length of time required to construct federal buildings, which resulted in "great wastefulness and loss of money to the Government." According to the report, the intent of the McKaig Bill was to make the supervising architect the "supervisor of the architects of the Government's works."[32]

O'Rourke read the report:

> with astonishment, and with the deepest regret: astonishment that so many errors and mis-statements [sic] could have found their way into so brief a paper, and regret, which I believe you will fully share, that you and the Committee should have been misled into endorsing with your high authority, and even publishing as your own, gross mis-statements [sic] as facts, for which there is not now, nor has there ever been, a shadow of evidence or justification.[33]

The McKaig Bill provided for a "commission on public architecture" to consist of three architects and two officers from the Corps of Engineers. The commission would adopt procedures for conducting competitions. Competing architects would be limited to five in number and would be selected by ballot. Competitions would be open only to practitioners who had worked for at least ten years as "architect-in-chief."[34]

The architectural presses presented extensive coverage of the legislative proceedings and encouraged its readers to try to exert influence over their Congressmen to support the bill. By the end of 1894, however, the bill had not moved beyond being reported out of the House Committee on Public Buildings and Grounds. On the other side of the Capitol, the chairman of the Senate Committee, Senator John Hollis Bankhead of Alabama, refused to move the bill out of committee. The death of the McKaig bill was pronounced in March 1895 by the *Inland Architect*. Its demise was ascribed to a "most baleful influence in the present administration, that which has its head in the Secretary of the Treasury, and ramifies every department to which his influence has appointed a relative or friend."[35] The architectural profession's need for a Washington, D.C., presence was evident again.

It was also clear that the McKaig Bill inspired little support from the Cleveland administration. Later, O'Rourke claimed that he had favored the McKaig Bill, but the report that accompanied the bill was "wretched" and made "many gross errors and misstatements of which constituted such a reflection on the common sense and intelligence of the members of the Committee on Public Buildings and

Grounds that it antagonized every one of them—Republicans as well as Democrats." Because of the McKaig Report, O'Rourke thought it was his duty to "traverse and expose them [the errors and misstatements]."[36]

O'Rourke's departure in September 1894 and Charles E. Kemper's holding of the Supervising Architect's position on an acting basis provided Treasury Secretary Carlisle with an opportunity to try to reach an accord with the AIA by offering the position of supervising architect to one of the profession's leading figures—John M. Carrère. In sounding out Carrère as to his willingness to accept the position if offered to him, Carlisle evidently "was prepared to grant the appointee a much fuller control and more absolute power over the working forces and administrative functions of the bureau than has been enjoyed by any previous holders of the office." Carlisle even offered to allow Carrère to manage his office on the lines suggested in the McKaig Bill and the Tarsney Act. Almost perversely, the *American Architect* breathed a sigh of relief when Carrère turned down the position:

> [W]e feel that his acceptance of the place, though in itself guaranteeing an improvement, would put a definite stop to all chances that the method of Government building could ever be put on a proper basis and carried out on a plane of elevated and sustained effort. With so good a man in the office as Mr. Carrère, the movement for an improved method would stop—half way, and it would be almost impossible to induce the political official mind to grasp the fact that the pinnacle had not been reached.[37]

New reports questioned Carlisle's commitment to finding a rapprochement with the AIA because a reorganization of the Supervising Architect's Office had put O'Rourke at the mercy of his own chief executive officer, Charles E. Kemper, a close friend of Secretary Carlisle's son, Logan Carlisle. Logan Carlisle served as the chief clerk of the Treasury Department. Kemper and Logan Carlisle, together with law clerk Fleming, were the threesome who ran the Supervising Architect's Office and "mean to perpetuate their authority by securing the defeat of the McKaig bill."[38]

In the absence of a specific plan of the Cleveland administration, rumored alternative means of action spread through the architectural press during the period 1895 to 1897. One scheme was to have officers from the Corps of Engineers superintend the construction of

all public buildings across the country. The Army engineers had supervised the construction of the State, War, and Navy building and
the Library of Congress building, and they had executed their work
efficiently. The *American Architect* thought little of this idea. The publication felt that the rapidity with which the work had been carried
out was:

> due as much to the energy with which the officers cut off
> Congressional interference, and demanded appropriations, as to
> any hidden capacity of the military mind for making bricks and
> stones jump into their places without assistance. . . . The fact is
> that the people who can build most rapidly, skilfully [*sic*] and beau-
> tifully are the people who have devoted their lives to learning how
> to do so, namely, the architects; and the sooner the public stops
> dodging around them, and trying to utilize politicians and gener-
> als and carpenters and what not, in place of them, the better off it
> will be.[39]

The appointment of William Martin Aiken as supervising architect on 1 April 1895 did not quiet the urgings of the architectural
presses. The *Inland Architect* responded to the appointment by expressing confidence that because:

> no architect, no matter his ability for designing, construction and
> for business detail may be, can in any way fill the requirements of
> the office, it is hardly possible for us to congratulate Mr. Aiken
> upon his appointment. It cannot increase his standing in the pro-
> fession, and observation has shown that it does not add to an ar-
> chitect's volume of practice after he has again returned to private
> life.

However, the publication thought Aiken was the most able architect
to fill the position since William A. Potter.[40] In its own perverse way,
the *American Architect* remarked on Aiken's selection with, "for our
own part, a more undesirable choice would have pleased us more, as
it would have been more in keeping with the real deserts of a country which allows itself to be disgraced by maintaining its present system of public building."[41]

The new Chicago post office was a major building project that
stood on the horizon in the mid-1890s. Thwarted in its attempts to
force the Treasury Department to implement the Tarsney Act, the

AIA searched intently for another means to make the Chicago project an exception to the prevailing practice of the Supervising Architect's Office. With the Chicago project, Congress set a precedent. When funds were appropriated for the building, a provision was made directing the secretary of the treasury to establish a "Chicago Department" under the Supervising Architect's Office. The secretary was also directed to hire a Chicago architect to prepare designs for the building. While these directives may have warmed the hearts of the members of the AIA, the AIA noted the limit on funds for draftsmen and expert services and declared that the architect would receive little else but glory.[42] The view of the *American Architect* was more positive. It felt that the arrangement formed "a precedent for future Government work." The appointment of a Chicago architect would guarantee a building:

> constructed with full knowledge of our local materials, methods, etc. . . . Also everyone hopes and expects that as an example of design it will do much toward putting the Government architecture on a thoroughly artistic and satisfactory basis and be at the same time a model to which the city and profession may point with pride.[43]

With this precedent established, rumors began to fly throughout Chicago that Henry Ives Cobb (1859–1931) would be selected architect of this building (the building designed by Cobb is shown in figure 6.1). A native of Massachusetts, Cobb was a prominent architect in Chicago and an intimate of Potter Palmer. He had been architect of the Fisheries Building at the World's Columbian Exposition, one of the few fair buildings—other than Adler and Sullivan's Transportation Building—that was not designed in the classical mode. He had also designed other buildings at the fair, including the Indiana State Building, the Indian Building, the "Streets of Cairo," and the Marine Cafe. With his firm of Cobb & Frost, he was also architect of buildings at the University of Chicago, the Newberry Library, and many other buildings throughout the Midwest.[44]

In late 1895, Congressman James Franklin Aldrich of Illinois reintroduced the McKaig Bill. The Aldrich Bill, a virtual duplicate of the McKaig Bill, made its way through the congressional system. By the end of 1896, the House committee reported favorably on the bill. The Senate had taken no action. The AIA's efforts, through its

Figure 6.1
U.S. post office, Chicago,
Illinois, designed ca. 1895,
Henry Ives Cobb.
Courtesy National
Archives.

Legislative Committee on Government Architecture, on behalf of the Aldrich Bill were becoming expensive. At the AIA's thirtieth annual convention in Nashville, Tennessee, the committee asked for small contributions from members to defray the expenses of its work. At this critical point, the AIA felt that the legislation had never had a better chance of passing. There was no opposition now from Treasury Secretary Carlisle or from Supervising Architect Aiken. The Congress was more Republican, a situation favorable to the passage of the bill. The committee had also organized supporters of the Aldrich Bill to include a variety of private citizens, contractors, material men, and bankers, as well as architects. From the annual convention, George B. Post urged all members to go forward and "see that their Congressmen and Senators understand the bill and its purposes perfectly, and the result which it is expected to obtain from the bill. They should do this not only once, but they should do it persistently."[45]

The AIA viewed the Aldrich Bill as "defective in minor points," but changes in the bill could be made after its passage and after the "commission on public architecture" began its work and investigated the "difficulties of the problem." The main objective was the employment of "the very best architectural talent of the country." The bill was an "opening wedge" in doing away with the Supervising Architect's Office. The next legislative step envisioned by the AIA was the creation of a "department of architecture" separate from the Treasury Department.[46] However, the AIA felt that the establishment of a separate and independent "Bureau of Architecture" should await a future date. The AIA feared that should it be created in 1896, a prominent civil engineer, such as General Edward P. Casey, would be appointed to head it. Should the "commission on public architecture" later recommend independent status for the federal architecture program instead, the commission would then be in a position to "suggest the character and qualifications of the incumbent," most likely an architect.[47]

The AIA ascribed its success in Congress in moving the Aldrich Bill to its current status to:

> the object lesson in Chicago [which] has done more toward the passage of this bill than all the members of the American Institute of Architects and its supporters, and this object Mr. Burnham always had in mind when he would point out the buildings of the World's Fair and compare them with Government buildings, much to the disadvantage of the latter.[48]

The presidential election of 1896 brought the Republican party back to power. The resulting change at the Treasury Department promised more concrete results for the AIA than the waning Aldrich bill. By late 1896, the *American Architect* observed many applicants lining up for the position of supervising architect. The position was expected to be vacant in March 1897 with the presumed departure of William Martin Aiken, who did not leave until May of that year. However, in Aiken, the architectural profession found a man with "developed qualities and capacities which deserve the recognition and demand the support of his fellow members in the profession." The *American Architect* urged that president-elect William McKinley reappoint Aiken to the job:

> Far more than any of his recent predecessors, [Aiken] has been willing to sacrifice his personal ambitions and a desire to make a name, and has devoted himself to the execution of his many-sided duties in the spirit of a good executive official. He has been willing to introduce into the office several men who very likely are much better designers than he is himself, and has not, like his predecessors, given chief attention to "impressing his own individuality" on every design prepared in the office.

Also, Aiken was aware that with AIA and public pressure, the Supervising Architect's Office likely was in a state of transition and would remain so until it was "permanently modified, reformed and improved in consonance with the demands of an awakened and educated public demand."[49]

The arrival in March 1897 of Lyman J. Gage (figure 6.2) as secretary of the treasury filled the architectural profession with great expectation as "Mr. Gage's connection with Mr. Burnham during the 1893 fair was one of the closest and most cordial nature."[50] The *Inland Architect* described Gage as a "broad-minded, intelligent business man. He is not a politician and will look at the needs of his office from a business stand point, and supply them with the most competent men without regard to political interest." The publication then incorrectly predicted that Aiken would be retained.[51]

Later that year several architects, including some who participated in the World's Columbian Exposition, met with Gage in New York City at the inauguration of the Grand Memorial Arch. Gage spent an afternoon with the architects and stated that he intended to implement the Tarsney Act.[52] To this, the AIA declared:

Figure 6.2
Secretary of the Treasury
Lyman J. Gage. Courtesy
National Archives.

All honor to Lyman J. Gage, Secretary of the Treasury of the
United States, and Honorary member of this Institute! If successful in this undertaking his name will shine in history most bril-
liantly as the rescuer of Government Architecture from the in-
cubus by which it has been crushed for years.[53]

The War of Words

The lobbying activities that the AIA carried out during the 1890s were
presented against a backdrop of the private architects' perception of
the Supervising Architect's Office. This perception had been developing since the late 1860s when the AIA first focused on the activities
of Alfred B. Mullett. In retrospect, the AIA's arguments on behalf of
their cause were intended to convince their colleagues, politicians,
and the general public of the validity of their vision. The arguments
took on tones of black-and-white and good-and-evil so as to heighten
the disparity between what existed and what would result from the
success of the AIA's cause.

In order for the lobbying to be successful, the "facts" cited by the
AIA were necessarily exaggerated beyond actuality. It was no wonder
that Treasury Department officials and the occupants of the supervising architect position were offended by the pronouncements of
the AIA in their effort to open federal architecture projects to competition. It is also not surprising that with the nearing completion of
the World's Columbian Exposition in Chicago, the AIA's arguments
appeared to have visual credibility and that the Tarsney Act was
passed just months before the fair officially opened. So powerful were
the visual "lessons" of the fair and so strongly stated were the opinions of the AIA regarding the federal government architecture program that they endured well into the early decades of the twentieth
century.

While there were many issues that divided the AIA and the numerous supervising architects, they generally agreed on the *objective*
of the "official architecture" of the United States government. Both
sides agreed that federal government buildings should "serve as
models and standards of excellence and superiority for the works
of private ownership."[54] The standards of public architecture in
Europe were frequently the measuring stick for judging the condition of American public architecture. However, foreign standards
most often were cited in vague terms. Supervising Architect Jeremiah

O'Rourke agreed with the AIA that public buildings in the United States reflected great mechanical and material progress. On the other hand, early in his administration, O'Rourke felt that the federal government had "almost wholly neglected the development of Architecture and the Fine Arts, leaving this latter almost entirely to the public spirit and munificence of private citizens."[55] Later, with his back pressed to the wall by the McKaig Report, O'Rourke reversed himself in:

> asserting confidently that the public buildings now designed and erected by this office will compare favorably even with European public buildings, and that in design, arrangement, construction and cost they are fully equal to the best buildings erected either by states, municipalities or private enterprise, and far superior to the great majority of such buildings.

Turning his other cheek to the attacks of the AIA on federal building design, O'Rourke pointed to "sky scraping monstrosities" and "architectural aberrations" produced for private enterprise, much of which he contended was disgracing the streets of the nation's cities and towns, "debauching public taste as to correct architecture, and provoking the condemnation of educated taste and criticism."[56]

No doubt, O'Rourke would have agreed with Daniel H. Burnham's declaration:

> [I]t is a fact that public buildings badly designed depress and injure the artistic sense of the whole people, instead of inspiring a better taste as good ones would. The national structures are the landmarks of our professional horizon, they are most prominent when men are gathered together, and no one can help but see them. So for good or ill, we are all profoundly affected by them.[57]

How the nation intended to reach the goal of improving federal government architecture was the crux of the differences between the Supervising Architect's Office and the AIA. O'Rourke felt that in the Office would be found the embryo of all that would be required for the "development of our national architecture to its highest expression." In fact, O'Rourke thought that with the encouragement and cooperation of Congress, the Office was capable of "being made the nucleus of a National Academy of Architecture and Fine Arts, which in a comparatively few years would equal, and probably surpass anything of the kind that now exists in Europe, or has existed in modern times."[58]

Supervising Architect Will. A. Freret questioned the AIA's assertion that securing designs through competition would improve the quality of federal building design. In June 1888, Freret wrote to Treasury Secretary Charles S. Fairchild:

> [T]he offer of a premium in cases of public competition is rarely an inducement sufficient to secure competition between architects of ability or reputation, and even where competition has been secured and the bonus awarded, it frequently happens that the administration and execution of the work is entrusted to architects who were non-competitors.[59]

The press of work in the Supervising Architect's Office and the sameness of the functions led to buildings that appeared to be similar from one location to another. This apparent replication of styles provoked the AIA to accuse the Office of functioning like a "plan factory." To this suggestion, Supervising Architect O'Rourke remarked, "It would seem unnecessary to produce proof of the fact that Government buildings are not duplicated, as the fact must be patent to any persons who have eyes to see the buildings themselves." The only similarities O'Rourke observed were their "general architectural expression which necessarily marks the taste and preference as to style of each successive Supervising Architect." In fact, O'Rourke argued that designs for federal government buildings were more varied than in private practice:

> Each building erected from this office varied from all others in design, dimensions, arrangement and material, each case being governed by the limit of the appropriation, the amount and character of the public business to be accommodated, and the location and surroundings of the site, and indeed it would be absurd to think that any other method could be procured.[60]

A frequent refrain of the AIA in its depiction of the Office was that federal buildings were being designed by clerks, copyists, and non-architects. To these assertions, O'Rourke stated that "thoroughly competent architects, engineers and draughtsmen," who possessed all necessary qualifications, carried out the design and technical work. O'Rourke contended that the personnel of the Office were equal if not superior to those found in most private firms. The Office operated as a "first class architectural establishment; it being the most extensive in this country—probably in the world." The high caliber of the staff was evident from "the fact that very many names could be given of architects and engineers now successfully conducting private practice and bearing high reputations, who have from time to time, as opportunity invited, gone out from this office to assume their present positions."

O'Rourke regarded himself as an example of the excellent qualifications possessed by the staff of the office. He had "enjoyed the advantage of a regular architectural and art education and training in one of the best schools of Europe, fully equal to that of any private architect in our country, without exception, and superior to the great majority." In addition to his training, O'Rourke thought that the length, scope, and variety of his professional practice had made him fully qualified to "develop Federal architecture to its highest legitimate character and expression."[61]

While O'Rourke expressed great confidence in the Supervising Architect's Office, the AIA thought that the mere existence of the Office was a mistake. The AIA pointed to the several good men who had held the position of supervising architect and their ultimate powerlessness to do good. As the AIA deduced:

> This is conclusive evidence that the system is radically bad. Its failure is another proof that architecture is a fine art, that it must be treated as a fine art and not as a mere business, that a successful design must be the result of the concentrated effort of one mind, and that the moment that conflicting demands on the controlling mind are such that its proper functions must be delegated to others, in that moment all art leaves the work and it becomes stale, flat and unprofitable.[62]

The AIA viewed the system of procuring designs for federal buildings as inherently wrong because no one person, no matter how talented, could ever fulfill both the artistic and administrative requirements of the position. For example, the requirements of the job included maintaining all federal government buildings already occupied. George B. Post felt that building maintenance was "all that one can do. . . . With the mass of work which comes to the Supervising Architect it is absolutely impossible for him to do one good thing unless he neglected all the rest of the work to do it."[63]

The evils of the system, according to the report that accompanied the Tarsney Act, resulted in "designs and plans [that] fall so far behind the standards of the age that they are obsolete almost before they are drawn, and are always wasteful and extravagant." The system had been created during a time when the small scale of the building program was "within the scope of the capacity of one man." According to the report, the Supervising Architect's Office was created in order to:

> obtain the exclusive benefit of the artistic skill and scientific knowledge of one learned and eminent in the profession of architecture for the planning of the buildings to be erected for its use. The main purpose in the creation of the office was that its incumbent should be the artistic designer of such buildings.

Instead, the heavy administrative workload required learned architects to be occupied with clerical work.[64]

While the AIA took pains to avoid pinning public blame for the ills of the federal government architecture program on the individuals who held the position of supervising architect (except for Alfred B. Mullett), they took aim at the qualifications of the design staff. In the report accompanying the Tarsney Act, the designs for federal buildings were ascribed to "clerks and copyists" who possessed "no architectural skill or learning." The "clerks and copyists" produced designs for buildings by the "simple system of copying the drawings and specifications of a structure constructed in one locality to be used as the design for another in a different locality, and this regardless of the differences in geological or atmospheric condition or space requirement." This system of design precluded the possibility of "progress in architectural design."[65] And a journalist wrote, "the subordinates in the different departments are often such as would not be tolerated in the practice of a good private architect; and when capable and efficient men are in the office they are hampered by the regulations and circumstances so as to well nigh destroy their usefulness."[66]

The staff at the building site also came under attack. The Tarsney report characterized the local superintendents as:

> some local carpenter or builder who never made any pretense to architectural knowledge or study, and whose appointment was secured, not because of his skill or knowledge of the work, but be-

cause of the political influence he could marshall to secure him employment, and whose greatest solicitude is to prolong the tenure of his employment in delaying the completion of the work.[67]

Then there was the issue of the private architects' right to prepare designs for federal government buildings. It was felt that successful architects, "as the culmination of their labors," should be rewarded with commissions for federal buildings.[68] "The nation has a right to expect that the public buildings should at least be fair examples of the architectural talent of the country, while the profession has no less right to the government patronage."[69] The enhancement of the architectural profession and its leaders was felt to be inherent in the implementation of the Tarsney Act and the passage of the McKaig and Aldrich bills. The *American Architect* regarded the provisions of the McKaig Bill as establishing:

> [a] means of making an open distinction between the real leaders of the profession and the rank and file, and will give to those who are in the ranks merely because of present youth and inexperience a reason for greater exertion, in the hope of attaining, finally, the distinction of having been entrusted with Government work—a distinction which, at present, few true architects crave.[70]

Architects also desired the opportunity to design major public buildings. As John M. Carrère stated:

> No architect can have a higher ambition, than to successfully design and execute a public monument, and it is my belief that nothing could be more educational or more improving to the profession at large in this country, than this opportunity to study monumental architecture. Twenty-two story buildings are expensive and quite elevated, but not at all elevating.[71]

The AIA also viewed its members as possessing special insight into the importance of the Tarsney Act and the McKaig and Aldrich bills. Congressmen "did not realize the widespread influence of architecture in educating the masses. . . . We do. We know how important it is. You cannot expect the average Congressman to take the artistic view of the subject."[72] Press coverage of the ongoing legislative process depicted Senator James Henderson Berry of Bentonville,

Arkansas, as representative of the legislation's opponents. Senator Berry, from a town of 1,600 citizens, held the local courthouse as an architectural ideal. The Bentonville courthouse was a small red-brick building with a red cupola. Berry came from a tradition that believed that "civic dignity cannot be expressed architecturally save as their courthouse expresses it." The little courthouse inspired "simple reverence and patriotism."[73]

James Windrim credited the American people with possessing an educated taste that was "not satisfied with the mediocrity in art." Their cultivated taste made them demand beauty in architecture.[74] This growing taste of the American people was noted by the correspondent for *The Southern Architect*, C. H. Read Jr., who stated:

> To those who visited the recent Columbian Exhibition at Chicago, and who travel with their eyes open, these buildings [U. S. government buildings] speak for themselves. Attention has at least been drawn to them and a comparison between the classes challenged, and the architects of the country without fear await the people's verdict.[75]

A change in the system of procuring designs would "raise the standard of the art, create new incentive, bring forth new men, new opportunities, and result in covering this country with monuments which will eventually compare with those of other countries, and in time perhaps excel them."[76] The AIA committee charged with promoting the McKaig Bill predicted that if the bill passed:

> federal buildings would then be under the charge of leading architects in the different sections of the country where they are to be erected. They would become individual to the locality and the outgrowth of the same, not only in design, but in construction and materials. They would also receive constant supervision, and would be built as promptly and as economically as buildings for private individuals.[77]

The appointment of Lyman J. Gage as secretary of the treasury in 1897 silenced the war of words between the AIA and the Treasury Department. In retrospect, the heated arguments on both sides were a measure of their efforts to sway public opinion in favor of their cause. Once the Treasury Department set its mind to implement the Tarsney Act, the war was "won." The struggle served as an educational experience for the AIA and convinced them of the necessity of maintaining a presence in Washington, D.C., in order to lobby Congress on their views on federal government architecture as well as on other matters. (The AIA moved its headquarters to the nation's capital in 1899.) The protracted hostilities also served as a warning to current and future treasury officials that the AIA could wield important congressional support in favor of its causes. The "victory" of the AIA in 1897 provided an opportunity for its members and the public to measure the correctness of the institute's vision of the federal architecture program under a competitive process. A new era in public architecture was inaugurated and the AIA claimed credit for the transformation.

7

PROPONENTS OF "ACADEMIC CLASSICISM"

1895–1925

Trends rooted in earlier decades—a renewed interest in the classical language of architecture and in creating a more coherent urban landscape—spurred the transformation of American public architecture in the 1890s. These trends were unified into a single image at the World's Columbian Exposition. The picturesque styles faded into obscurity during the 1890s but did not completely disappear. Classicism gained in popularity during this decade and dominated the sympathies of architects and building clients for the next five decades.

Whether or not the implementation of the Tarsney Act was essential to the progression of federal government architecture from the picturesque to the classical style is open to debate. The American Institute of Architects (AIA) claimed that this act alone was responsible for the "improvement of federal architecture" beyond what it had been since the creation of the consolidated federal architecture program in the early 1850s. As AIA lobbyist Glenn Brown contended, "Under the Tarsney Act it must be conceded that the work is immeasurably superior to any building done by the government from 1860 to 1896." Brown also credited the act with serving as "a material factor in uplifting the character of work" that the staff of the Supervising Architect's Office still carried out.[1] These benefits for the Tarsney Act were still claimed after the act was repealed in 1912 and throughout the 1920s and 1930s.

The classicism of the late nineteenth and early twentieth centuries was based on an educated knowledge of classical styles as adapted during the Italian Renaissance and as French and European countries further developed it. It also paid homage to America's colonial architecture which provided the inspiration for neocolonial and Georgian revival styles. The colonial style was felt to be particularly appropriate to American architecture because it was "sufficiently allied on the one hand to the Classic and Renaissance formulas to admit of any degree of refining study, while on the other it impinges enough on the style of the Louis, the Jacobean and Queen Anne to allow of expansion in the direction of any exuberance that may suit the whim of the designer or client." For this reason, the *American Architect and Building News* predicted that the colonial style "will always remain the standard type in this country."[2]

The adaptation of these styles to new buildings could be considered eclectic, because the overall style, details, and motifs were derived from a number of sources. However, there was also a concern with correct proportions, massing, and dimensions based on mastering the language of classical forms. The aim of the classical movement was to "look to wisdom embodied in precedent in order to solve contemporary problems."[3] As public buildings during this period were almost invariably of the classical or neocolonial style, this phase in the history of the federal architecture program can generally be placed under the umbrella of "academic classicism."

While architecture of this period was often considered backward-looking because of its references to historical forms, some observers felt that classicism blazed the trail to a modern style that was uniquely American. As Theodore W. Pietsch noted:

> Our too great prepossession for the picturesque and exaggerated silhouette has been tempered, and we have been taught to consider more wisely the values of mass and proportion. This is a healthy check to an active and robust imagination, and, far from blighting our natural individuality, will serve to nourish and cultivate the same, along firm and mature lines, and prepare the way for the coming of that day that shall print upon the face of our buildings as clearly as upon our bales of merchandise, the words of national stamp: "Made in America".[4]

Although the administration of Supervising Architect Willoughby Edbrooke is most often associated with the picturesque period in federal government architecture, several designs that emerged under his name were harbingers of buildings to come. For example, the post office and court house for Fargo, North Dakota, designed during Edbrooke's period, was classical in massing proportions and in details, even if it supported a picturesque tower at one end. It was unlike most of the other federal government buildings of Edbrooke's, and later O'Rourke's, period. It signified that the Office was aware of the new architectural wave about to break over the nation and had experimented with the new forms.

William Martin Aiken

The administration of William Martin Aiken (1855–1908) marked a significant break with the picturesque past. Aiken was a native of Charleston, South Carolina. He received his architectural training from the Massachusetts Institute of Technology and worked for several years in various Boston area offices, including that of Henry Hobson Richardson. In 1885, Aiken moved to Cincinnati where he practiced architecture and taught at the Cincinnati Academy of Design. He was respected by the AIA and the architectural presses. Upon his appointment in April 1895, the *Inland Architect* asserted that, "With the exception of Mr. Potter, no architect with equal training has filled the Office of the Supervising Architect." The publication expressed confidence that the Supervising Architect's Office "will be elevated as far as its conditions will allow."[5]

Aiken's architectural sympathies were in keeping with those of the AIA and its leaders. He professed great admiration for the architecture at the 1893 World's Columbian Exposition, which he felt was a triumph for the École des Beaux Arts in "the general arrangement, proportions, details of the chaste and beautiful Art building and those magnificent structures forming the Court of Honor." Aiken viewed the architectural success of the fair as an important step in addressing the problem of evolving an "American Style of Architecture."[6]

Simply stated, Aiken's philosophy of public building design was:

> thorough but simple construction, using the most substantial and fireproof materials permissible within the limit of appropriation, elaboration of design being of secondary importance, and the use of local material has been taken into consideration whenever suitable for the purpose.[7]

Aiken's public statement belied the emphasis he placed on architectural and interior design as represented in his buildings. The illustrations that accompanied his annual reports presented romantic depictions of urban life, with parks, promenades, church spires, and a benign industrial presence. The interiors of federal buildings were never before depicted in annual reports, but Aiken's pride in interiors caused him to include illustrations of them (figure 7.1). The perspectives for the annual reports received special attention. Architects and engravers, such as Julius A. Schweinfurth of Boston and Albert Bierstadt of New York City, prepared them.

Federal buildings designed under Aiken were in keeping with the new interest in classical and American colonial forms. For the U.S. Mint in Denver, Colorado, he devised a simple Italian Renaissance exterior (figure 7.2), with elaborate interior detailing. The custom house and post office in New London, Connecticut, was one of the office's first colonial-revival buildings, with Georgian details and forms adapted to a building of a scale larger than that of the eighteenth century (figure 7.3). The design for the classical style U.S. Mint

Figure 7.1
Law library, U.S. courthouse, St. Paul, Minnesota, 1893–1900, William Martin Aiken. Courtesy National Archives.

ELEVATION ON COLFAX AVE.

STATE STREET ELEVATION.

in Philadelphia provided a building on a scale that was later typical of buildings included in "City Beautiful" plans (figure 7.4). The post office for Pueblo, Colorado, included decorative motifs from Spanish-American buildings integrated into a building of classical proportions (figure 7.5). These were buildings that recalled the standards set by the 1893 fair in design and adaptation to local traditions.

Some of the inspiration for the buildings designed under Aiken's administration can be ascribed to the sizable corps of "temporary draftsmen" hired to handle the design workload. During the nineteenth century, the title of draftsman was ascribed to a range of design professionals in the Supervising Architect's Office. In most cases, the draftsmen were the architects of the federal buildings. The drafts-

Figure 7.2 (*top*) U.S. Mint, Denver, Colorado, 1896, William Martin Aiken. Courtesy National Archives.

Figure 7.3 (*bottom*) U.S. custom house and post office, New London, Connecticut, 1896–1898, William Martin Aiken. Courtesy National Archives.

SPRING GARDEN STREET ELEVATION
Scale: 1/16"=1'-0"

Figure 7.4 (top)
U.S. Mint, Philadelphia,
Pennsylvania, 1896–1901,
William Martin Aiken.
Courtesy National
Archives.

Figure 7.5 (bottom)
U.S. post office, Pueblo,
Colorado, 1896–1898,
William Martin Aiken.
Courtesy National
Archives.

men under Aiken included accomplished architects such as Frank L. Averill, Francis B. Wheaton, George Oakley Totten, Jr., Edward A. Crane, and James Knox Taylor.

A native of Decorah, Iowa, Averill worked in the Office for periods during the late nineteenth and early twentieth centuries before leaving permanently in 1904 to take up a private practice.[8] Wheaton had worked for the firms of Van Brunt and Howe and for McKim, Mead & White before employment with the Office in 1895. He resigned in 1905 to become advisory architect to the War Department.[9] Totten, described as one of Aiken's protégés, was sent to represent the United States at the International Convention of Architects at

Pueblo, Colo.
July 6, 1900.

Brussels in 1897. The *American Architect* felt that he was too young to speak for the architectural profession in a gathering of "old world celebrities."[10] After his departure from the Supervising Architect's Office as the chief designer in 1898, Totten became a well-known architect in Washington, D.C.; the firm of Totten & Rogers designed many residential structures throughout the city. Crane was recommended to Aiken by Wheelright and Haven, where he served as head draftsman. Crane later became chief of the Engineering and Drafting Division in the Supervising Architect's Office but resigned in 1903 to join the Philadelphia firm of Rankin, Kellogg and Crane.[11] In his application to the AIA for membership, Crane claimed credit for the design of the custom house and post office at New London, Connecticut; the Philadelphia Mint; and the U.S. Government Building at the Trans-Mississippi Exhibition at Omaha, Nebraska.[12] Taylor entered the Supervising Architect's Office in April 1895 and quickly rose through the ranks to become supervising architect in October 1897.

Aiken's design interests were also reflected in the architectural books purchased for the Office's library. These books included *Colonial Architecture in Charleston and Savannah, Colonial Details in Philadelphia, Colonial Furniture and Interiors,* and *The World's Fair.* Aiken also requested photographs of American Indians from the Bureau of Ethnology for "purposes of design in this office."[13] Aiken allowed his architectural staff freedom in the preparation of designs for federal buildings, and he was relieved from much of the routine administrative responsibilities. The chief executive officer, Charles E. Kemper, handled the business side of the Office's work. Rather than viewing this position as a threat to his authority, as O'Rourke expressed it, Aiken viewed Kemper's role as freeing him "as much as possible from routine checking and signing of mail matter which has already received the supervision of the Chief Executive Officer." This arrangement allowed Kemper to proceed with matters that had no relation to architectural or technical matters. Aiken then had additional time for "those things that are strictly in the line of my profession."[14] The *American Architect* applauded Aiken's willingness to subordinate his design authority to the talented design staff. The publication lauded the buildings turned out during his administration as "markedly superior to recent governmental buildings in all that concerns propriety, sobriety and common sense."[15]

When Aiken departed from the Treasury Department in June 1897, the *American Architect* lamented:

Of Mr. Aiken, the retiring incumbent, architects will speak only
with praise. Whatever might have been his other qualifications for
an office which demands tact and discretion, as much, perhaps, as
professional skill, it can be truly said that he brought to it high
training and perfect integrity, and that he labored earnestly and
successfully to make the Government building-work a creditable
feature in the artistic development of the country.[16]

Aiken centered much of his postgovernment career in New York City,
where in late 1901 he was appointed consulting architect and chief in-
spector of the Building Department of New York City.[17] Upon his
death in December 1908, his former colleagues in the Treasury
Department remembered him as instrumental in bringing about a
new era in the design and construction of public buildings.[18]

Early Steps to Implement the Tarsney Act

The architectural presses were gratified to learn that Treasury
Secretary Lyman G. Gage had issued an order to put into force the
provisions of the Tarsney Act. It was also reported that the position
of supervising architect would be filled by a competitive examination
in which the AIA would participate. It was anticipated that, with the
implementation of the Tarsney Act, the new supervising architect
would "devote himself mainly to the conduct of the business of the
office, while the designing of new buildings for Government will be,
so far as existing laws permit, entrusted to private architects, selected
by some form of competition."[19]

With Aiken gone, Kemper again became acting supervising architect. Kemper's legal background and his devotion to administrative
matters relieved the AIA of any fears that he would vie for the permanent position of supervising architect. With the advice of the architectural profession, Kemper developed the plan for carrying out
the Tarsney Act. The regulations for the competitive program provided for the secretary of the treasury to invite "at least five architects
of good professional standing" to submit plans, drawings, and
specifications for federal buildings.

A commission (jury) made up of the supervising architect and two
other architects would critique the merits of the designs. The successful competitor would be compensated with a percentage of the
cost of the building for professional services. The other competitors

would receive no payment. Soon after the issuance of the Tarsney Act regulations, the Treasury Department announced that the first building to be designed under the act was the court house and post office at Norfolk, Virginia. For this project, George B. Post and Daniel Burnham were selected to serve on the jury. In carrying out the wishes of Secretary Gage in regards to the Tarsney Act, the *Inland Architect* felt that Kemper had created such a good impression of executive ability that his retention as acting supervising architect might actually be in keeping with what the profession hoped for the position of supervising architect—that it be in the future "purely executive and supervisory."[20]

While the Tarsney Act regulations were being issued, Gage was searching for a new supervising architect. The announcement of the position in July 1897 inspired the *Inland Architect* to suggest that political influence with the position would soon be replaced by merit. However, the salary of $4,500 would not attract many "architects of well-established practice . . . but it will bring to the service of the country the best architectural talent obtainable for the money." Applicants for the position were requested to submit information on their education and work experience, examples of their work, and an essay describing their approaches to design and administration. Applicants were also required to "undergo a test in formulating a scheme for competition for a public building, and in criticizing designs submitted to them for their [the United States Civil Service Commission's] guidance and inspection."[21]

As could be predicted, no architects of major reputation applied for the position. The civil service examination, assisted by George B. Post, Daniel H. Burnham, Robert Peabody, Theophilus Chandler, and John M. Carrère, whittled down the list of sixty applicants to three finalists: Howard Constable and George M. Huss, both of New York City, and James Knox Taylor. It was reported that Taylor entered the competition more in the spirit of testing how well he stood in relation to his peers, but he had no expectation that he would be selected.[22]

James Knox Taylor

Speculation regarding prospective candidates for supervising architect was stilled on 20 October 1897 with the appointment of James Knox Taylor (1857–1929) to the position (figure 7.6). Taylor was a na-

Figure 7.6
James Knox Taylor.
Courtesy National
Archives.

tive of Knoxville, Illinois, and was educated at schools in St. Paul, Minnesota. He received his architectural training at the Massachusetts Institute of Technology and was a classmate of his predecessor, William Martin Aiken. Taylor's early architectural work include a position with the offices of C. C. Haight and later Bruce Price of New York City. In 1882, Taylor began his architectural practice in St. Paul. Two years later, he formed a partnership with Cass Gilbert, another former MIT classmate who had worked in the firm of McKim, Mead & White. Gilbert found Taylor an agreeable partner because the latter's practice was already established. In addition, Taylor offered "expertise in the business and technical aspects of architecture, unquestionable integrity, and prime social connections."[23] The firm of Gilbert & Taylor designed a large number of residences for prominent St. Paul families, churches, and office buildings.[24] While the two engaged in a successful and, one assumes, a harmonious partnership, there is some indication that Gilbert had a low regard for Taylor's artistic interests. As Gilbert reported to his friend and fellow architect in St. Paul, Clarence H. Johnston, in January 1879, "When I spoke enthusiastically of a sea, a sky, and a bit of sunlight he [Taylor] made me think that his artistic soul was thinking of a fat position in a comfortable office, rather than of artistic aspirations and delight."[25]

Taylor and Gilbert parted company in 1892 on friendly terms. The economic depression of 1893 hit Minnesota hard and building operations declined. Taylor chose to leave St. Paul on account of his wife's health, and they moved to Philadelphia where she had relatives. In Philadelphia, Taylor entered into a partnership with Amos J. Boyden to form the firm of Boyden & Taylor. However, the depression prevented the firm from flourishing and Taylor, weighed down by personal responsibility, wrote to Jeremiah O'Rourke inquiring about a position as a draftsman in the Supervising Architect's Office.[26] He received a perfunctory reply that his application would be placed on file. A few weeks later, Taylor wrote to O'Rourke again outlining his financial plight. He even considered leaving his profession and taking up another line of work.[27] Taylor succeeded in gaining a position as a temporary draftsman in April 1895 at $7.00 per day. By October 1896, Taylor had been promoted to the position of temporary principal draftsman at $8.00 per day. In 1897, he was appointed chief draftsman.

Taylor's ascension to the position of supervising architect caught the *American Architect* by surprise and rendered it nearly speechless. The publication announced the appointment but uncharacteristically omitted any comment on the event.[28] The *Inland Architect* thought that Taylor's appointment, the first civil service supervising architect, represented "the regular and well-merited course of promotion—the true aim of civil service—reform."[29] His selection, according to the publication, presented a "most convincing proof that there is as much and as high a degree of talent in that office as can be found outside; and that while there have been most execrable designs turned out from that office, the fault has always been with the men in charge, who generally were politicians, not architects."[30]

Many years later, in 1913, it was revealed that while Taylor was selected from the list of eligibles, he was not the first choice.[31] Taylor's successor, Oscar Wenderoth, speculated that while Taylor did not pass the examination with the highest marks, he was appointed because, as head draftsman in the Office, "it was considered that his knowledge of the work of the office gave him a special fitness for the place."[32]

In Taylor's essay, which was included in his civil service examination, he outlined his philosophy of public building design and of the administration of the Supervising Architect's Office. The *Inland Architect* reprinted portions of the text of his essay. According to Taylor, the selection of an architectural style for a public building should be guided by three considerations: first, that the style should have dignity; second, the public buildings should be pleasant to look upon and should be beautiful; and third, the style should permit a convenient interior arrangement. In the running of the Office, "the more closely good business principles and methods can be applied, the more satisfactory will be the work in the end."

Taylor thought that designs for public buildings should be secured by competition among U.S. architects:

> [I]t is impossible for any one man to have as intimate a knowledge of the requirements of buildings in all sections of this great country as have those of his profession who have devoted themselves to the acquisition of experience in the particular section in which any proposed building is to be. Even were it possible for any one man to acquire such knowledge, no one human brain is equal to the task of designing the large number of buildings that are necessary in a year, and turning them out perfect or even nearly perfect of their kind.

Should the supervising architect be relieved of much design responsibility, he would:

> become in reality what his title would seem to imply. He could devote his attention to seeing personally that the three general considerations stated in the beginning of this thesis were studied, and that the actual work of construction was honestly done. Another advantage gained would be the reduced liability of the designs for public buildings falling into a rut of similarity.[33]

At Taylor's appointment, his personal qualities seemed impeccable. The *Inland Architect* described his appearance in glowing terms. Taylor was characterized as "suave and genial, thoroughly liked by superiors, equals and subordinates; sympathetic, yet firm, in character; without political debts to pay."[34]

By the spring of 1898, Taylor had surrounded himself with loyal subordinates. They included Kemper, who continued to serve as chief executive. James A. Wetmore, a lawyer on the staff of the office since 1896, was the chief of the Office's Law and Records Division. According to the *Inland Architect*, Wetmore's job was to watch "day and night that Uncle Sam may not be outwitted by bad, *designing* men." The "Chief Constructor," H. R. P. Hamilton of St. Paul, oversaw the work of the draftsmen, tracers, and photographers. Under Hamilton were Edward A. Crane, principal draftsman, and Francis B. Stryker, assistant draftsman.

In order to avoid "cut and dried, stereotyped buildings," Taylor inaugurated a new system of building design within the office. The position of chief designer was abolished. In its place, Taylor held open four "designer" positions for which the draftsmen could compete. The competition took the form of an examination in which the draftsmen were to demonstrate their knowledge of architecture, its history and styles, construction methods, building materials, and the location and treatment of public buildings. In this examination, the draftsmen were required to "show versatility and rapidity in handling decorative problems, and also demonstrate their ability to quickly, truthfully and intelligibly represent a design by a rough study; and later they will be allowed to restudy and elaborate the design upon the lines already established by that sketch." Taylor was convinced that this system of "healthy rivalry" would result in better buildings and a "more diversified interpretation of his ideas."[35] The result of this system, according to the *American Architect*, was the creation of a "real atmosphere of an architectural studio, to have access to which a young man may now honorably be eager."[36]

The result of Taylor's administration of the office was a select number of federal buildings, usually those located in large cities, designed under the Tarsney Act provisions, and a larger number of modest government buildings, usually post offices, located in small communities, which were designed by the Office staff. Much to the surprise of the *American Architect*, "the average architectural worth of the designs for which Mr. Taylor is officially responsible has at least equalled the average worth of those prepared by private architects, under the workings of the Tarsney Act." The publication ascribed this development to Taylor's good sense, patience, and "self-abnegation to bring about the long-desired improvements" that attracted talented designers and draftsmen to government service."[37] The federal buildings for Annapolis (figure 7.7), Cumberland, Maryland (figure 7.8), and Muskegon, Michigan (figure 7.9), typify buildings designed under Taylor's supervision.

The Tarsney Act was first applied to the custom house in Norfolk, Virginia (figure 7.10). The jury, made up of Kemper, Post, and Burnham, selected designs prepared by the Baltimore firm of Wyatt & Nolting. The *American Architect* credited part of the success of the entry to the perspective drawings prepared by C. D. Maginnis.[38] The second competition was for the Ellis Island Immigration Station buildings. The New York firm of Boring & Tilden won the competition. In its entry for the Ellis Island buildings, the firm paid close attention to the immigration laws and the method in which the immi-

Figure 7.7
U.S. federal building,
Annapolis, Maryland,
1899–1901, James Knox
Taylor. Courtesy
National Archives.

grants would enter, be detained, and then be discharged into the United States. The buildings were outfitted with dormitories, facilities for medical examinations, and an information bureau. The *Inland Architect* praised the winning scheme as "away and above any submitted by other competitors."[39] The third Tarsney Act project was the post office and courthouse in Camden, New Jersey. The cost of the Camden building, $168,000, evidently was too small to inspire the creative juices of the firms invited to compete. The invited firms included Bailey & Truscott, Totten & Rogers, Edgar V. Seeler, Wilson Brothers & Co., Theophilus P. Chandler, and Rankin & Kellogg. The *Inland Architect* thought the entries were "somewhat disappointing," mediocre and commonplace, but that the winning entry by Rankin & Kellogg was unquestionably the best design.[40] Upon its completion, the Camden building was praised as having "one of the most refined and dignified exteriors in recent Governmental architecture."[41]

The biggest plum of the Tarsney Act program—and the most controversial for its outcome—was the New York custom house competition. The *American Architect* pronounced the building as "one of the most important buildings ever erected by the Government outside of Washington."[42] To this competition were invited the best

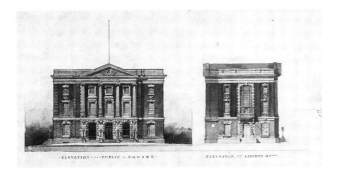

·ELEVATION·—·PUBLIC·SQUARE·   ·ELEVATION·—·LIBERTY·ST.—·

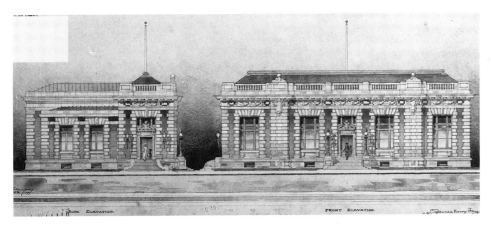

SIDE ELEVATION.   FRONT ELEVATION.

known firms in New York City, Boston, and Chicago, although it was assumed that a New York firm would be given preference. The jury consisted of Taylor, Philadelphia architect Frank Miles Day, and Omaha architect Thomas R. Kimball, described as a "former associate" of both Taylor and Gilbert. The jury first narrowed the competition to Carrère & Hastings and Cass Gilbert. Carrère & Hastings recently had won the competition for the New York Public Library. Gilbert, Taylor's former partner, had visited Secretary Gage in early 1899, accompanied by Senator Knute Nelson of Minnesota. Gilbert asked that his name be placed on a list of competitors for buildings to be designed under the Tarsney Act, particularly the New York custom house.[43] The outcome of the apparent "tie" was the selection of Gilbert.

Gilbert's selection raised an outcry in New York and the architectural profession. New York politicians challenged the decision because of Gilbert's appearance as "an interloping opportunist poorly

Figure 7.8 (*top*)
U.S. courthouse and post office, Cumberland, Maryland, 1901–1903, James Knox Taylor. Courtesy National Archives.

Figure 7.9 (*bottom*)
U.S. post office, Muskegon, Michigan, 1904, James Knox Taylor. Courtesy National Archives.

Figure 7.10
U.S. post office and
courthouse, Norfolk,
Virginia, 1898–1900,
Wyatt & Nolting.
*American Architect and
Building News,* 63
(March 4, 1899), No.
1210.

disguised as a New Yorker," the absence of a dome on the designed
building, and the "obscurity" of the men who served on the jury.[44]
Gilbert fought back with strong support from the Midwest, including a banker from Chicago who was acquainted with Secretary
Gage. The AIA, however, was reluctant to see the competition decision overturned, because the results could bode ill for the future of
the Tarsney Act. Various AIA chapters sent letters to Gage testifying
to Gilbert's fitness for the project and the procedures followed in the
implementation of the Tarsney Act. Architects who had initially
protested the decision then withdrew their objections. As the AIA observed, the New York custom house was only the fourth Tarsney
building, and there was no guarantee that more would follow.[45] With
support voiced from prominent business leaders and with professional protests diminishing, Gage approved the award of the New
York custom house project to Gilbert.

Cass Gilbert's custom house at Bowling Green in New York City
is one of the masterpieces of the Beaux Arts period (figure 7.11). As a
building standing at the entrance to the port of New York, Gilbert
thought that it should be of a large scale, but not so tall as to compete with nearby skyscrapers. "It should be so impressive by reason
of the majesty of its composition, rather than its *actual* size, that it

should be truly a monument." The adornment of the building should express the "wealth and luxury of the great port of New York." The customary architectural motifs of a dome and columnar portico were thought to be inappropriate for such a structure. The interior was richly finished with a "noble corridor," an elliptical rotunda, sculpture, and decorative paintings. The paintings illustrated commerce through history. At the base of the main facade were four seated figures, representing America, Europe, Asia, and Africa, the "four great continents which contribute to the commerce of the world." At the cornice were placed figures representing the "great commercial nations of the world."[46]

Other notable Tarsney Act projects included the federal government building in Indianapolis, the invited competitors for which were divided between local firms and the profession at large. The firm of Rankin & Kellogg won the competition with a design marked by a long Greek Ionic colonnade along the building's facades (figure 7.12). The second success of the firm with a Tarsney Act project led some to speculate that the program might foster the growth of a

Figure 7.11
U.S. custom house, New York, New York, 1899–1907, Cass Gilbert. Courtesy National Archives.

Figure 7.12
U.S. federal building,
Indianapolis, Indiana,
1901–1905, Rankin &
Kellogg. Courtesy
National Archives.

"privileged clique" of architects who would be selected to design federal buildings.[47] The competition for the new custom house in
Baltimore was won by the Washington, D.C., firm of Hornblower &
Marshall (figure 7.13). This Beaux Arts building was designed with a
continuous arcade fronted by Ionic pilasters. The interior was richly
adorned with a variety of marbles and a ceiling painting by Frank D.
Millet. Upon its completion in 1908, the *American Architect* praised the
building as leaving "nothing to be desired, and the result achieved by
the intelligent cooperation of architect and artist stamps Baltimore's
new Custom House as among the most successful public buildings
erected in this country."[48]

Out of the glare of press coverage of the large Tarsney Act projects, the Supervising Architect's Office continued to design many
smaller federal buildings, mostly post offices, located in small communities throughout the country. The division of responsibility between private architects and the Office was not what the AIA had expected with the implementation of the act. That Taylor's Office
continued to design federal buildings may have been the result of the
"experimental nature" of the Tarsney Act implementation. The cost

Figure 7.13
U.S. custom house,
Baltimore, Maryland,
completed 1908,
Hornblower & Marshall.
Courtesy National
Archives.

of running competitions may also have been a factor; the cost could be justified with major buildings, but not with smaller buildings.

The active design work of Taylor's Office may also have been the result of a concerted effort on his part to retain control over a large number of (albeit modest) buildings. The change in Taylor's stated position regarding the inability of one man to do justice to the many federal building projects that fell under his jurisdiction was evidenced early in his administration. In November 1897, the *Inland Architect* reported that Taylor "candidly admitted that they [his views on competitions for public work] had changed radically since entered into departmental service." Since taking the position of Supervising Architect, Taylor saw the "difficulties, the complications, that render that mode of procedure as unsatisfactory as the old way, and [he] has about concluded that there must be some other solution of the difficulty, so that he has earnestly set himself to studying what to devise and suggest."[49]

In his annual report for 1899, Taylor indicated a reluctance to open all federal building projects to competition. He referred to buildings authorized in the last session of Congress and suggested that "several" be selected to be designed under the Tarsney Act, while "retaining buildings of like extent and location for design, erection and completion under this office." The outcome of this process was to "determine as to which method is the better to adopt for the Government's interests, giving due consideration to cost of construction, suitability for required use and character and treatment of design."[50]

The AIA was hesitant to criticize Gage for allotting such a limited number of federal buildings to competition, because he possessed the authority to exercise his discretionary powers *not* to place building projects under the Tarsney Act. In 1901, AIA President Robert S. Peabody gently prodded Gage with the suggestion that a "wider circle of architects" as well as "younger and less experienced men" might be involved in federal architecture work if:

> some of the smaller Government buildings were offered in competition as has been done with those of great importance. If the provisions of the Tarsney Act could be extended to some of these buildings, I believe the Government would gain good results, and possibly greater variety and more local character in the buildings than if all this work were done in the Government office.

Gage demurred with a vague but bureaucratically correct response:

> The Department has never decided to withhold the smaller buildings wholly from competition, but must continue, as in the past, to consider and decide each case according to its conditions, as related to remoteness of locality, limit of appropriation and other attending difficulties affecting the probability of securing satisfactory results by the competitive method.[51]

During the fifteen years of the Tarsney Act (1897 to 1912), only thirty-one buildings were designed according to its provisions. Private architects, selected directly and not through competition, designed another six buildings. These designs were procured when authorizing legislation specifically designated an architect or firm to perform the work. An example of this method of design procurement included the U.S. Post Office building in Washington, D.C., which (like the adjacent Union Station) was designed by Daniel H. Burnham's firm. Also, during the period 1897 to 1912, designs for four buildings in Washington, D.C., were obtained by competition, although not under the Tarsney Act. These four ultimately unexecuted designs were for buildings that would house the Departments of Justice, State, Commerce, and Labor.[52] When viewed against the

more than 400 federal buildings that were designed during this period, the number of Tarsney Act projects was small. In addition, the
number of architects and architectural firms that participated in the
federal architecture program was even smaller because several firms,
such as Rankin & Kellogg, were selected to design more than one
building. The benefits of the Tarsney Act reached only a small, elite
group of architectural firms.

As already mentioned, the bulk of the design work during Taylor's
period was still under the control of the Supervising Architect's
Office. Most of these buildings were modest post offices, while a
smaller number contained judicial, customs, and other federal functions. It included modest-sized buildings such as the courthouse and
post office in Altoona, Pennsylvania (figure 7.14) as well as major
structures, such as the courthouse, post office, and custom house in
Los Angeles (figures 7.15 and 7.16). Appropriations for their construction provided for whole groups of buildings, which were justified according to levels of postal receipts and federal activities in the localities. Nearly all the federal buildings designed under Taylor can be
classified as classical or colonial revival. By the turn of the century,
these styles were well entrenched in the architectural vocabulary
throughout the country. The early buildings designed under the

Figure 7.14
U.S. courthouse and post
office, Altoona,
Pennsylvania, 1900–1902,
James Knox Taylor.
Courtesy National
Archives.

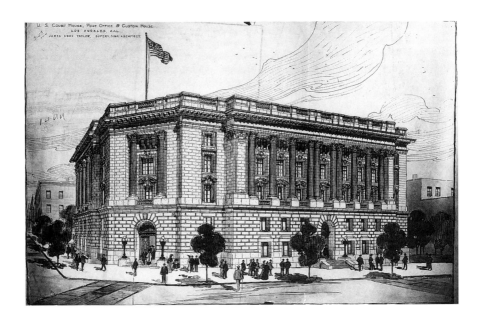

Figure 7.15
U.S. courthouse, post
office, and custom house,
Los Angeles, California,
designed 1906, James
Knox Taylor. Courtesy
National Archives.

Tarsney Act may have influenced the actual application of the styles
to federal buildings. These buildings themselves were reflective of
the predominant national taste in architecture.

The great number of smaller federal buildings designed under
Taylor tended to appear highly standardized. In 1911, Treasury
Secretary Franklin MacVeagh accelerated this trend and instructed
Taylor to use his plan for the Grand Rapids, Michigan, federal building for the building in Dayton, Ohio. The two cities "are almost identical in area, population, and in the requirements of the several
Departments of the Government, and from the fact that the appropriation for the one is identical with the authorization for the other."
Representative James Middleton Cox of Dayton, Ohio, was also
agreeable to having a replica of the Grand Rapids building in his district.[53]

MacVeagh further encouraged standardization of smaller federal
buildings with a competition to produce a design for the new $75,000
post office in Waukegan, Illinois. MacVeagh appealed to the architects' patriotism, love of good architecture, and professional pride in
inviting their participation in this competition. As MacVeagh stated:

I feel that you will agree with me that no specimens of good architecture in the country are better fitted to exert a beneficial in-

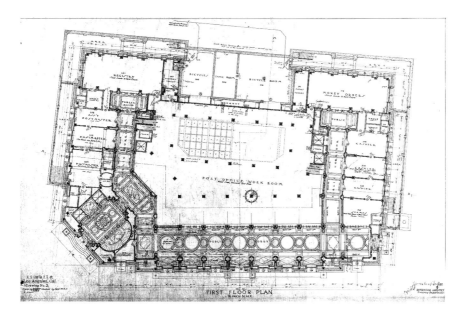

Figure 7.16
U.S. courthouse, post
office, and custom house,
Los Angeles, California,
First Floor Plan, designed
1906, James Knox Taylor.
Courtesy National
Archives.

fluence upon the general development of our building than these post-office buildings of the less important classes placed in the smaller cities where they are often the most important structures in their neighborhoods, so that they stand as examples of what we should like to see done by the cities and by the citizens themselves.

The winning design would serve as a "type which shall stand in its absolute simplicity, dignity and justice of proportion an example that will lead and foster the development of American architecture."[54]

Taylor's administration of the Supervising Architect's Office attracted a good deal of positive press coverage. During the period 1899 to 1904, Taylor assembled a team of talented architects who later pursued distinguished careers in the private sector. All had received formal training in architecture, were active in professional associations, and were recommended by leading figures in the AIA. These men included Percy Ash, Edward W. Donn Jr., Theodore W. Pietsch, and Nathan C. Wyeth.

Appointed in 1900, Ash had been educated at the University of Pennsylvania's engineering school and studied at the American Academy in Rome. Previous to his work at the Supervising Architect's Office, he was an architectural draftsman in the Department of Yards and Docks at Philadelphia's Navy Yard and had served as an officer with the T-Square Club in Philadelphia. While at the Office, Ash was credited with the designs for the U.S. Government and Fish Commission buildings at the 1904 St. Louis Exposition and the post office buildings in Seattle, Washington, and Charlottesville, Virginia. Ash resigned from the Office in late 1904 to assume the position of "Head Professor of Architecture" at George Washington University. He left GWU in 1910 to become professor of Architecture at the University of Michigan. He later taught at the University of Illinois and Pennsylvania State University. During a brief period during 1912–1913, Ash returned to Washington, D.C., to prepare an unexecuted design for a mountain retreat for Gordon Strong at Sugarloaf Mountain in nearby Maryland. He was also in partnership with William D. Hewitt of Philadelphia in the early 1920s.[55]

Edward W. Donn Jr. was the son of a draftsman connected with Thomas U. Walter and the extension of the Capitol building. He was educated at MIT and did postgraduate work at Cornell. Donn's early professional work was with Frank W. Chandler of Cabot & Chandler of Boston and with the Capitol Architect's Office under Edward Clark. In 1900, Donn was appointed to the Supervising Architect's Office, where he stayed until 1902. He left to "enter upon the private practice of my profession." He went on to form the successful Washington, D.C., firm of Wood, Donn & Deming. In the 1920s and 1930s, he embarked on a career as a restoration architect, working on historic houses in Virginia such as Woodlawn Plantation at Mt. Vernon, and Kenmore in Fredericksburg.[56]

A 1898 graduate of the École des Beaux Arts, Theodore W. Pietsch entered the Supervising Architect's Office in 1902 as a "designer." He stayed only two years, leaving in 1904. During his tenure at the Office, he enjoyed a special status; he signed his name to his designs, such as the one for the post office at Perth Amboy, New Jersey. He later formed his successful Baltimore firm of Simonson & Pietsch, in partnership with another former employee of the Office, Otto G. Simonson.[57]

Chicago-born Nathan C. Wyeth also was educated at the École des Beaux Arts. He was a designer at Carrère & Hastings in New York from 1899 to 1900. In 1900, he was appointed to the position of "designer" in the Supervising Architect's Office. He stayed with the Office until 1903, when he took a job with Elliott Woods, architect of the Capitol. In the following year, Wyeth commenced his private practice in Washington, D.C., designing a great number of buildings throughout the city. From 1934 to 1946, he served as municipal architect of the District of Columbia and oversaw the design and construction of the Municipal Center, public school buildings, and the D.C. Armory.[58]

Other noted architects associated with the Office during this period include Frank L. Molby, Francis B. Wheaton, Theodore F. Laist, Walter G. Peter, and Robert Beresford. Two other architects in Taylor's Office, Oscar Wenderoth and Louis A. Simon, later played important roles in the evolution of the Supervising Architect's Office through the early decades of the twentieth century. Women continued to occupy clerical and "copyist" positions but were not employed as draftsmen or designers. Taylor felt that the appointment of women to the drafting force "is not considered advisable."[59]

These young designers were active in the Washington Architectural Club, an organization founded in 1892. The club attracted younger members of the architectural profession, whereas the Washington Chapter of the AIA tended to be composed of and led by the more established architects. The Washington Architectural Club sponsored meetings, undertook architectural competitions, organized architectural exhibitions in the Corcoran Gallery of Art, and embarked on outings to historic sites. Many of its officers were drawn from the younger ranks of the Supervising Architect's Office and the work of the Office was frequently included in the club's annual exhibition. Its events attracted many of those who "had been students together in Paris."[60] The club flourished until the outbreak of World War I, when it was disbanded.

In 1902, the Washington Atelier was founded with Theodore W. Pietsch as its patron. It was a center of activity for the younger designers in the Office. The atelier was modeled after those in Paris and New York, as an association of ateliers was viewed as a "smart stimulant of rivalry and vigorous esprit des corps." In such an organization, the individual success is "shared by all the members, who strive by their joint work to outrank rival institutions. Such conditions pushed even to the extreme are invaluable to art, where the strongest convictions and bitterest antagonisms produce the most happy results." The Washington Atelier members, together with members from ateliers in other cities, hoped to find a common ground at the American Fine Arts Building in New York City, where the Society of Beaux Arts Architects would judge their work.[61]

Another institution closely allied with the Supervising Architect's Office was the Architecture Department at George Washington University. Members of the Office's staff taught courses, served on award juries, or were students in the school. Instructors included

Percy Ash, Louis A. Simon, Theodore Laist, Frank L. Molby, Edward Donn Jr., and Bedford Brown (son of Glenn Brown and an employee of the Office during the first decade of the twentieth century). Many of the courses were offered in the late afternoon so that working architects and draftsmen could supplement their office work with special training in design, rendering, and other technical subjects. The university abolished the architecture school in the late 1930s.

Taylor's reputation rode a high wave among the private architects and the architectural presses during his tenure as supervising architect. His standing was briefly but badly shaken during the period in 1904–1905 when the failure of Congress to make appropriations for new federal buildings forced Taylor to reduce his drafting force drastically. Lyman Gage retired as treasury secretary in 1902. While willing to carry out the provisions of the Tarsney Act, his successors, first L. M. Shaw and then G. B. Cortelyou, did not command the respect of the AIA accorded to Gage. The election of William Howard Taft as president in 1908 and the appointment of Franklin MacVeagh as secretary of the treasury promised support for the Tarsney Act, although not necessarily at the high level that President Theodore Roosevelt and Secretary Gage had provided. In fact, the departure of Roosevelt in early 1909 prompted the *American Architect* to remark, "Not since the time of George Washington has a President possessed in like degree both an appreciation of the value of art in our national life and the courage to throw the full weight of his influence to its forward movement."[62]

The reaction of Congress to the AIA's aspirations was disheartening and did not bode well for the future. Congressman James Beauchamp Clark of Missouri was quoted as saying that Taylor's practice of supplying individual designs and specifications for every public building under his charge was merely a pretext for employing a larger drafting staff than necessary. He suggested that Taylor prepare "uniform plans and specifications for, say, $30,000 buildings, $40,000, $50,000 or $60,000 buildings and just keep them in stock." The AIA was also mortified to hear that Congress thought that the new House and Senate Office Buildings were designed by the Capitol architect, with John M. Carrère and Thomas Hastings acting as mere assistants.[63]

Shortly after taking office, Franklin MacVeagh hired the accounting firm of Arthur Young & Co. to make a study of the various offices within the Treasury Department. The firm was instructed to report on conditions and outline recommended actions. When the firm reported on the Supervising Architect's Office, it recommended a "thorough and drastic reorganization," in order to provide savings in money and time to the government. The firm's view that the Treasury Department was harboring a "defective organization" was based on its assessment of the executive capacities of the Office's top staff members. The conclusion was also due to the inefficient handling of the mail and the "segregation of the work under the six so-called divisions which had resulted in a practical elimination of all team work among the different branches of the office."

The Arthur Young firm was especially critical of Taylor's declaration that he had developed a "one-man office" because he claimed he was unable to find a subordinate able enough to whom to delegate responsibility. The firm felt that Taylor was lacking in executive ability:

> From policy or temperament, he appears incapable of letting go any details, and as a natural consequence, he is wading in a mass of detail, "unable to see the woods for looking at the trees." With him, it appears to be rule or ruin, and his office shows the inevitable result of such a policy in its abysmal disorganization.

Several of Taylor's subordinates were subject to adverse criticism. William Windom, son of the former treasury secretary, was found to hold the position of architectural draftsman, but his only duties were to care for the Office's small library. Charles Kemper's lack of technical qualifications rendered him unfit to serve as the right-hand man of the supervising architect. "As the condition of the non-technical division reveals an entire lack of executive control on the part of anybody, Mr. Kemper's activities appear to be of a negative character." While Wetmore was criticized for the system of handling mail and keeping files, the firm commended him for his system of following up on legislation. Louis A. Simon appeared to have the work of the drafting division under control, even if his office seemed "unduly littered up with miscellaneous papers."[64]

The result of the report was the replacement of Kemper with Wetmore as executive officer. Evidently Taylor's hold on his position weakened and he submitted his resignation in June 1912. His removal was likely being contemplated for some time, because Oscar Wenderoth was waiting in the wings at Carrère & Hastings should the resignation occur.[65] Until Wenderoth could conclude his work in New York and move to Washington, D.C., in July 1912, Wetmore served as acting supervising architect.

Nearly coincident with Taylor's departure was the repeal of the

Tarsney Act. Considerable dissatisfaction was expressed regarding the expenditures devoted to paying private architects while the federal government continued to employ a sizable number of architects on the staff of the Supervising Architect's Office. In June 1911, Congressman William E. Cox of Indiana introduced the bill to repeal the act. Although the Treasury Department protested the bill, as did the AIA, the repeal measure was included as a clause to the Sundry Civil Bill and the repeal became effective in August 1912.

The AIA *Journal* predicted that the Tarsney Act repeal would "produce a degrading effect upon the architecture of the United States. . . . Not only architects . . . but the whole community should resent this repeal of a law which has accomplished so much for the advancement of the nation in well-designed buildings."[66] Philadelphia architect Milton B. Medary Jr., Chairman of the AIA's Committee on Government Architecture, suggested that a department within the federal government be created with the authority "to veto in the name of the people, any public work proposed for the nation by any department whenever such a work could not be regarded by this department as a worthy monument to this generation and a factor in the education of the next."[67] The New York Chapter of the AIA felt that the repeal would return the federal government back to "rubber-stamp" architecture and represented a "backward step of twenty years in Government architecture."[68] The AIA vowed to have the Tarsney Act, or another bill like it, reenacted.

After his departure from the federal government, Taylor became professor of architecture at MIT and later director of the architecture department. While at MIT, he also served with Cass Gilbert and Glenn Brown on the AIA's Committee on Conservation of Natural Resources. He left MIT in October 1914 and was replaced by Ralph Adams Cram. Taylor's career then followed a circuitous and obscure path through Philadelphia; Northampton, Massachusetts; Yonkers, New York; and finally Tampa, Florida, where he died in 1929 at the age of 72.[69]

Oscar Wenderoth

Taylor's successor, Oscar Wenderoth, was born in Philadelphia in 1871 (figure 7.17). At the age of fifteen, he entered the office of a local architect. He worked in Philadelphia until 1897 when he was hired as a senior architectural draftsman in the Supervising Architect's Office.

Figure 7.17
Oscar Wenderoth.
Courtesy National
Archives.

In September 1897, Wenderoth was transferred to Philadelphia to work on the new mint building. Wenderoth was reappointed senior architectural draftsman in the Office in 1903, but he left the following year to become head draftsman under Capitol Architect Elliott Woods on the new House and Senate Office Buildings, both of which had been designed by Carrère & Hastings on a consulting basis. In this position, Wenderoth also prepared the drawings and specifications for the tunnels connecting the two buildings with the Capitol Building, the central power plant, and the court of appeals building at Judiciary Square. In 1909, he became head draftsman at the firm of Carrère & Hastings in New York City, where he was working when he was called upon to be supervising architect.[70]

Wenderoth approached the position of supervising architect with a sense of openness and wisdom. He was also devoid of the defensiveness that gripped other supervising architects when the office was attacked for producing poor designs, mismanagement, or inefficiency. As Wenderoth stated to Paul Gerhardt, county architect for Cook County, Illinois: "This office welcomes any investigation that any committee with proper authority cares to make. The more our methods are investigated and the more suggestions are given us, the more will it become possible to increase the efficiency of this office."[71] Wenderoth's even temper permitted him to regard his position as similar to that of state and municipal architecture operations which oversaw the design and construction of public buildings within their jurisdictions. Consequently, he devoted considerable effort to learning about the operation of these other public works offices throughout the country. Some of these offices provided for the use of private architects and engineers as consultants on public building projects. Other government architects performed design services for a government entity on a project basis, and, at the same time, provided services to other clients.

The repeal of the Tarsney Act provided Wenderoth with an opportunity to discuss how the federal architecture program might be revised so that a similar act could be reinstated. Wenderoth's view on the subject was that the Tarsney Act was defective because private architects were asked to provide services which the Office could handle as well. However, the services of private architects were desirable in working out the solution to problems in design on all federal government buildings, especially those in smaller cities. He saw little value in hiring private architects for building in a city like New York "where the Government spent several million dollars to build a Post Office in the rear of a railroad station [designed by McKim, Mead & White]."[72]

In an effort to provide for a way for private architects to participate in the federal architecture program, several methods were suggested. One plan was to place every building valued at $250,000 or more under the design of private architects. Wenderoth opposed this idea as he believed that private architects could render a greater service with smaller buildings. Taken together, the smaller buildings were "seen daily by thousands who have but little opportunity to feel the influence of the great architectural works in the large cities, and their collective potentiality for aiding in the development of a national appreciation of the beautiful is correspondingly greater."[73] Another method to involve private architects was to parcel out the entire work of the Office to the private sector; yet another suggestion was to create a Department of Public Works or a Bureau of Public Buildings and Grounds that would absorb the work of the

Office along with that of other federal offices and bureaus engaged in building construction. Wenderoth felt that parceling out all of the Office's work would lead to a confusing variety of methods and processes, which ran counter to the stated desire of the Treasury Department for standardization. The separate department or bureau idea was one that was discussed during Wenderoth's period and throughout the 1920s and 1930s.

In 1913, Senator George Earle Chamberlain of Oregon introduced Senate Bill 3063, providing for the discretionary employment of private architects in a consulting capacity to the supervising architect. Wenderoth favored this method of involving private architects, because it reflected his personal experience on the new Senate and House Office Buildings (where John M. Carrère and Thomas Hastings served as consulting architects). Even though his recent professional association may have rendered him biased, Wenderoth felt that the cooperation between the federal government and private architects as represented in these congressional buildings produced "the finest public structures in the last quarter century."[74] Wenderoth thought that while the legislation "may not be the final solution of what is conceded to be a problem of national importance, it is believed that it is worthy of serious trial."[75] The bill was never enacted.

The push toward standardization that was initiated under Treasury Secretary Franklin MacVeagh gathered greater strength between 1913 and the U.S. entrance into World War I in 1917. Treasury Secretary William G. McAdoo was a proponent of standardization, in conjunction with Congressman Cyrus Cline, chairman of the House Committee on Expenditures on Public Buildings. Wenderoth himself was a party to this effort; he was critical of Taylor's practice of taking up each building "de novo," as an independent problem. As Wenderoth stated, "a great deal of time was expended in seeking variations in details or modifications in type instead of attempting to refine and perfect a sufficiently diversified range of acceptable types."[76] Much of the heating, ventilating, sanitary work, and the production of specifications could be standardized, and Wenderoth preferred to invest the efforts of his staff in producing "correct and perfect architectural models." Wenderoth also recognized that local sentiment could force exceptions in the efforts of the Office to standardize, as such demands were made for extra entrances, for a review by the locality of preliminary sketches, or for other alternatives to a proposed architectural design. He also noted that no two sites for post offices were absolutely identical, that post office building types would continue to evolve, and that climatic conditions required adjustments in architecture.

To enforce the policy of standardization, the Public Buildings Act of 1913 created the Public Buildings Commission composed of the secretary of the treasury, the postmaster general, the attorney general, and four members from the House and Senate Public Buildings and Grounds Committees. The commission was instructed to prepare a "connected scheme involving annual appropriations for the construction, in a reasonable time, of all public buildings heretofore authorized, as well as to frame a standard or standards by which the size and cost of public buildings shall, as far as practicable, be determined."[77]

Figure 7.18
Secretary's Office, U.S. Department of the Interior building (old), 1915–1917, Charles Butler. Courtesy National Archives.

After the repeal of the Tarsney Act, the role of private architects in the federal architecture program was much reduced. A few architects or firms were selected under the terms of the legislation that authorized the projects. For example, Charles Butler of Carrère & Hastings was hired to prepare plans for the new Interior Building in Washington, D.C., which was constructed 1915–1917 (figure 7.18).

The repeal of the Tarsney Act naturally provoked a heated discussion in the architectural presses. The spate of articles denounced
the congressmen who spearheaded the repeal movement as having no artistic sensibilities. Wenderoth thought the articles to be
"founded upon profound ignorance of the situation" and "undigni-
fied where it is not stupid." Wenderoth warned Thomas Hastings
that the impression created by the articles was such that he felt dis-
inclined to make any effort to assist the architectural profession in its
quest for recognition. "So long as the profession will permit its leading magazines to indulge in blackguardism, just so long do I think the
most dignified thing for Congress to do is to see that the profession
is excluded from any participation in public work."[78]

By late 1914, tempers had moderated. The AIA *Journal* of November
1914 remarked that the federal architecture program was "going
through a tentative stage, preparatory to being established on a different, and on a much better, basis—better than even that existing when
the Tarsney Act was in operation." The AIA apparently was content
to stand ready to "help when help is desired."[79] Wenderoth suggested
that a first step was for the AIA members to obtain:

> [a] complete knowledge of what is being done in the Department,
> of the limitations placed around us by statutes and by regulations,
> and that, after making such a study, if they thought they could
> suggest means of cooperation which might be helpful to the
> Department, it might be possible to consider such suggestions.[80]

In spite of the cooperative spirit exhibited by Wenderoth and the
AIA, the possibility of friendly gestures emanating from top Treasury
Department officials was dim. William McAdoo and his Assistant
Secretary Byron R. Newton were not interested in reaching a quick
rapprochement with the private architects—beyond the concession
that under certain conditions the employment of architects and engineers on a consulting basis might be advantageous. Newton declared the policy of distributing architectural commissions to private
architects under the Tarsney Act a "decided failure." Newton blamed
the Tarsney Act for causing project delays, unnecessary duplication
of work, and enlarged expenses. Newton also expressed the opinion
that the act did not have "any appreciable effect upon the standard of
public architecture; in fact, since the repeal of the Tarsney Act the
standard of endeavor in the Office of the Supervising Architect has
appreciably risen."[81]

Wenderoth resigned his position in April 1915 and became super-vising architect with the Weary & Alford Company of Chicago, a firm that specialized in designing bank interiors. Why Wenderoth should have left his Treasury Department post is unclear, other than his statement that "the contrast between the comparative freedom of private employ and the restrictions of Government service is so great that I cannot contemplate the latter without a shudder. I cannot be-lieve that anything would tempt me to re-enter the public service."[82] Later, there was speculation that Wenderoth was ill and unable to at-tend to his work at the Treasury Department on a full-time basis. He later practiced architecture in New York City; he died in 1938.

James A. Wetmore

Upon Wenderoth's departure, James A. Wetmore (figure 7.19) again rose to the top of the Office. Although he was not an architect, he dominated the federal architecture program for nearly twenty years from 1915 to 1934. He entered federal service in 1885 as a court stenog-rapher and in 1893 transferred from the Interior Department to the Treasury Department. He attended George Washington University's Law School for evening classes, receiving his degree in 1896. He served as head of the Treasury's Law and Records Division from 1896 to 1911 when he became executive officer to James Knox Taylor. This position gave him charge of all the nontechnical operations of the Office.[83] He continued in this position under Wenderoth. When Wenderoth resigned, Wetmore became acting supervising architect, a position he relished, but he never presumed to be named "perma-nent" supervising architect because of his respect for the work of ar-chitects. His hold on the position for a long period of time can be as-cribed to what was later said of him: "His knowledge of the workings of his organization and his shrewd understanding of the mental pro-cesses of the gentlemen before whom he talked made his testimonies masterpieces of clarity and tact. The legislators admired and re-spected him."[84]

To outsiders, a lawyer serving as head of the federal architecture program seemed incongruous. Indeed, many inquiries were made re-garding whether Wetmore might ultimately be replaced with a per-manent supervising architect. However, by 1915, even Wetmore felt that the administrative duties of the supervising architect precluded him from doing more than directing policy in architectural design.

"It is the draftsman, then, and not either the Supervising Architect or the assistant in charge of the drafting room, who is the real designer."[85] Wetmore filled the administrative bill so well that successive treasury secretaries felt comfortable leaving the situation alone. While Wetmore left the matter of architectural design to his staff, he was acknowledged as having "an uncanny facility for knowing the intent and purpose of the architectural and engineering actions of his organization."[86]

Wetmore's assumption of the position of acting supervising architect marked the end of one era and the dawn of a new. Whereas in the mid-1890s, classicism was perceived as novel and refreshing, by 1915, it was the most common style for public buildings as well as other building types. Contrary to the widely held belief of the AIA, the style had been adapted to federal architecture before the implementation of the Tarsney Act in 1897. During the Tarsney era, however, the classical style pervaded nearly all of the federal architecture projects the private architects had undertaken, as well as those projects retained under the control of the Supervising Architect's Office. To many observers, the buildings designed by the private

Figure 7.19
James A. Wetmore.
Courtesy National
Archives.

firms and the government architects appeared to be of comparable quality in design. This consistency of architectural design raised the question of the expense incurred in administering the Tarsney Act. The push toward standardized public building design under Wetmore's regime underscored doubts surrounding the wisdom of the Tarsney Act. Instead, official federal government policy viewed the most efficient way to enforce a policy of standardization was to have the Supervising Architect's Office prepare all the designs.

McAdoo's Classification System for Federal Government Buildings

By the time James A. Wetmore assumed the position of acting supervising architect in 1915, the federal government's role as purveyor of classical designs and as federal contributor to "City Beautiful" plans in American cities had lost their air of novelty. In the place of lofty aspirations for aesthetic pleasures, the Treasury Department turned to businesslike determinations of a federal building's size and architectural garb. Public buildings could now be turned out with near factorylike precision. Wetmore proved to be a willing agent of Treasury Secretary William McAdoo's desire to standardize federal building design (figure 7.20). In 1915, McAdoo sponsored the development of a classification system for federal buildings. This system categorized buildings according to the level of annual receipts, their location within a city, and their inclusion of a post office of the first or second class. As Assistant Treasury Secretary Byron R. Newton stated, the system provided for expenditures to be made in proportion to the revenue the government derived on its investment.[87] For example, the "Class A Building" was defined as one with annual receipts of $800,000 or more, sited as part of a city development or situated on a major thoroughfare of a large city, and adjoining property of high value. These buildings were intended to have marble or granite facing, marble interior finish, ornamental bronze, and special interior light fixtures. At the other end of the scale, buildings with a post office having annual receipts of less than $15,000 were to have brick facing; stock sash, frames, and door; and resemble an "ordinary class of building, such as any businessman would consider a reasonable investment in a small town."[88] With the classification system, McAdoo expected that "we shall be able to save a sufficient amount

under our present policy to make the 100 buildings cost no more, or very little more, than 75 buildings under the old policy."[89]

Anticipating the objections to this standardization program, Assistant Secretary Byron R. Newton stated:

> opinions vary through a wide range as to just what constitutes a proper Federal building, i.e., whether such buildings stand for only the utilitarian purposes which they serve, and therefore may approach a factory type, or whether Federal buildings have other functions which would be best fulfilled by structures of monumental character.

Newton ascribed the inconsistent limits of costs for buildings to the lack of an "established point of view as to the architectural character suitable for Federal buildings under different conditions." Newton felt that the classification system placed the Treasury Department's policy somewhere between the factory and the monumental type,

Figure 7.20
Secretary of the Treasury
William McAdoo.
Courtesy National
Archives.

and that the system applied the principles of sound business investment.[90]

Wetmore praised McAdoo's classification system as a way to "provide a rational system of uniformity and business economy in designing and constructing Federal buildings, suitable in each instance to the public needs, and without calling for waste in Government money." Wetmore also anticipated that the design of a "master type of building for small communities" could be used in about thirty locations during the 1917 fiscal year.[91] In fact, Wetmore's enthusiasm for standardization extended to furniture and methods of building maintenance. The following year, however, Wetmore noted that even with the classification system, costs for buildings in communities widely separated ranged from $38,000 to $57,000 for buildings constructed from practically identical plans. Nonetheless, Wetmore claimed that the results of the classification system justified its continuance "in the interest of economy and the equitable treatment of the communities in which public buildings have been authorized to be constructed."[92]

Wetmore's defense of the Treasury Department's public buildings policy won him the respect of department officials. As Byron R. Newton wrote to J. H. Moyle, his successor at the Treasury Department, "You will find Mr. Wetmore a very sound and safe advisory. In my four years at your desk we passed through some rather trying times and I never once had reason for questioning his loyalty or doubting his sound judgement."[93]

After gaining experience in standardization, Wetmore eased his position somewhat. In 1923, he noted that each individual building required a separate set of drawings and specifications because of variations in functions, location, topography, availability of materials, and the cost limit fixed by Congress:

> Furthermore, the method of handling Government business, especially of the Post Office, makes continued study necessary in order to meet the changing requirements in a satisfactory manner, and for this reason standard drawings are subject to changes at any time when an improvement in methods makes this advisable.[94]

The AIA's opinion of Secretary McAdoo's approach to federal building design was highly negative. At the 1916 convention of the AIA, the participants blamed McAdoo's system on the poor advice he received from Oscar Wenderoth, who was described as "not an architect in any sense of the word . . . his vision was limited and un-sympathetic to an unfortunate degree." Wenderoth was also blamed for contributing to an environment in which the Tarsney Act was re-pealed. Wenderoth's successor, Wetmore, was described as an assis-tant "outside of the profession and unsympathetic with radical re-forms."[95]

Architect Breck Trowbridge said that McAdoo's classification sys-tem was likely to produce "public buildings of a standard factory type." When compared with the great homes of the nation's mil-lionaire class, the common peoples' public buildings would look pale by comparison:

> A government which fails to recognize the right of its people to enjoy the benefits of the great heritage of art; which fails to culti-vate and encourage in its people the love of beauty; and which does not recognize, as one of its legitimate functions, the orderly and sympathetic development of the fine arts, is no true democ-racy.[96]

Some members of the general public did not share the AIA's atti-tude toward the Treasury Department's program. For a series of ar-ticles prepared for the *Ladies' Home Journal,* journalist John Elfreth Watkins of Philadelphia requested from Wetmore photographs of small post office buildings. Watkins felt that the illustrations would reflect "a great deal of credit on your office, the purpose of these ar-ticles being to illustrate what Uncle Sam is doing to beautify the coun-try."[97]

A Proposed Bureau of Fine Arts

The absence of a "permanent" supervising architect and dissatisfac-tion with the direction of the federal architecture program prompted proposals for a reorganization of the Supervising Architect's Office along with related public works functions. During the first decades of the twentieth century, two possible plans were considered. One was the effort to create a Bureau of Fine Arts with responsibilities of a national scope. The other was to form a Department of Public Works. Throughout these discussions, the AIA paid close attention to the role of AIA members in advising the proposed bureaus and de-partments.

The initiative for a Bureau of Fine Arts emerged out of the experience of the alliance of architects, landscape architects, and artists at the World's Columbian Exposition. In 1897, the Public Art League had sought legislation, largely crafted by AIA lobbyist Glenn Brown, to "establish a body of experts to decide upon the merits of art and architecture to be commissioned or acquired by the Government."[98] Although the law never was enacted, the idea lived on. A confederation of art societies and organizations, with the National Academy of Art as its foremost leader, promoted the notion. In 1906, the AIA drafted a bill to provide for a National Advisory Board on Civic Art. The intent of this board was to oversee the development of the fine arts (such as buildings, parks, and monuments) by the federal government throughout the nation.[99]

In order to promote support for the national advisory board, Glenn Brown wrote an explanation of the problem the bill would address. He viewed the problem of obtaining beauty in federal buildings, parks, and monuments as "the most important artistic problem in the United States yet to be solved." Whereas the first fifty years of the nation's history was marked by a striving to obtain the beautiful, "a dark period in Federal Art began about 1850 and continued without a ray of light for nearly fifty years." According to Brown, this problem was especially evident in Washington, D.C.[100] Despite Brown's best efforts, the bill for a national advisory board did not pass.

Three years later, President Theodore Roosevelt acceded to the wishes of the AIA and issued an Executive Order creating a Council of Fine Arts composed of thirty leading architects, painters, sculptors, and landscape architects. He directed the heads of the federal government's departments to submit to the council "any plans formulated for any building or grounds, or for the location and erection of any statues." The body's advice was to be followed unless "for good and sufficient reasons the President directs that it be not followed." The supervising architect was appointed the executive officer for the council.[101] It met only once, to consider the site of the Lincoln Memorial.

Almost simultaneous with Roosevelt's Executive Order was legislation of Senator Frances Griffith Newlands of Nevada to rename the Supervising Architect's Office the "Bureau of Arts and Public Buildings." Newlands's legislation also called for the creation of an advisory council known as the Council on the Arts. This would be composed of thirty "eminent architects, painters, sculptors, landscape architects, and laymen" all to be drawn from a list of names submitted. The council would advise the director of the new Bureau of Arts and Public Buildings on "matters of general artistic character," on the matter of competitions, and "make recommendations for the conservation of all historic monuments." The president would appoint the director of the new bureau from names the Council on the Arts submitted. Nothing came of this legislative proposal.

When William Howard Taft became president in 1909, he abolished Roosevelt's Council of Fine Arts because he believed that Congress should establish such a body, not the president. The following year, Congress established the Commission of Fine Arts to advise on buildings, parks, monuments, and statues in the District of Columbia only. The new body also became the custodian and defender of the McMillan Commission Plan of 1901–1902 for Washington, D.C. Named for Senator James McMillan of Michigan who authorized its development, the McMillan Plan was a farsighted document on coordinated groupings of public buildings and monuments and on the improvement of the park system for Washington, D.C. The commission's responsibilities were later broadened to include buildings constructed by the District of Columbia government and areas bordering on the major parklands in the city.[102]

The idea of a national bureau of fine arts sprang to life again in 1913 with a bill to create a Bureau of Buildings and Grounds. Again drafted by Glenn Brown of the AIA, this proposal sought to recoup from the repeal of the Tarsney Act. The proposed national bureau would undertake all matters related to architecture, painting, sculpture, and parks. It would also be responsible for all questions related to education in the fine arts as well as the collection and administration of the proposed National Galleries of the Fine Arts. All design work would be open to competition. In the scheme of things, the bill bestowed the Commission of Fine Arts as the superior council, whose decisions on matters of design "shall be binding on the Director of the Bureau."[103] When viewed in the context of the Tarsney Act's repeal, this bill represented an attempt not only to reinstate the practice of competition with federal buildings, but also to enlarge the educational role of the federal architecture program and "invest the whole subject of the fine arts with appropriate dignity, to encourage the establishment of proper schools, to stimulate the universities in this much neglected branch, and to educate the people."[104] If this act proved to be an impossibility, the AIA hoped for a law similar to the Tarsney Act.[105]

A Proposed Department of Public Works

The other proposed reorganization of the federal government's architecture program was the consolidation of all the federal design and construction activities, including those of the Army Corps of Engineers, into a Department of Public Works. This new agency would include the responsibilities of the Supervising Architect's Office as well as bridges, parks, and roadways.[106] This idea was discussed as early as 1909, but it did not result in congressional activity until after World War I. In 1919, the Jones–Reavis Bill was introduced to create a federal Department of Public Works. The idea was supported by a number of technical, construction, and business organizations joined together to form the National Department of Public Works Association. The AIA passed a resolution to support this effort. There was some speculation that this department, if created, would be placed under a reorganized Department of the Interior.

With the proposed reorganization of the federal government's architecture program, hopes were raised among AIA members once again that a means could be found for the employment of the services of private architects. As Milton B. Medary Jr., chairman of the AIA's Committee on Public Works, stated:

> We believe when such an agency of the Government is created, it will be possible through its investigations to develop and use local talent in architecture and engineering, and that we can stimulate a greater interest in Public Works by calling on the various regions in the country to use their own available forces to execute the public works within their District.[107]

A major obstacle to the formation of the Department of Public Works was the Corps of Engineers. This agency of long historical standing was contemplated for inclusion in the proposed department. Lieutenant-Colonel C. O. Sherrill remarked to the 1924 annual convention of the AIA:

> One of the fundamental errors made by the proponents of this matter was that they undertook to destroy a really valuable organization of the Government in order to create something else larger and more widespread. . . . That organization [the Army Corps of Engineers] has had an honored career of one hundred and thirty years of construction work with but one isolated case

of peculation, and no matter what the individual's views of the pork-barrel may be, no one can claim that the Corps of Engineers has not been well-conducted and economically administered.[108]

The formation of the Department of Public Works fell victim to the general effort to reorganize the entire federal government. The proposed general reorganization would have materially changed many departments, the sweeping character of which precipitated a great deal of opposition. The AIA felt that its only interest in the reorganization studies lay with the location of public architecture within the department that ultimately resulted, and that the director of the public architecture program be placed at a level high enough to deal directly with Congress and with other department heads. By 1925, the prospect of a major reorganization of the federal architecture program appeared likely, because major legislation was being considered in Congress to provide funds for new public buildings in Washington, D.C., as well as the rest of the country. One version of the legislation provided for the employment of private architects under the direction of the Supervising Architect's Office. In the end, however, when major public buildings legislation was passed in 1926, no new agency or department was created to handle the work and only discretary authority was provided for the employment of private architects on these projects.

World War I and Return to Peace

The effect of World War I on the work of the Supervising Architect's Office was to bring its programs to a virtual standstill. The demands of the war placed a strain on the financial, industrial, and transportation resources of the country such that Secretary of the Treasury William McAdoo directed the postponement of public building construction except in cases where the "public interest would suffer."[109] Work went forward on marine hospitals and quarantine and immigration stations required for wartime use. Buildings already under construction were completed. The low level of construction left the staff of the Supervising Architect's Office with a minimal level of work. It was suggested that the employees of the Office be farmed out to other agencies for the duration of the war. However, McAdoo did not want the organization to "break up or dissipate" because of the level of work and directed Wetmore to outline a method by which the office could be kept together and used to good advantage."[110] Despite Wetmore's best efforts, the technical and clerical force became depleted due to the entry of staff members into the armed services and other war services. Some staff members transferred to other agencies concerned with military construction.

After the war, the Office returned to its construction program. By this time, the increase in the cost of labor and materials had pushed the cost of construction beyond the estimates made during the prewar period. The Treasury Department estimated that "not many of the buildings for which there are authorizations can be constructed within the present limit of cost."[111] However, by 1922, Wetmore reported that the activities of the Office had returned to a normal level of activity. New buildings were underway. Investigations and estimates were being prepared for the nearly 700 bills for new buildings, extensions, and site acquisitions. Despite this return to a high level of operation, the pent-up demand for new buildings called for a major public building program.

Into this discussion stepped the secretary of the treasury under Presidents Warren G. Harding and Calvin Coolidge, Andrew W. Mellon (figure 7.21). Mellon was one of the most architecturally sophisticated treasury secretaries during the entire time the Supervising Architect's Office was housed in that department. Mellon viewed the work of the Office as a reflection of his interest in the subject. He held sway over the federal architecture program during a time when it was felt that authorizations for federal buildings were ten years behind and that larger cities, including Washington, D.C., were in urgent need of new buildings.

Despite Secretary Mellon's interest in architectural matters, he did not feel compelled to fill the position of supervising architect on a permanent basis because he thought Wetmore had been ably performing the duties for several years.[112] When demands arose again from the architectural profession that private practitioners be employed on federal architecture projects, Mellon stated that additional legislation was required before the Treasury Department could employ outside architects and engineers.[113] Wetmore reinforced Mellon's position by arguing that the use of private architects was appropriate:

> only in exceptional cases. Generally, satisfactory designs are obtainable through organizations like that of the Office of the Supervising Architect, and the administration and execution of

the work by such an organization is superior to that obtainable through private architects.[114]

Paralleling discussions of the need for new federal buildings across the nation were studies of public building needs in Washington, D.C. The Public Buildings Commission studied the subject in a systematic manner in 1916. The AIA hoped that as public buildings were constructed they would follow the recommendations of the McMillan Plan. The placement of the first few buildings were crucial as they would foretell the location of subsequent buildings. The new Department of Agriculture building, which the firm of Rankin, Kellogg & Crane designed, was important for guaranteeing the configuration of the Mall. So too was the construction of the Natural History Museum, which the firm of Hornblower & Marshall designed, located along the northern boundary of the Mall. The construction of Union Station had previously fulfilled the desires of many to remove the railroads from the Mall.

The proposed Executive Group building complex around the

Figure 7.21
Secretary of the Treasury
Andrew Mellon (seated at
center) and assistants.
Courtesy National
Archives.

White House was another matter. Although the presence of the Treasury Building and the State, War, and Navy Building offered precedents for an executive grouping, some members of Congress thought that large government buildings surrounding Lafayette Square would "dwarf and belittle the White House." The alternative appeared to be to develop the square with large office buildings and apartment houses. Milton B. Medary Jr. of the AIA's Committee on Public Works voiced the opinion that this possibility would result in "buildings of various heights developing congestion and confusion in the streets serving them and destroying forever the possibility of preserving the dignified setting of these [existing] buildings." Even the presence of the new Treasury Annex at the southeast corner of the square did not guarantee the completion of the grouping (figure 7.22). The Chamber of Commerce Building on the north side of Lafayette Square, intended to harmonize with the intent of the Executive Grouping, might "eventually [be] surrendered to the government as part of the governmental development of Lafayette Square."[115]

Figure 7.22
U.S. Treasury Annex
building, 1917–1918, Cass
Gilbert. Courtesy
National Archives.

In the AIA's eyes, the Treasury Annex building redeemed the reputation of Secretary McAdoo from the considerable depths into which it had fallen with the classification system for federal buildings.

Although the first section of the Treasury Annex building covered only the southern third of the block diagonal from the White House, it was originally intended to cover the entire frontage along Madison Place. This section was designed with a view to enlargement. By an act of Congress in 1917 that provided funds for the Treasury Annex, the secretary of the treasury was authorized to "secure special architectural and expert services." Architect Cass Gilbert was selected to design the building in a style in harmony architecturally with the White House and the Treasury.[116]

That the Treasury Annex was designed according to the dictates of the McMillan Plan was testimony to the power of that document. In a discussion among senators regarding the Treasury Annex, Senator Frank Bosworth Brandegee of Connecticut argued that to design a building with "no artistic finish at all" across from the Treasury Building—a building described as the "finest example of pure Grecian art" in the country—would be a "public calamity." He also noted that on the block facing the Treasury Building, several new bank buildings recently had been constructed, "all buildings of artistic merit, with fine granite columns, and all buildings, I have no doubt, designed with some respect and some attention to the old Treasury Building." The alternative to the Treasury Annex was an "ordinary office building."[117]

McAdoo's selection of Gilbert as architect and his interest in maintaining the spirit of the McMillan Plan won him praise from the AIA. As the organization's own *Journal* noted:

> Deliberately, and with conviction, Secretary McAdoo built according to the Plan of Washington, having in his mind, as he himself expressed it, "the adoption of a logical and continuous building program, not only for the adequate housing of all Departments, but also the harmonious development of Washington."

For McAdoo's turnaround on the matter of public architecture, it was written "whereas he was blind to aesthetic values, he came to see how deep and genuine and reasonable was the interest of the people of the United States in the proper development of their capital. From a persecutor of the saints he became their chief apostle."[118]

The acclaim that accompanied the selection of Cass Gibert to design the Treasury Annex underscored the wild swings in editorial opinion on the part of private architects. Their views of Treasury

Department officials blew according to the favors granted them. Where they denouced individuals for pursuing policies contrary to their interests, their opinions of the same individuals could radically change with a single building project assigned to own of their own. The triumph of classicism and the improved architectural designs were no longer the major issues with the private architects. The aesthetic arguments were tossed aside. The private architects' campaign was now more baldly one of financial gain. Perhaps this issue had been at the heart of the argument all along.

THE PUBLIC BUILDINGS PROGRAM IN
ERAS OF AFFLUENCE AND DEPRESSION

1926–1939

The horizon of the 1920s promised great things for the federal architecture program. A large public buildings bill was making its
way through Congress, authorizing an ambitious multimillion dollar
building program that would take ten years to complete. This legislation would provide hundreds of federal buildings for the nation's
cities and towns. The Office of the Supervising Architect would administer this large program, which required an enlarged staff for the
Office—certainly a plus to a bureaucracy that prided itself on fend-
ing off efforts to chip away at its authority. The "acting" supervising
architect, James A. Wetmore, had held onto his position for a longer
time than any of his "permanent" predecessors. Not only was he entrenched in the Treasury Department and commanded the respect of
members of the U.S. Congress, he was highly protective of his staff
and its prerogatives. The decade also appeared bright as the country
rode the high wave of prosperity and optimism for the future.

Against this apparently rising sun for the Office, the efforts of the
American Institute of Architects (AIA) to gain a position for private architects with federal building projects comparable to the Tarsney Act
appeared dim. In part, the AIA's failure to reinstate comparable legislation can be ascribed to the boom in private building activity that
brought affluence to the construction industry. Some of the leading
private architects were too preoccupied with private business to devote much effort to reformulating and lobbying for legislation. The
clash of architectural design philosophy that had marked the 1890s

was not repeated in the 1920s. Although the International style and other modern styles were seeping into the American architectural consciousness, the established private architects were not proponents of this new wave. Both the federal government architects and private practitioners preferred updated adaptations of classicism, particularly for public buildings.

But at the very close of the 1920s, the onset of the Great Depression shattered the spirit of optimism. The once prosperous building industry slid into a sharp decline; private practitioners scratched hard for the next job. Designers and draftsmen, who had once scoffed at the idea of ever working for a federal bureaucracy, now lined up to apply for positions. The enlargement of the Supervising Architect's Office to handle the work authorized by the public buildings legislation was viewed as an example of government intrusion into an area that private enterprise ought to dominate. The Office was depicted as contributing to the economic hardships of private architects.

During the period from the 1920s to the 1930s, the purpose of the public buildings program was transformed. Whereas the program of the 1920s was intended to provide accommodations for federal activities and represent the best in public building design, by the 1930s the program was recast as a vehicle for providing jobs to unemployed construction workers to help lift the country out of the economic depression. This role pitted the architectural profession, anxious to help its members find work, against the Supervising Architect's Office, which wanted to move building projects quickly to the construction phase in order to create jobs for the building trades. The old rivalries between the Office and the AIA reached a level comparable to those in the 1890s. While the balance of influence over federal building design weighed in favor of the Supervising Architect's Office in the 1930s, in actuality the Office was moving into its sunset years. Once a proud tradition in the Treasury Department, in 1939 the agency suffered the humiliation of being removed from its home base in the department and transferred into the new independent Federal Works Agency. This was only a stopgap before another reorganization of the federal government in 1949, when the federal building program was made part of the General Services Administration.

The Public Buildings Act of 1926

At the outset of this period, the mid-1920s, the major crisis facing the Office of the Supervising Architect was the need to provide federal

buildings to the nation's cities and towns. The delay in federal building construction that World War I and its aftermath occasioned postponed many projects authorized in the Public Buildings Act of 1913.
Congress took note of this need and prepared drafts of public buildings legislation. The question was not whether Congress would act,
but what form the legislation would take.

Of great interest to the architectural profession were provisions
that would be made for the employment of private architects on new
building projects. The private architects were suspicious of circulars
distributed by the U.S. Civil Service Commission soliciting applications from architects to the Office in anticipation of the passage of
the public buildings bill and of a need to staff up to handle the work.
Architect A. Ten Eyck Brown of Atlanta wrote to Congressman
Thomas M. Bell suggesting that the pending legislation include a provision to restructure the Supervising Architect's Office to limit its
work to the handling of repairs and alterations, to the supervision of
the selection of independent architects, and to the administration
of the construction process. Brown urged that such a restructuring
of the Office and the distributing of the design work to private architects would "tend to minimize local criticism of Government
work, as its main production would be in the hands of local people."[1]

The response of the Treasury Department was consistent with its
earlier views. Assistant Treasury Secretary McKenzie Moss cited the
increased costs associated with delegating design work to private architects. Moss also noted the problems inherent in dividing responsibility for federal buildings and the "many unavoidable conferences
[which] would take up so much time of the supervising force that a
slowing up of the building program might result."[2]

Private architects were also concerned about possible language in
the public buildings bill that might require standardized buildings.
The desire for standardization was one of the contributing factors to
the repeal of the Tarsney Act in 1912. The architects' fears were
justified; in his defense of the Office, Assistant Secretary Moss noted
that the need to produce standardized plans would make the employment of private architects "exceedingly difficult if not impracticable."[3]

The Public Buildings Act was passed on 25 May 1926. Its implementation was left to the Treasury Department and the Office of the
Supervising Architect. The bill gave the secretary of the treasury "authority to reinforce this architectural machinery by employing others outside of the Office of the Supervising Architect when in his
opinion it is necessary or useful to do so."[4] In the year after the pas-

sage of the act, little was done to implement its provisions because additional authorizations for buildings both inside and outside of Washington were tacked onto the original legislation. The prospect of an even larger building program required that the dust settle before action was taken.

The lack of clarity on the matter of hiring private architects on buildings authorized by the 1926 act caused considerable anxiety among private architects. The AIA's Committee on Public Works cautioned the organization's members not to repeat past patterns of protest:

> Our present duty [is] to use the influence which we have towards improving the machinery of making plans. This will not be brought about by an insistent demand upon our Representatives and the Treasury Department that trained architects shall be employed. This may be very well a result but that result will be best accomplished if these Representatives are approached with something other than a seeking spirit. If it can be shown that architects have an understanding that exceeds that of their Representatives their services will appear valuable.[5]

In pursuit of its goal, the AIA held several conferences with officials of the Treasury Department. The organization made suggestions related to the selection of architects. According to William Adams Delano, the idea of using able architects throughout the country "appealed" to the Treasury Department. By 1930, the AIA and the Supervising Architect's Office agreed to the compilation of lists of architects in the sections of the country where federal buildings were to be built. Delano reminded the AIA that:

> [the] prime consideration is to get the best possible results for the Government, not only for the large buildings, but for the smaller ones which are of relatively greater importance in their communities, and that such lists should include the outstanding men in the various sections of the country, whether or not they are members of the Institute.[6]

This low-key approach proved successful, to some extent. Several large building projects across the nation were assigned to private architects. In terms of the cost of these buildings, the projects represented a large portion of the annual output of the federal building program. However, because these were larger buildings, when measured in terms of projects and private architects who benefited, the numbers were much smaller. The dispersed nature of these building projects left many observers with the impression that the Supervising Architect's Office still dominated the design of federal buildings. The one exception to this impression was the design for the Federal Triangle project, the most massive endeavor of this period. Here the private architects saw a vindication of their exhortations that the design abilities of private architects were superior to those employed in a federal bureaucracy.

The Federal Triangle Project

The Public Buildings Act of 1926, which provided $50 million for the construction of new buildings in the city of Washington, D.C., made possible the Federal Triangle project. Half of the appropriated amount was to be spent on the triangular piece of land, later known as the Federal Triangle, bounded by Pennsylvania Avenue, Constitution Avenue, and Fifteenth Street, while the other half was to be spent on the U.S. Supreme Court building and the Government Printing Office extension.[7] The buildings of the Federal Triangle comprised what the Committee on Public Works of the AIA considered to be "one of the greatest building projects ever undertaken." Washington architect Horace W. Peaslee represented the sentiments of the AIA in expressing concern for "the extent to which what might be called the genius of the country at large will be employed; in other words, whether the building program will be entirely handled in the Office of the Supervising Architect, or whether architects of national reputation will be associated in the development of the scheme."[8]

The scope of the Triangle project did not appear initially to affect the way in which Wetmore and his staff went about their business. They set about the preparation of plans for the Triangle area. According to Peaslee, the Office prepared plans and many of the working drawings for a "block-by-block design development in the Triangle, without any regard to group planning."[9] Peaslee referred to the buildings the Office planned as "parked instead of grouped."[10] AIA President Milton B. Medary Jr. jumped into the fray, arguing that a bureau:

> which is limited to the employment of designers who can be brought to Washington for a salary of $3,800 is not equipped and should not be expected to be equipped to continue the traditions

established by the Capitol and the group of early buildings on the one hand, and the development of the Mall to create a setting for the Lincoln Memorial, and the Lincoln Memorial itself, and the Arlington Bridge, on the other.[11]

In an article intended for the AIA readership, Louis A. Simon presented a different view of how the Supervising Architect's Office initially approached its task. The highest ranking architect in the Office, Simon represented the agency on major design matters, such as the Federal Triangle project. He recalled:

> When the space-needs of the Federal Government had reached such proportions that the Congress was moved to authorize some relief from the growing congestion, the first intention was to construct a few Federal buildings, regarded at that time as unrelated. For that purpose there were to be utilized several sites then owned or to be acquired for the location of buildings to furnish a given number of square feet of floor area for offices, etc.

According to Simon, this original condition changed radically by the act of Congress on 13 January 1928, which authorized the Secretary of the Treasury to acquire all of the remaining land in the Triangle area. Given this new situation, "the aims now expressed point to the creation of an impressive, monumental group of buildings that will take its place in the larger possibilities which the opportunity provides."[12]

The protests from the AIA had their desired effect. The plans of the Supervising Architect's Office were scrapped and steps were taken to turn over the Triangle project to private architects. While the Office hung onto the design responsibility for the Internal Revenue Service building, Peaslee thought that the building when completed was not up to the standards of the other Triangle buildings.[13]

The first step in the direction of what the AIA envisioned for the Triangle area had already taken place. In October 1926, at the urging of Charles S. Dewey, his assistant secretary, Treasury Secretary Andrew W. Mellon hired Edward H. Bennett as "Consulting Specialist (Architectural)" to "act in an advisory capacity in matters affecting the location of Public Buildings and related matters bearing on the Public Building Program of the District of Columbia."[14] As an employee of Daniel Burnham in the early part of the twentieth century, Bennett had worked on the 1905 plan for San Francisco and the 1908–

1909 plans for Chicago. In 1909, Bennett struck out on his own. In 1924, he formed the architectural and planning firm of Bennett, Parsons and Frost.

Coinciding with Bennett's studies, the Commission of Fine Arts, through its secretary Charles Moore, made suggestions to Secretary Mellon. The commission's plans provided for "a practically continuous line of buildings from the Capitol to Fifteenth Street, connected by arched passageways on the upper stories." One of the major features of the Commission plan was the creation of a great plaza at the intersection of Pennsylvania Avenue and Fifteenth Street. The arrangement was to be similar to that of the Louvre and Palais Royal in Paris, with long public buildings, measuring 1,500 feet or more in length (figure 8.1). These should be of the "highest possible character" and "represent the dignity and the power of the nation." According to the Commission, the treatment of the Federal Triangle area involved a "virtual extension of the Mall to Pennsylvania Avenue, so the great central composition shall have harmonious treatment throughout the entire area." In order to accomplish this plan, the commission recommended that language in a pending deficiency bill make a provision for the treatment of the area from Third Street to Fifteenth Street as a single entity.[15]

After Bennett had completed several studies of the Triangle area, the Treasury Department determined that "the problems involved were of such a nature that it would be wise to create a Board of Architectural Consultants to deal generally with the various situations which might arise." The board was composed initially of Arthur Brown Jr. of San Francisco; Milton B. Medary Jr. of the Philadelphia firm Zantzinger, Borie & Medary; William A. Delano of the New York City firm Delano & Aldrich; Louis Ayers of the New York City firm York & Sawyer; and Louis A. Simon of the Supervising Architect's Office. Later John Russell Pope of New York City was

Figure 8.1
Proposed new federal buildings, Federal Triangle, Washington, D.C., Board of Architectural Consultants. Courtesy National Archives.

added to the board. When Medary died in 1929, his partner C. C. Zantzinger was appointed in his place. In 1933, two additional architects, Hal F. Hentz of Atlanta and William W. Watkin of Houston, were added to the board.[16]

As the plans for the Triangle developed, designs for the individual buildings were divided among the members of the board. Ayers was contracted to design the Department of Commerce building; Brown the Department of Labor and the Interstate Commerce Commission buildings, and their connecting wing; C. C. Zantzinger the Justice Department building; Delano the Post Office building; Bennett the Apex building (later called the Federal Trade Commission building); Pope the National Archives building; and Simon the Internal Revenue Service building (figure 8.2).

The employment of Bennett and the other architects on the board provided the AIA with hope that the federal government might soften its stance on the employment of private architects on other building projects. With the Triangle project, the secretary of the treasury demonstrated his recognition of the magnitude and importance of the problem. Congress received the board's report with enthusiasm. With these developments, the AIA Public Works Committee waxed expectant: "It is the Institute that has done this thing and those parts of Congress and of the Administration which have to do with public buildings developments are beginning to recognize the architectural profession as their advisors when they are seeking public opinion toward the solution of these problems."[17] The success of the Triangle

Figure 8.2
Internal Revenue Service building, Washington, D.C., 1928–1935, Louis A. Simon. Courtesy National Archives.

plan led Medary to suggest that the functions of the board might extend beyond the capital city to embrace the federal building needs of the nation. Medary also recommended that the functions of the board become a permanent feature of the federal government, possibly as an extension to the Commission of Fine Arts.[18]

Although the AIA basked in the sunlight of congressional approval of the private architect's contributions to the Triangle plan, Louis Simon reminded the institute's members of the key role the Supervising Architect's Office played in the Triangle design. In the 1926 act, the Office was the government agency through which the various projects would be carried forward. Even the Board of Architectural Consultants for the Triangle project was to coordinate their work with the "regular establishment."[19]

The ultimate appearance of the Triangle group was derived from a number of sources. One was the "City Beautiful" movement, which had been given one of its earliest expressions at the World's Columbian Exposition in 1893. This movement encouraged the placement of classically designed public buildings in formal landscape settings. Another source for the Triangle plan was the model of Whitehall in London, where government department buildings were concentrated in a single area and related to one another by harmonious architectural design and proximity to parkland and water frontages. Models for the individual buildings in the Triangle group could also be found elsewhere in London, with such hemicycle buildings as the London County Hall building by English architect Ralph Knott and the Anglo-Persian Oil Company Building designed by famed English architect Edwin L. Lutyens. Both buildings were completed in the early 1920s, publicized in the United States, and admired by members of the AIA.

The concentration of monumental buildings in the Federal Triangle, covering seventy-four acres, also had a psychological effect on those who encountered it. As Louis A. Simon related, the Triangle created "an environment thoroughly suited to express the dignity and sovereign power of the United States government as it comes into contact with its workers and its citizens, and with those representatives of foreign governments located in Washington."[20]

The Triangle group was more than a grouping of monumental public buildings. It was intended to have an elaborate landscape treatment, the most distinctive features of which were a rectangular plaza facing Fourteenth Street and a circular plaza intersected by Twelfth Street. Louis Simon referred to the Triangle plan as a "reasonably

Figure 8.3
Model of Federal
Triangle project,
Washington, D.C.
Courtesy National
Archives.

open plan," with two principal open spaces framed by buildings of monumental character."[21] These landscaped areas were viewed as settings for gardens, fountains, and trees. At the center of the Twelfth Street axis, a monumental shaft was suggested (figure 8.3).

The largest of the Triangle buildings was the Commerce Department building, which covered three city blocks. It was described as the "largest monumental building yet erected by the Government, and materials in staggering quantities went into its construction."[22] The Commerce Department building, together with Louis Simon's Internal Revenue Service building, were two of the first Triangle buildings to be constructed.

The National Public Buildings Program

While the Federal Triangle project was being handled as a special and separate endeavor, the Supervising Architect's Office prepared to increase its staff to handle the national program. Wetmore viewed the

staff as a "skeleton organization" and that 150 additional men were required. He described the desirable qualifications for recruits as
"young men graduates from technical colleges with a few years of
practical experience."[23] One method of recruiting architects and
engineers was through a fifteen-minute radio program called "Architectural Outposts of Our Government" produced by the U.S. Civil
Service Commission. The radio spot appealed to architects and engineers, stating that no one would be required to take an examination. Applicants would be rated on education, training, and experience.[24]

Three years later, in August 1929, the U.S. Civil Service accelerated
its appeal to young architects. In another radio spot, the attractions
of the Supervising Architect's Office were spelled out:

> The work is very congenial, there being a wide field for indepen-
> dent judgement, for the development of talent, and for advance-
> ment to the higher grades. It is recognized that the Office of the
> Supervising Architect produces work of the highest character and
> uses the best methods of construction so that young men with
> technical training obtain experience which enables them later in
> life to carry out their professional careers successfully and gives
> them a background of which they will always be proud.[25]

While applications from engineers were sufficient to fill the vacancies, the application level for architects was not. Members of the
architectural profession cited the salary range of $2,000 to $5,000 per
year as too low to attract capable architects. Philadelphia architect
Andrew C. Borzner thought that because the salary offered would attract only "mediocre inexperienced men, their mistakes and loss of
time will cost the Government thousands of dollars, which could be
applied to increased salary, thus getting real men."[26] Chicago architect V. A. Matteson offered his observation that it was "due to the
large demand in private work among architectural firms . . . that inexperienced men are receiving relatively large compensation."[27]
Reflecting on his own experience in the Office as a young man,
Boston architect Henry H. Kendall wrote to John T. Doyle, secretary
of the U.S. Civil Service Commission: "the salaries offered are so inadequate to the present times and the character of service demanded
that you will always find it very difficult to secure men willing, even
if capable, to take up drudgery and isolation of a government position where the end is not any better than the beginning."[28]

The difficulty experienced in recruiting architects led some private practitioners to conclude that the federal government should not be in the architecture business at all. To counteract this impression, the U.S. Civil Service Commission produced another radio spot, "The Construction of A Million Dollar Federal Building by the Office of the Supervising Architect." This time, the agency attempted to illustrate that architectural work in the federal government was substantially different from that in the private sector. The spot led the listener through the steps required in the construction of a federal building from congressional authorization to maintenance. Of the Architectural Division, the radio spot noted that "in order to handle a great many projects simultaneously, there are five group chiefs (full grade architects), each of whom has charge of from 6 to 10 buildings, directing a number of associate and assistant architects and draftsmen varying from 12 to 20." The "Million Dollar Federal Building" was assigned to "one of these architects who studies and restudies the problem under the supervision of the group chief and the Superintendent of [the] Division until finally satisfactory floor plans and an attractive and suitable architectural composition is produced."[29]

Providing Employment to the Private Sector

By early 1930, the effects of the stock market crash and the onset of the Great Depression made their mark on the building industry. The ambitious public building program, justified at the time of its passage on the grounds of efficiency and increased savings to the government, was now viewed as a means of promoting employment. The Treasury Department program was one of the ways in which the federal government fostered construction work. In January 1930, Treasury Secretary Andrew W. Mellon wrote to Commerce Secretary R. P. Lamont that every effort was being made to comply with the wishes of President Herbert Hoover to expedite the construction work under the Supervising Architect's Office. As an example, "for the smaller buildings standard sets of drawings are being utilized with such modifications as are required by topography of sites and service facilities." Standardized designs provided for a faster means of letting smaller buildings out for construction contracts.[30]

As a concession to the private architects lobbying for participation in the public buildings program, an amendment to the 1926 act passed in 1930, known as the Keyes–Elliott Bill, provided for increased authority to the secretary of the treasury to enter into contracts with private architects for full professional services.[31] Because of the pressures to move building projects to the construction phase, the Supervising Architect's Office contemplated the employment of private architects for "only a few of the larger projects."[32] Only large projects were considered for private architects because "as the work [of the Supervising Architect's Office] is only slightly more for a large building than for a small building, it is evident that it is advantageous to make a contract for say a $5,000,000 building than ten contracts for buildings costing $500,000 each."[33]

By late 1930, private architects had been awarded contracts for the design of large federal buildings in San Francisco; Chicago; Pittsburgh; Detroit; Portland, Oregon; Fort Wayne, Indiana; Hartford; and Boston. By November of that year, the Treasury Department reported that private architects were enjoying a hefty share of the design work on federal buildings. Whereas the Supervising Architect's Office had taken on the design of ninety-two projects at a cost of $51,480,647, private architects were responsible for the design of twenty-two buildings (including the Federal Triangle project) at a value of $111,667,000.[34]

The Treasury Department envisioned a limited role for private architects, despite the hard times that had arrived at the doorsteps of the nation's architectural firms. A debate ensued over the scope of the Supervising Architect's Office. The level of the debate had not risen to so high a level since the 1890s, the period when the Treasury Department failed to implement the Tarsney Act.

Because of the conditions the Great Depression presented, the arguments set forth by the AIA and private architects regarding federal architecture projects differed somewhat from those of the late nineteenth century. In late 1930, the AIA board of directors passed a resolution noting that the "AIA feels a deep obligation to offer constructive service in the present condition of business depression and widespread unemployment." The solution to the problem, according to the AIA, was the reorganization of the Supervising Architect's Office so that it would serve only a supervisory function rather than continue as a "gigantic unit for the design of Government Buildings." The AIA also warned that without reorganization, construction projects would be delayed and thus not aid in the relief of unemployment. The continued concentration of design work in the Office was viewed as producing stereotyped and mediocre results and constituting an unwarranted intrusion of the federal government into private business activity.[35]

The AIA chapters put forth these basic arguments in lobbying with the Treasury Department. The Rhode Island Chapter of the AIA also argued that the wider employment of private architects would lead to a:

> more living and vital architecture appropriate to the regions in which our federal buildings are to be erected. We claim that to restrict the designing of our federal buildings to a single department, no matter how efficient, must inevitably narrow and stereotype the expression of our architectural ideals.[36]

Even the President's Emergency Committee for Employment questioned the ability of the Supervising Architect's Office to administer the public building program. The committee noted that "public welfare and the present objective of Federal architectural establishments seem inimical to one another." The American Telephone and Telegraphic Company (AT&T) offered a standard of measurement. In 1931, AT&T was undertaking a building program figured to be seven times the size of the federal building program. "They [AT&T] have a system of delegating architectural work [to private architects] throughout the country under the supervision of their Supervising Architect, Mr. Voorhees. His advice might well be sought." At the report's end, the committee concluded, "the men are competent, but the method is wrong. The Supervising Architect's Office is so busy that it is not able to correct its point of view, and see itself as others see it."[37]

Members of Congress picked up on this line of argument and protested the methods of the Supervising Architect's Office. Senator James J. Davis of Pennsylvania complained to Treasury Secretary Ogden Mills that the Office's preparation of designs took food from the mouths of architects and their families, delayed the awards of contracts to builders, and withheld much needed income from the citizens of Pennsylvania. Davis added, "I furthermore feel that the Treasury's policy has a tendency to too greatly standardize the architecture of our federal institutions through the duplication and repetitious use of drawings. In other words, we are Babbitizing our National Architecture."[38]

While the Treasury Department officials received these protests, the staff of the Supervising Architect's Office was working at a break-neck speed to move building projects to the construction phase. As the President's Emergency Committee described the pace of work, "it has been running its blueprint department night and day, three shifts, and its committee on the selection of sites has been holding night sessions."[39]

In order to develop a camaraderie among federal architects, the Association of Federal Architects founded the quarterly publication *The Federal Architect*. In the first issue, published in July 1930, editor Edwin Bateman Morris stated that the publication was intended to respond to the great interest throughout the country in the large building program of the federal government. Although the prime movers behind the magazine were from the Office of the Supervising Architect, the magazine also presented projects designed by the Construction Division of the War Department, as well as those of the Veterans Bureau, the Bureau of Yards and Docks of the Navy Department, and the National Capital Park and Planning Commission. Morris thought that *The Federal Architect* would serve to improve the morale of the organizations that produced buildings.[40]

The reaction of the Office to the protestations of the private architects was predictable. As the editors of *The Federal Architect* wrote, "The Federal Architectural offices are weaned and reared on criticism."[41] The Office took issue with the figures quoted regarding the AT&T architecture program and voiced the opinion that the federal government's program, in terms of numbers of buildings, was many times the size of the program the telephone company handled. The Office claimed that it had studied the methods of the telephone company and had employed some of the architects associated with the telephone company's program, but thought that "their methods would cause much greater dissatisfaction among the architects of the country than the methods the Treasury Department is pursuing." The accusations, according to the department, stemmed from "selfish interests which, whether they are right or wrong, cannot possibly be satisfied."[42]

By 1932, the AIA protests regarding the federal architecture program resulted in the introduction of legislation in Congress, H.R. 6187. Known as the "Green Bill," it called for the placement of all federal building design into the hands of private architects. Several building contractors who had undertaken the construction of Treasury Department building projects flocked to the support of the Office. W. D. Lovell of Minneapolis protested the bill based on his belief that the design of government buildings was a highly specialized area of architecture with which the Supervising Architect's Office was adept:

> The average run of architects are not specialists and the architecture of Government buildings is highly specialized, as anyone who is acquainted with those buildings knows. At the very best the work of private architects must be thoroughly checked over in the Office of the Supervising Architect and in most cases must be entirely re-vamped in certain features where the private architect has not been acquainted with the specialized requirements of the various Departments of the Government which are to occupy the building.[43]

H.R. 6187 provoked a highly defensive reply from the Supervising Architects' Office. An unnamed source in the Office described the bill as a result of a "movement [that] has been fostered by a comparatively small number of people who have stirred up considerable propaganda for over a year, and supported by people engaged in construction work for these people." The source also thought that the arguments presented in favor of the legislation were "so extravagant and erroneous and the motives so selfish that it was thought unnecessary to dignify the question by giving it attention."[44]

The intense lobbying by the AIA did not succeed in extracting a more flexible posture from the Treasury Department during the Hoover administration. However, with the election of Franklin Delano Roosevelt as president, the architectural profession saw an opportunity to influence a new group of Treasury Department officials. In a telegram to Treasury Secretary William H. Woodin, the editor of the *American Architect*, Benjamin F. Betts, called attention to the fact that Acting Supervising Architect James A. Wetmore was not an architect. Betts urged Woodin to select a man for this position, "who is thoroughly conversant with building practice" in order to achieve public buildings expressive of the highest ideals in architecture.[45] In a follow-up letter to Secretary Woodin, Betts appealed for a reorganization of the Supervising Architect's Office "to remove its activities from competition with architects in private practice."[46]

Betts capped his campaign with a letter to Director of the Budget Lewis W. Douglas containing a recommendation that all federal building activities, then located in several different agencies, be consolidated into a single office "functioning in a fact-finding supervisory capacity, utilizing as needed the services of numerous established offices of architects, landscape architects, and engineers throughout the country. This office should be directed by an executive who is conversant with building design and construction."[47]

The Procurement Division

Upon taking office, Roosevelt instructed Secretary Woodin to withhold all expenditures of unobligated funds for public building projects until the administration had formulated a national program for public works and unemployment relief."[48] The promised reorganization was announced in June 1933 with Executive Order 6166. With this order, the Procurement Division was created within the Treasury Department; the division was responsible for all the federal government's properties, facilities, machinery, equipment, stores, and supplies. The reorganization did not include the Army Corps of Engineers or military property. The Supervising Architect's Office was transferred to the Procurement Division under Assistant Secretary Lawrence W. Robert and renamed the Public Works Branch. Rear Admiral Christian Joy Peoples became the director of the Procurement Division. Assistant Director W. E. Reynolds, an architect, would oversee the Public Works Branch. Reynolds directed five units, headed by the supervising engineer, supervising architect, office manager, chairman of the board of award, and the chief of the legal section. The building administration functions were divided between the Procurement Division for Treasury Department buildings; the Post Office for post offices; and the National Park Service for public buildings, monuments, and reservations in Washington, D.C.[49]

Of the placement of the Supervising Architect's Office, the editors of *The Federal Architect* wrote, "We saw the good old Supervising Architects' Office, the oldest architectural office in the country, with its fine record for achievement and ability, buried without flag or volley in the Procurement Division." Noting that the Procurement Division was conceived as a gigantic purchasing agency, the editors lamented, "it is perhaps unfortunate that architecture should be submerged under the purchasing of coal and typewriters."[50] Adding salt to the wound, the new Public Works Branch was moved out of the Treasury Building because of the expansion of the Treasury Department during the Depression years. The branch was moved into the Federal Warehouse Building at 9th and D Streets, S.W. (figure 8.4). Because of its remoteness from the "seething marts of trade,"

Figure 8.4
Procurement Building,
Home of Public Works
Branch, Washington,
D.C. Courtesy National
Archives.

the editors of *The Federal Architect* remarked that the location can be reached by "boat on the Potomac River, by oxcart, and in other ways."[51]

While the federal bureaucracy was reorganized to address the conditions of the Great Depression, new relief funding programs were initiated to allocate and supplement the level of funding for public works. The federal emergency administrator of public works, Harold L. Ickes, allotted funds to the Treasury Department for the construction of federal buildings under the provisions of the National Industrial Recovery Act of 1933. In August 1933, for example, Ickes made two allotments, one of $6,971,648 and the other of $13,799,550.[52] Other funds for emergency construction projects were appropriated and distributed to generate jobs in various parts of the country.

Within a year's time, Ickes complained to Peoples that work under the Treasury Department had been progressing at a very slow pace. "The Department's record of men employed per million dollars allotted is among the lowest."[53] Director Peoples defended the work of his division, ascribing the delays to the changing levels of allotments for buildings and the continued increase in construction costs.[54]

The press of the workload caused internal reorganizations within the Public Works Branch. One of these reorganizations was the decentralization of the engineering force into eight districts, each headed by a district engineer. According to Peoples, the regional office plan allowed for "greater flexibility and expedition in the field service."[55]

The arrival of Henry Morgenthau Jr. as secretary of the treasury in early 1934 portended more changes to the federal architecture program (figure 8.5). In June of that year, Morgenthau ordered that all future federal buildings designed in the Treasury Department would be designed under the supervising architect. Morgenthau thought that because most of the buildings to be designed in the foreseeable

Figure 8.5
Secretary of the Treasury
Henry Morganthau Jr.
Courtesy National
Archives.

future were valued at less than $60,000 each and were adaptable to "standard characteristics of design," it was not economical for private architects to handle work of this smaller size. He thought that the department's first priority was to place the buildings under contract, put men to work, and thus facilitate employment in the construction field. The advantages to the nation's employment picture through this plan were greater than the benefits to a "comparatively few architectural organizations."[56]

The small number of larger building projects would be assigned to individual "consulting architects" who would be assigned to Washington, D.C., on a temporary salaried basis. These consulting architects would take charge of the design and preparation of drawings and specifications. This consulting arrangement was made based on the belief that the federal government would enjoy the "enlightening effect of fresh thought in the development of building design." At the same time, the work was performed under the supervision of the trained personnel in the Supervising Architect's Office.[57]

According to the assistant director of the Public Works Branch, W. E. Reynolds, "These architects will be assigned two or more buildings geographically grouped in the general locality of their home office."[58] In order to dampen the inevitable complaints from the private architects regarding this new policy of federal building design, the Procurement Division convened an Advisory Committee on Architectural Design, composed of private architects—Henry Shepley, Charles Z. Klauder, Philip B. Maher, Aymar Embury II—and Louis Simon of the Public Works Branch.

The AIA questioned how closely the Treasury Department followed the $60,000 guideline. The president of the St. Louis Chapter of the AIA, W. Oscar Mullgardt, noted that a list of building projects the federal government undertook showed buildings with values ranging from $60,000 to $1,500,000. Mullgardt predicted that the policies of the Treasury Department would have a "most demoralizing effect on the architectural profession." The most that architectural firms could hope for in the face of hard times was "small residential work," because private building activity was virtually nonexistent. He accused the federal government of serving as "an agency in the elimination of those offices which have, through their continuous experience and development, made American architecture the foremost in the world today."[59]

While the Washington, D.C., residency requirement for private architects who wished to design federal buildings struck many as unreasonable, some felt that the work was worth the inconvenience. Among those who agreed to the terms of the Treasury Department and took up temporary residence in Washington, D.C., was Ralph H. Deane of Boston, who accepted the assignment to design federal buildings in Worcester, Arlington, and Somerville, Massachusetts, and St. Albans, Vermont. John P. Almand of Little Rock, Arkansas, agreed under similar terms to design the federal buildings in Anadarko, Oklahoma; Columbia, Missouri; and Ft. Smith, Arkansas. Gilbert Stanley Underwood was assigned the federal buildings at Huntington, California, Flagstaff, Arizona, and Provo, Utah. He later designed the Moderne style U.S. post office and courthouse in Los Angeles (figure 8.6). Each consulting architect was given the right to sign the plans as "designing architects. This privilege was granted with the definite intention that because of certain advantages the credit of designing these buildings might give them in the future, this would compensate them in a degree for the sacrifice they have made in coming to Washington to take part in this program."[60]

The long continuity in the federal architecture program provided by James A. Wetmore was broken in 1934 with his retirement at the age of seventy-one. After nineteen years as acting supervising archi-

Figure 8.6
U.S. post office and courthouse, Los Angeles, California, 1938–1940, Gilbert Stanley Underwood. Courtesy National Archives.

tect, Wetmore had become an institution in the Treasury Department and to members of Congress. Consideration of age doubtless
dictated his departure, but he later wrote from his retirement home
in Florida, "I have found it difficult to adjust myself to the new conditions resulting from the reorganization." He also recalled the pace
of work of the Office: "I have but one sore spot and that results from
the unreasonable demands that were made on us at times for a rate
of speed that was impossible."[61] He also recalled that the Supervising
Architect's Office was regarded by the Treasury Department as a
stepchild, a condition that made the Office's accomplishments all the
more remarkable.[62] Wetmore continued to stay in contact with the
staff of the Office with an occasional column in *The Federal Architect*
in which he reminisced about the Office in the good old days. Upon
his death in March 1940, Edwin Bateman Morris remembered
Wetmore as "symbolic. Just as his choice, not being an architect, to
make no effort to use the title of Supervising Architect was symbolic
of a desire to do rather than to be, so was his whole life devoted to
accomplishment rather than publicity."[63]

Louis A. Simon

At the age of sixty-six, Wetmore's successor was "no longer young"
and had also attained something of an institutional status. Louis A.
Simon had worked with the Supervising Architect's Office for nearly
four decades and was well known to the architectural community
(figure 8.7). Simon was born in Baltimore in 1867 and was educated
at the Massachusetts Institute of Technology. After an extended tour
of Europe, he opened an architectural office in Baltimore in 1894.
Two years later, he was brought into the Supervising Architect's
Office by Edward A. Crane. His energy, enthusiasm, and persistence
attracted the attention of his superiors and resulted in his rapid rise
through the organization. In 1915, Simon was appointed chief of the
Engineering and Drafting Division. Between 1915 and 1934, with
Wetmore at the administrative reins, Simon was responsible for "all
phases of architectural work" in the Office. He was equally at home
with the AIA, which he joined in 1908. He was elected a fellow of the
AIA in 1937.[64]

Although his long association with the federal architecture program may have made him antithetical to the aspirations of the AIA,

private architects respected Simon, although somewhat begrudg-
ingly. In his AIA fellowship proposal, the submission stated:

> While it is unquestionably true that buildings designed by a large
> federal agency, such as the Supervising Architect's Office, handi-
> capped as it is by many controlling influences in the selection of
> personnel, will never, as a rule, rise to the high standards of per-
> fection in design achieved by architects in private practice who are
> qualified by natural ability, training, travel and experiences to do
> outstanding work and who faithfully accept their responsibility to
> do so, nevertheless the average quality of design is in all probabil-
> ity higher than the average in private practice. Particularly has this
> been true under the guidance of Mr. Simon as Supervising
> Architect, largely because of his culture and broad experience and

his sympathy with all that is fine in the profession of architecture.[65]

The 1933 reorganization of the federal architecture program placed the newly named Public Works Branch at a lower level within the Treasury Department bureaucracy than the old Office of the Supervising Architect had enjoyed. However, Simon retained the title of supervising architect as well as control over the architectural design of federal buildings designed within his office. Simon's architectural philosophy was reflected in his buildings. His contemporaries felt that his work was "characterized by an effort toward simplicity and restraint and the attainment of pleasing results, by a studied consideration of mass and proportion, rather than by excess of elaboration or non-functional expression, such as characterized some of the early work of the Supervising Architect's Office."[66]

His fellow member of the Advisory Committee on Architectural Design, Aymar Embury II, came to know the workings of Simon's Office. As Embury stated:

> Most architects think of the Office of the Supervising Architect as a kind of combination assembly line and slot machine, into one end of which Congress pours money to be transmuted by internal and invisible processes into designs for buildings, which come out at the other end neatly wrapped in cellophane and untouched by human hands.

After working with Simon, Embury gained a new respect for the position of supervising architect. He marveled at the freshness of view that Simon brought to his work after nearly four decades with the Office. He felt that once Simon became the "sole responsible official" (after Wetmore's retirement), the work turned out by the Office:

> changed very materially, became freer, bolder, with a sort of wisely conservative experimental quality; (this may sound like a paradox, but it is also a fact) and under his administration, the government architect has ceased to follow, and has taken its rightful place of leadership in the forward movement of this greatest of the American arts.[67]

The design of federal buildings under Simon was described as a "suitable bromide" to the exuberance of the French renaissance promulgated by his predecessors. "In its place, under Mr. Simon's guiding hand, came more the subdued, more sentimental architecture of the Italian Renaissance and the Colonial."[68] The federal buildings for New Philadelphia, Ohio (figure 8.8), Arlington, Virginia (figure 8.9), and Clarksburg, West Virginia (figure 8.10), are typical of Simon's designs. An in-house Board of Consulting Architects, composed of staff and consulting architects, was set up in 1934 at the suggestion of LeRoy Barton, an assistant to Treasury Secretary Morgenthau, who felt that the exterior design of standard post offices should be improved and that a general committee on design should review "all existing type designs and suggest changes and improvements."[69]

With the formation of the Procurement Division and the allotment of funds to the Treasury Department made possible through the National Industrial Recovery Act, Administrator Ickes's subordinates advised him that the budget for each federal building was extravagant and should be reduced. According to Reynolds, the result was "cheese-box construction and chaos" and the subsequent congressional decision to make available funds for the augmentation

Figure 8.8
U.S. post office, New Philadelphia, Ohio, 1927–1928, Louis A. Simon. Courtesy National Archives.

Figure 8.9
U.S. post office,
Clarendon Branch,
Arlington, Virginia, 1937,
Louis A. Simon. Courtesy
National Archives.

of previous allotments. Reynolds asked the Board of Consulting
Architects to develop a short paragraph recommending a policy that
would govern the design of public buildings.[70]

This the board did. In a brief and general statement, the board recommended that federal buildings should be:

> (1) of simple governmental character in consonance with the re-
> gion in which they are located and the surroundings of the specific
> sites; (2) materials shall be such as to require no excessive mainte-
> nance; and (3) the buildings shall be of sufficient capacity to rea-
> sonably meet the needs of the Federal Government as may be an-
> ticipated for a ten-year period.[71]

Later this general policy was given detail. Rather than selecting
one of a number of "so-called 'type designs,'" federal buildings were
designed to meet the conditions peculiar to the site:

> Architectural traditions, as well as the utilization of natural or
> manufactured products of the vicinity, are given every practicable

Figure 8.10
U.S. federal building,
Clarksburg, West
Virginia, 1931–1932,
Louis A. Simon. Courtesy
National Archives.

consideration. Thus, in New England will be found examples of Colonial architecture with exterior facing of brick or stone; in the Southwest, many of the buildings designed for that locality will reflect the Spanish influence in elevation and materials; and in sections of more recent traditions, buildings of contemporary character have been designed. In the larger centers of population, design tends toward monumental structures, expressing the strength and dignity of the Federal Government rather than local color.[72]

The federal buildings for Colusa, California (figure 8.11), and Amsterdam, New York (figure 8.12) illustrate the "architectural traditions" approach. The federal buildings for Minneapolis, Minnesota (figure 8.13) and Baton Rouge, Louisiana (figure 8.14) represent the "monumental" approach.

Despite the respect private architects held for Simon and the efforts Simon and his staff invested in producing and overseeing quality designs, the AIA fought on with its effort to open more federal architecture projects to private practitioners. In 1935, the AIA passed resolutions, made statements, and held conferences to address this problem. Among the assertions the AIA made was that the architectural profes-

Figure 8.11
U.S. post office, Colusa,
California, 1937, Louis A.
Simon. Courtesy
National Archives.

sion has "never been able to look to it [government architecture] for inspiration and leadership in these qualities [highest type of service in planning, design, and construction that the talent of the country can furnish]; and that its influence on the taste and culture of the people has rarely been helpful or inviting." The AIA ascribed these failings to an "inevitable result of the methods of designing federal buildings" and stated that the preparation of plans for buildings "at high speed and under great pressure is not in the Government's interest."[73]

Even Frank Lloyd Wright entered the fray: His observations confounded both sides. In a speech to the Association of Federal Architects, Wright addressed the question of who should design government buildings: "Certainly not government employees, because no employee is free to do creative work. And I am not so sure about private architects as they stand at present." He concluded that perhaps builders should be designers of government buildings because "their hands were in the mud of the bricks."[74]

These discussions of ideals and abstract situations were in reality a smoke screen for what was really ailing the architectural profession. Architects were suffering from the severe trials and hardships of the Depression, a situation that was exacerbated by their perception that

the government was doing little to grant the profession relief. Francis P. Sullivan, chairman of the AIA's Committee on Public Works, noted in 1935 that many architects had been forced to give up their profession and "take up in middle life some entirely new kind of work for the sake of a bare subsistence."[75]

The unrelenting pressure of the AIA placed on the Treasury Department officials had its effect. Treasury Secretary Morgenthau expressed a strong interest "in seeing that the government buildings were properly planned and designed" and that they represented a high standard. However, he also expressed "surprise and incredulity" at the assertion by the AIA that, except for two brief periods, government architecture did not represent the "highest attainable standard of planning and design."[76] Despite Morgenthau's puzzlement at the AIA's protestations, he encouraged the organization's representatives to remain in contact with him. As he wrote to Sullivan, "I am desirous of affording the responsible officials of the AIA a full opportunity to be heard."[77]

The Treasury Department officials followed up their stated concern for the status of federal government architecture by creating a joint committee representing the Procurement Division and the AIA

Figure 8.12
U.S. federal building, Amsterdam, New York, 1935–1936, Louis A. Simon. Courtesy National Archives.

Figure 8.13
U.S. post office,
Minneapolis, Minnesota,
1932–1935, Leon Arnal of
Magney & Tusler.
Courtesy National
Archives.

to consider this question. The members of the committee included LeRoy Barton, Cornelius V. R. Bogert, N. Max Dunning, Clair W. Ditchey, Louis A. Simon, and Francis P. Sullivan. Surprisingly, members of the joint committee found themselves in agreement over the potential role of private architects in the federal architecture program. The report of the committee stated that the staff of the Procurement Division was highly efficient in the "routine work" of the building program. On the matter of architectural design, private architects were able to produce "work of greater freedom of expression and virility not always obtainable in a large, permanent organization." Private architects possessed this ability because of "their greater freedom from restraint in adopting new materials, methods, and philosophies of design and their greater opportunity for discussion of their problems with their fellow practitioners." The joint committee recommended that private architects play a role in the federal architecture program "not only for his value in the specific building or buildings at hand, but as a source of inspiration for the continuing work of the government bureau."[78]

In order to bring about the greater involvement of private architects in the federal architecture program, the committee recommended a "direct selection method based on prequalification and selection" rather than competition programs. The establishment of a
board of five qualified persons, three of whom would be architects,
abetted this system. From time to time, the board would submit
names of architects or architectural firms that were qualified to undertake design work.[79]

Although the Procurement Division had participated in the discussions of the joint committee, the Treasury Department did not
agree fully with the recommendations contained in the report.
Procurement Director Peoples proclaimed himself to be a "firm be-
liever in the principle of competitions," and he observed that this
method was being carried out with success by the Section of Painting
and Sculpture. Peoples recommended that the plan of competition
be limited to exterior designs only, and that the remainder of the
work would be carried out by the Procurement Division. This competitive program could be implemented by an amendment to the law

Figure 8.14
U.S. post office and
courthouse, Baton
Rouge, Louisiana, 1931–
1933, Moise H. Goldstein.
Courtesy National
Archives.

governing professional services, allowing the secretary of the treasury to "purchase on any large government building which may
thereafter be authorized, say three sets of architectural designs, the
prices to be fixed, in order of merit."[80]

Secretary Morgenthau echoed People's inclination toward competitions. He also defended the record of the Procurement Division
during the period since 1933 when federal architects handled all design work, except for the few buildings that were designed by temporary consulting architects. Morganthau was of the opinion that,
during the period from 1933 to 1937:

> there has resulted a real evolution in the architecture of federal
> buildings, in that extravagance in design, waste in space, unusual
> individualistic idealism, and delays in the prosecution of the work,
> have been largely avoided. The buildings designed and constructed
> in the Public Buildings Branch have dignity and originality, econ-
> omy in design, with strict adherence to the utilitarian purpose for
> which the building is to be used.[81]

The federal buildings for the Roseland station, Chicago, Illinois,
(figure 8.15) and the Forest Hills Station, Queens, New York (figure
8.16) were among several exceptional and widely admired Moderne
federal buildings of the Simon period.

Despite the defense of Treasury Department officials of the past
record of their in-house architects, the direction toward greater participation by private architects was clear. By 1937, the building program had reached and passed its peak. Director Peoples looked into
the future and predicted that "we cannot expect a building program
of more than about $25,000,000 per annum, if that."[82] If the federal
building program leveled off, this would then relieve pressure on the
Treasury Department to interpret the program as a primary method
of bringing employment to the construction industry. President
Franklin Roosevelt ordered a slowdown in the construction program
in mid-1937 as a way to reduce the demands on the federal treasury.
The order affected not only small post office projects throughout the
nation, but it also postponed major projects in Washington, D.C.,
such as a new War Department building, the Thomas Jefferson
Memorial, and the Social Security building.[83]

By the late 1930s, the federal government was not only easing off
on the civilian construction program, it was also beginning to prepare for wartime demands. In June 1938, Congress passed an act pro-

UNITED STATES POST OFFICE

U.S. POST OFFICE, CHICAGO, ILL.
9-14-36
ROSELAND STA.

viding for the transfer of funds to the Procurement Division to carry out needed construction work. Many of these projects were facilities for the Navy Department and were already contracted out to private architectural and engineering firms.[84]

Figure 8.15
U.S. post office, Roseland station, Chicago, Illinois, 1935, John C. Bollenbacher. Courtesy National Archives.

By 1939, the Procurement Division had cast a wide net through a variety of building projects. It was associated with preparing working drawings and specifications for airports, embassies, hospitals, zoo buildings, and laboratories. Peoples boasted that the Procurement Division could handle such work quicker and more economically. The division's staff could also easily confer with departments and agencies in Washington, D.C., as to the requirements of the occupants of federal buildings. Citing examples such as the work done for eleven large federal buildings in Washington, D.C., Peoples stated that the working drawings had been done at a cost of $345,000 less than if comparable work had been carried out by private architects. As if advertising the capabilities of his staff to other agencies, Peoples claimed that this efficient and economical production of work could be done only by "an experienced expert force of technicians and architectural draftsmen which are now available." Peoples then challenged the conventional view of the talents of the Procurement Division. "Every private architect, if he is honest about the matter, as

Figure 8.16
U.S. post office, Forest
Hills Station, Queens
New York, 1937–1938,
Lorimer Rich. Courtesy
National Archives.

certain architectural journals have pointed out [should acknowledge] that the architectural work done by the Public Buildings Branch in the last few years has been revolutionary, and of superior standards."[85]

The comparative leisurely pace of the civilian building program, plus the interest of Treasury Secretary Morgenthau and Procurement Director Peoples in architectural competitions, led to specific plans to carry out such a program. As a first step in testing the waters of architectural competitions since the repeal of the Tarsney Act in 1912, Morgenthau announced in May 1938 two competitions. One was for designs for a typical small post office. Out of a general competition, ten designs would be selected. Each architect of the winning designs would receive a prize of $1,000. Should any of the designs be used by the federal government, working drawings and specifications could be prepared in the Supervising Architect's Office. If any one design was used more than once, the architect would receive $100 each time the design was used within one year of the award. The other competition was for a $450,000 post office and courthouse building in Covington, Kentucky. As with the small post office project, Louis Simon's office would undertake the working drawings and specifications. Underscoring the high level that this effort involved, the jury was made up of stellar figures: Charles Z. Klauder and Paul P. Cret of Philadelphia; Aymar Embury II and Gilmore D. Clarke of New York City; Philip B. Maher of Chicago; Henry R. Shepley of Boston; Richard J. Neutra of Los Angeles; and Edward Bruce of Washington.[86]

Following up on this limited experiment with competitions, the Treasury Department decided to carry out a broad program of regional competitions for the architectural design of federal buildings. The working drawings and specifications would continue to be prepared under the direction of Supervising Architect Louis Simon.[87] The Treasury Department maintained control over working drawings and specifications because it was thought that government work required that drawings and specifications must be prepared in minute detail "in order that competing construction contractors may be properly advised and may bid on an equal basis." The Treasury Department also cited "Government practices and legal requirements."[88]

For the purpose of the competition, the country was divided into eleven regions. Participation in the competitions was limited to architects in the region in which the projects were located. In March 1939, Secretary Morgenthau announced four post office projects that would be designed under this program. Winning architects would secure a design prize and would be retained as consultants to ensure that the "spirit of the design might be maintained in the development of the working drawings."[89] With this method, Morgenthau hoped to obtain "the nation's best architectural talent for Government construction."[90]

Morgenthau's actions regarding competitions went a long way toward rapprochement with the community of private architects. The AIA, however, felt that the secretary had not gone far enough. AIA President Charles D. Maginnis cited Morganthau's belief that exterior design for a building could be separated from its construction, and that good architectural results could be obtained by having one person prepare preliminary sketches and another the working drawings and specifications. Maginnis felt that this method of designing federal buildings was contrary to the competition code of the AIA which stated that "the object of a competition is to select an architect to design a building and carry it through to completion." He urged

Morgenthau to expand the terms of the competition so as to restore the architect to his traditional relationship with a building project and to ensure that the "final result will be a perfect expression in concrete form of the original intention."[91]

Despite the best intentions of both the Treasury Department and the AIA, the initial results of the new competition program fell short of their aspirations for federal building design. Cincinnati architect Charles Cellarius wrote to the chairman of the AIA's Committee on Public Works recounting his recent experience as a member of the jury that judged the competition for a post office in Leavenworth, Kansas, which William B. Ittner, architect with the St. Louis Board of Education, won. According to Cellarius, the jury was "tremendously disappointed by the quality of designs submitted, and I imagine the Treasury Department was also. There were not a large number of designs and it is my opinion . . . that none of the designs were as good as could have been executed by the Treasury Department itself." He concluded that the architectural profession was not cooperating in the competitions or was unaware of the opportunity presented by these competitions.[92]

The enthusiasm of Secretary Morgenthau and Director Peoples for competitions was carried out into the work of the staff of the Procurement Division. In 1939, an Office competition was held for a design of a small post office. The purpose of the competition was to select a "certain number of designs which may be used as types." Each entrant had one day in which to prepare a sketch. The jury of award included three private architects and three senior members of the Procurement Division. Of the 189 submissions from the staff, twelve designs were selected. One of the designs (figure 8.17) was submitted by Leonard L. Hunter, who was a central figure in federal government architecture in the 1950s.[93]

Preparing for World War II

The gearing up of the federal government for wartime demands lifted the nation out of the Great Depression. In order for the federal government to meet the challenge of war, various agencies were realigned. In July 1939, the Public Works Branch of the Procurement Division was taken out of the Treasury Department altogether and became part of the Public Buildings Administration of the Federal Works Agency under John M. Carmody. Under this reorganization,

the former assistant director of the Procurement Division, W. E. Reynolds, became commissioner of public buildings. Louis A. Simon retained the title of supervising architect and was subordinate to Reynolds. Simon's counterpart as supervising engineer was Neal A. Melick. In addition, the building management functions of the National Park Service were consolidated into the Public Works Administration. The remainder of the Procurement Division was left in the Treasury Department.

The charge of the Public Buildings Administration was to design and construct all new federal buildings, exclusive of those for the War and Navy departments and the Veterans Administration. With the postmaster general, the Public Buildings Administration was also responsible for the development of a "progressively expanding national plan" that would distribute future federal buildings in an equitable fashion.[94] Commissioner Reynolds envisioned that architectural work for the federal building program would be performed by the regularly employed staff of the Supervising Architect's Office, an arrangement that he felt precluded the award of commissions to architects or architectural firms in private practice. However, the Public Buildings Administration proceeded with a series of regional competitions for federal building design that had been initiated by the Treasury Department under Morganthau.[95]

Figure 8.17
U.S. post office, Type Buildings Office Competition, 1939, Leonard L. Hunter. Courtesy National Archives.

End of an Era

The removal of the federal architecture program from the Treasury Department marked the end of an era. The Office of the Supervising Architect left the department that had nurtured, sustained, and defended it. When the inventory of federal buildings consisted of a few dozen custom houses and marine hospitals, it was natural that the design and construction work for these buildings should have come under the purview of the Treasury Department, which collected the revenues. When the federal building program expanded to encompass thousands of federal buildings intended to house the activities of the judicial system, the postal system, and other federal functions, the Treasury Department appeared to be an illogical location for a major public buildings program. By 1939, few observers could justify the continued role of the Treasury Department in weighty architectural matters. In January 1940, from his Florida retirement home, Wetmore wrote his last letter to his former compatriots. He could not become accustomed to the idea that his old architectural office was no longer a part of the Treasury Department. But he was gratified that the Office did not leave the Treasury Department with a whimper; because he considered Robert Mills to be the first supervising architect, he felt the Office was "hale and hearty at the advanced age of 100 years."[96]

Attempts to move the Office of the Supervising Architect out of the Treasury Department were alluded to during the period leading up to the Tarsney Act of 1893. In theory, such a move would result in the loosening of the traditional methods of operation—including the way in which architectural designs were obtained. The private architects hoped to benefit from changed methods in procuring designs. Throughout the first three decades of the twentieth century, possible reorganizations of the federal building program would have placed the architectural functions in a bureau of fine arts or a department of public works. A "public works department" turned out to be the new home of the program, with the creation of the Federal Works Agency in 1939.

It was ironic that the 1930s marked both a high point in the fortunes of the Office of the Supervising Architect as well as its demise. Never before had the Office undertaken a building program of such enormous proportions. Under Louis A. Simon, the buildings received praise (albeit reluctant) from private practitioners. Except for a select number of major federal buildings that were designed by private architects, the Office still maintained control over the vast majority of design projects.

Despite these accomplishments, the omens of change were present early in the decade. High-minded discussions of public architecture gave way to businesslike calculations of a building's adornment and form and its job-creation potential. Then, architecture became part of a vast procurement bureau, reflecting an attitude toward public buildings that would take root in 1949 with the creation of the General Services Administration. The consolidation of the public buildings activities into the Federal Works Administration was a temporary expedient. It dashed any hopes that the federal architecture might be placed in a fine arts bureau. Idealism had run its course. Pragmatism now guided the federal architecture program.

EPILOGUE

1940–PRESENT

At first glance, the transfer of the Public Buildings Administration from the Treasury Department to the new Federal Works Agency (FWA) did not dramatically affect the character of the federal architecture program. The architectural staff was transferred as a whole to the new agency. Louis Simon's continued position as supervising architect promised stability and continuity in the new order. Even the 1949 transfer of the public buildings program to the General Services Administration (GSA) was not viewed as disruptive because, in some ways, the new agency resembled a throwback to the Treasury Department's old Procurement Division.

However, 1939 marked the gradual beginning of the inevitable engagement of the United States in World War II, which changed the country in ways that World War I, twenty years before, had not. For a populace with the Great Depression still fresh in its mind, every effort was made after 1945 to foster employment for returning veterans and maintain private enterprises as the nation returned to peacetime concerns. Private architectural practitioners reaped the benefit of this national mood. The backlog in new public buildings construction, created during the nation's build-up for wartime requirements, became a vehicle for sustaining the nation's economy. Even with the tremendous demand for new public buildings, the supervising architect and his staff would not likely return to "business as usual" after combat concluded.

The post-World War II era also ushered in the atomic age and fear of nuclear war. Efforts to protect the vital workings of the federal government led to a further decentralization of federal functions to regional locations throughout the country. In the nation's capital, plans were made to disperse major federal installations beyond a fifteen-mile radius from the city's center. This dispersal plan operated under the assumption that an attack on the city would leave intact most government functions in the outlying areas. Defending the nation from atomic attack also influenced the design of federal buildings and of an expanded national transportation network.

The growth of the military and defense infrastructure during the post-World War II era paralleled a similar increase in the investment in federally subsidized civilian housing and urban development. No longer could the architectural profession isolate the Supervising Architect's Office as the most important architectural bureau in the federal government. Federal architectural activities were diffused throughout military and civilian agencies. Embedded in the Public Buildings Administration (and later the Public Buildings Service), the supervising architect and his staff constituted only one of a sizable universe of federal agencies to which the private architects could direct their attention.

The expansion of the federal government, which the Depression era and wartime programs presaged, continued into the postwar era. The role of public works in propping up the national economy during the 1930s served as an important model for postwar federal planning. The GSA's first administrator, Jess Larson, depicted the agency's role in this area. He suggested that the federal government keep on hand a large number of fully blueprinted plans ready for immediate contract letting, "should that action become necessary." Stockpiling projects was not linked solely to addressing economic concerns. Larson also argued that "an adequate shelf of completed blue prints would permit a more orderly progression of public construction."[1]

During the postwar era, new federal programs emerged that increased not only the size of the federal government but its complexity as well. Where one federal agency spawned public works programs, other federal programs were created to prevent those activities from needlessly destroying natural and cultural resources. Federal public works now contributed to a broad range of social goals, such as providing access for the handicapped to public services.

The participation of minority contractors in the design, construction, and maintenance of public works was another social goal that developed in the post-World War II era.

The important design functions that the supervising architect so jealously guarded gradually dwindled through the 1940s and 1950s. From the late 1950s through the following decades, the once-proud design staff was concerned primarily with the administration of design contracts let to private practitioners. The question was no longer the maintenance of high design standards through the employment of talented architects, but the encouragement of such standards through the careful development of buildings requirements and the selection of capable architects. The success of new federal architecture also required that elusive element—the commitment of a president and his administration to quality buildings.

The glories of the design bureaucracy known as the Supervising Architect's Office lay in the past. This past was recalled through the preservation and continued use of federal buildings designed by the Office. General Services Administration architects also found respectability in recalling the name of Robert Mills, the first architect to claim the title of "Architect of Public Buildings." Whether or not the Public Buildings Service of the GSA was the legitimate heir of Mills was beside the point. Federal government architects needed a tradition to guide their future activities and Mills's reputation provided artistic respectability.

The Federal Works Agency

The Federal Works Agency's first annual report, in 1940, represented a first step in a break with the past. The agency described itself as "primarily an organization for building." Its engineers and architects were concerned with the provision of facilities, the economies of construction, and the role of construction projects in providing for the common welfare. Because of its far-reaching activities, the policies of the FWA also contributed to the maintenance of employment levels and safeguarded labor standards.[2]

The commissioner of public buildings, W. E. Reynolds, headed the Public Buildings Administration (PBA). Under Reynolds was Supervising Architect Simon and the design staff. The PBA retained its authority over the design and construction of public buildings. The design staff of the bureau continued to feel the effects of the expansion of the federal buildings program that had started in the 1930s. A pool of "well-known designers and consulting architects, engaged both part time and full time, abetted the work of the bureau's still sizeable staff."[3] A limited number of building projects outside the capital city were designed by private practitioners selected through competitions.

Simon continued to serve as supervising architect until 1941. Upon his retirement, the *Federal Architect* praised Simon for his leadership and insistence on quality designs. "Louis A. Simon will have a thousand or more buildings throughout the land, some bearing his name, some not, which are tokens of his architectural ability. Words concerning that ability are relatively ineffectual. It is the buildings themselves which are the best commentary of his judgement and his service to the country."[4]

George Howe, a prominent Philadelphia architect, succeeded Simon. Howe had established a national reputation for his work undertaken as part of the firms of Mellor, Meigs and Howe; Howe and Lescaze; and Howe, Stonorov and Kahn. Howe and Lescaze's work on the Philadelphia Savings Fund Society secured his name in the modern movement in architecture. His work with Stonorov and Kahn on government-sponsored housing projects expanded his reputation in the public sector. Howe served as supervising architect for the duration of World War II. Because the war years were not an active period for traditional federal government buildings, Howe was unable to explore the possibilities of the position fully.[5]

Two of the most important projects of the early 1940s were the Social Security Board and the Railroad Retirement Board buildings (figures E.1 and E.2). The two buildings were located on adjacent lots in the southwest quadrant of the city just south of the Mall. The FWA contended that this location would "relieve and disperse traffic congestion in the other areas [of the city] and help stimulate widespread civic improvements in that section."[6] The buildings, described as in the "modern classic" style, were designed with light courts in order to provide for maximum light and ventilation.[7] These buildings were designed to relieve the two retirement agencies of severe overcrowding conditions in more than a dozen different locations. However, because of the national emergency, the two buildings were loaned to the National Defense Advisory Commission and the War Department for the duration of the war.

For a location directly behind the Social Security and Railroad Retirement buildings, the Public Buildings Administration designed

and superintended the construction of the first "General Federal Office Building." The Federal Works Agency hailed the development of the Federal Office Building as a "new solution to the constantly pressing office-space problem in the District of Columbia." The standard materials required in the Federal Office Building allowed it to be built "with the speed of a warehouse." When completed, the space could be divided as needed by movable partitions with offices of varying sizes. "Functional both in purpose and design, such a building could be made available to any Government agency, temporary or permanent, whose space needs justified the use of the building."[8]

Another major PBA project of the era was the building for the War Department in the northwest section of the capital. Gilbert Stanley Underwood and William Dewey Foster were the designers of record for the building, which was completed in 1941 (figure E.3). When the War Department moved to the Pentagon Building across the Potomac River in Arlington, Virginia, the State Department occupied the building. The War Department building was described as being in the "modern classical style" with simple wall surfaces of buff lime-

Figure E.1
Social Security
Administration building,
Washington, D.C., 1940,
Louis A. Simon. Courtesy
National Archives.

Figure E.2
Railroad Retirement
Board building,
Washington, D.C., 1940,
Louis A. Simon. Courtesy
National Archives.

stone with a "shot-sawn finish to provide a greater play of light and shadow." The Section of Fine Arts within the Public Buildings Administration provided for the free-standing sculpture and bas-reliefs to adorn the building.[9]

Outside Washington, D.C. the PBA continued to design hundreds of small post offices in communities throughout the country. In FWA's design, the agency aspired to have all "conform to the dominant style in the locality." Where no such style could be discerned, a simple contemporary design was created. Many post offices were one story in height with a standard arrangement of public lobby, arrangement of work spaces, and loading platforms. The Section of Fine Arts sponsored competitions for the artwork that adorned these post offices.[10]

Elsewhere in the country, other federal buildings were constructed to house appraisers' stores and immigration stations. The Public Buildings Administration constructed and renovated hospitals that were operated by the Public Health Service, forestry buildings, and federal reformatories. The PBA also assisted with the design and construction of the Franklin Delano Roosevelt Presidential Library in Hyde Park, New York.

After the entry of the United States into World War II, the Federal Works Agency concentrated its full efforts on the war program, especially in the construction of temporary office buildings, hospitals, and dormitories:

> With the possible exception of the routine maintenance and operation of public buildings, not a single activity of the Federal Works Agency escaped the influence of the war. Its programs were so completely altered that not one single program in operation during 1940 was going forward in 1942; and hardly a program that was in operation during the last fiscal year had been commenced two years before. The transformation was complete.[11]

The supervising architect and his staff designed twenty-nine temporary office buildings throughout the capital city; each building was capable of housing from 45,000 to 53,000 workers. Construction of these "tempos" took only a few months to complete and were noteworthy "for their efficient plan, for their sparse use of critical materials, and for simple, straightforward beauty of design." They were generally constructed of cemesto board sheathing, a combination of Portland cement and asbestos, with flat composition roofs.

Figure E.3
U.S. War Department building (now U.S. State Department building), Washington, D.C., 1941, Gilbert Stanley Underwood and William Dewey Foster. Courtesy National Archives.

The Supervising Architect's Office also collaborated with the United States Housing Authority in the design of war housing and community facilities adjacent to military-related industrial plants, projects made possible under the Lanham Act.[12] Residence halls for single women were constructed in the Washington, D.C., area. With the change in building type from public to residential, the *Federal Architect* stated:

> Of later months, the organization has gone low-cost housing. Persons are discovered rushing about with papers concerning broom cabinets and linoleum. Intramural dissension arises over garbage cans. . . . Architecture becomes concerned with refrigerators, toasters, space heaters, plyboard and the painting of chimneys. That sort of thing doesn't carry all the inspiration of monumental architecture, but there is in it a certain poetic excitement. It is human.[13]

The crush of federal workers into the already crowded capital city was alleviated somewhat by the Presidential Order of 23 December 1941 that authorized the Public Buildings Administration to supervise the decentralization of nonemergency federal agencies to locations outside the Washington, D.C. "This work involved the removal of 18,746 persons to 43 cities; the establishment of branch offices for aiding employees in 11 cities; and the recapture of nearly 2,000,000 square feet of office space in the District." According to the Federal Works Agency, all removals were accomplished in approximately six months.[14]

During the period 1942 to 1943, the U.S. government prepared for possible enemy attack on its own shores. The Public Buildings Administration aided in the defenses of federal installations along the coasts by strengthening buildings, constructing air raid shelters, and moving records to bombproof repositories. Other buildings were equipped with blackout windows and baffle walls.

By 1943, much of the needed temporary construction was completed. The staff of the Supervising Architect's Office was substantially reduced from 202 to 121 employees. Some of the staff was transferred to war-related agencies. The construction of nonmilitary buildings was virtually at a standstill.[15] However, planning for a future federal construction program continued. With a knowledge of the building demands that arose after World War I, the Federal Works Agency initiated measures that would contribute to an orderly and considerate method of conducting a public works program after the war. In 1943, Congress appropriated $500,000 to the PBA for advanced planning studies. These studies included a review of the list of authorized building projects that were deferred because of the war. Studies were made of the character and suitability of building materials in present use, design and construction methods, and the adaptability of new materials and methods to the federal building program.

The conclusion of the war did not result in a return to peacetime business as usual. "Contrary to general opinion, the needs of Government agencies for space [across the nation] were not immediately reduced with the end of the war." Postwar activities also required space in the capital city. So too did the recentralization of the agencies that had been moved to the field.[16] However, the demand for new public buildings was not met with massive appropriations. Federal construction was deferred to focus on the construction activity on homes for veterans and on industrial, commercial, and utility plants. The relatively high cost of construction was another deterrent to public construction.[17]

In the absence of a major construction program, the remnants of the Supervising Architect's Office staff performed design work for individual building projects as they were approved by Congress on a piecemeal basis. Projects of the immediate postwar era in Washington, D.C., included the West Central Heating Plant in Georgetown, new hangers at National Airport, and the new building for the General Accounting Office. The design staff also undertook design work at the request of other agencies, such as new buildings for Howard University and the conversion of residence halls to officers' quarters at Fort Myer in Arlington, Virginia. Gilbert Stanley Underwood, architect of federal buildings in the West in the mid-1930s and living in the capital under the Washington, D.C., residency arrangement, served as supervising architect from 1943 to 1949. He was succeeded by Allan Stewart Thorn, who served from 1949 to 1954.

Postwar Planning and the General Services Administration

Postwar planning for a national building program reached a new threshold in 1949. In that year, new legislation provided direction for the national architecture program. Later in the year, the public buildings program was transferred to the General Services Administration.

The Public Buildings Act of 1949 authorized the appropriation of $40 million toward the purchase of sites and the preplanning of federal buildings. This initial program addressed 575 building sites, some of which were deferred from the late 1930s and others that were new. Many of these prospective buildings were post offices. This act provided for the stockpiling of a "shelf of construction projects for prompt release when a federal building is authorized by Congress."[18] The 1949 act empowered the commissioner of public buildings, at his discretion, to employ the services of private firms or individuals for any buildings project the Public Buildings Administration handled. The commissioner was also authorized to hold competitions for the design of any projects.

The 1949 Commission on the Organization of the Executive Branch of the Government, headed by former President Herbert Hoover, examined the disposition of the federal buildings program. The report on a proposed Department of Works, prepared under the direction of Robert Moses, noted that little building legislation had been enacted since 1939. The report recommended that the Public Buildings Administration be incorporated into the proposed Department of Works in order to reduce duplication of federal public works programs.[19]

Instead of following the recommendations of the Hoover commission, Congress placed the residual functions of the Federal Works Agency into the new General Services Administration. The creation of the General Services Administration was intended to "simplify the procurement, utilization, and disposal of Government property."[20]

W. E. Reynolds continued as commissioner of public buildings in the General Services Administration. His initial pronouncement on public building design reflected wartime experience and postwar planning. It also encapsulated the goals of the agency: standardization, direct purchase, mass production, and savings in initial cost. Reynolds predicted that the "design of future Federal buildings will be greatly simplified to achieve economy in construction and maintenance costs." Features of new federal buildings included standard details for all types of fixtures and equipment, elimination of exterior steps, and clean lines. One of the first building types to benefit from this new trend was the post office. Reynolds cited the standardization of post offices: lobby windows, counters, lockboxes, and letter drops. Reynolds contended that, in the past, many of these elements had been custom-made for each building.[21]

The General Services Administration implemented the $40 million planning program authorized by the 1949 legislation. While no construction funds had been appropriated for these projects, sentiment for initiating building activity was growing.[22] In anticipating the construction phase for these projects, each congressional district would benefit from the construction program.[23]

The selection of private architects to design small post offices resulted in designs that were appropriate for the highly mobile postal functions. Some post offices were financed by private investors and then leased to the Post Office Department. The flexibility of the design allowed for the building's owner to adapt the building to another tenant. A new branch post office in Denver, for example, was designed as a "bare box" which could be subdivided and rearranged as space requirement changed. The exterior was made up of glass panels and corrugated asbestos cement.[24]

The boxlike small post offices reflected the desire of the Postmaster General Arthur Summerfield for standardized "modern post office structures" designed for the job they were intended to do, with no extraneous frills such as flights of steps leading to entrances. What concerned Summerfield was adequate parking, tailgate space, rail sidings, and drive-in service.[25] The requirements for leased post offices were encouraged through the production of standardized drawings and specifications, placed in each regional office of the postal service. While prescriptive, the plans were also intended to be flexible. The architectural treatment of the exterior was left to the decision of the building owner and the architect. The interior spaces had to conform to the standards set by the postal service. The postal service believed that the standardized plans and specifications would expedite negotiations with building owners and facilitate contract drawings prepared by architects.[26]

The leasing program of the postal service was working so well that a plan for the lease-purchase of other public buildings was initiated in 1954. With the lease-purchase program, private investors financed and erected public buildings according to the requirements of the federal government. The government would lease the buildings for a specified number of years and then, according to a pre-arranged purchase contract, become the owner of the building. This program was intended to lessen the up-front commitment of dollars by the federal government to a massive national building program. Lease-purchase was developed to respond to urgent buildings needs and was not intended to supplant renting or the direct appropriation method of acquiring buildings.

Two important policy changes grew out of the lease-purchase program. One was that all projects undertaken by the Public Buildings Service (PBS) of the General Services Administration would be designed by private architects. As Peter Strobel, the second commissioner of public buildings, stated, his bureau was not staffed to handle a large building program. The second policy change was the removal of all exclusively post office projects from the GSA and their transfer to the postal service. The PBS was left with all other civilian federal buildings, including those that combined post office space with other federal functions.[27]

By the mid-1950s, the Public Buildings Service had evolved into an essentially administrative organization. The design staff had been depleted over nearly two decades of a lull in civilian federal building activity. The GSA expressed little appetite for augmenting its design staff. The transformation of the PBS was evident in the succession of appointments for the bureau's leaders. Commissioner W. E. Reynolds, an architect, served with the program from 1939 when the Federal Works Agency was formed to his retirement in 1954. He was succeeded by Peter A. Strobel, a Danish-born engineer from New York. Strobel served only a little more than a year. Upon Strobel's departure, F. Moran McConihe took over as commissioner of public buildings. McConihe was a realtor by profession. In 1959, Ralph G. Macy, an engineer experienced in construction work and public works projects, replaced McConihe.

The supervising architect served under the commissioner of public buildings. Beginning in 1954, this position was filled by Leonard L. Hunter, who had worked for the Supervising Architect's Office in the late 1930s and later in the Public Buildings Services since the creation of the General Services Administration in 1949. In 1956, Hunter's title was changed to "Assistant Commissioner for Design and Construction." With this change in title, another important symbol of the old Supervising Architect's Office evaporated. The position of assistant commissioner endures to this day and represents one of the highest positions an architect can hold in the federal government.

While the GSA developed its postwar policies relating to a national building program, its program for the national capital area also was taking form. The possible effects of an atomic attack prompted agency planners to propose moving 40,000 government employees out of downtown Washington, D.C., into new buildings fifteen to twenty miles from the White House. The location of these buildings required a new network of highways and other supporting facilities. The proposed dispersed structures were not designed to be bombproof because the Public Buildings Service considered dispersal to be the best defense. Instead, these buildings would be designed like other public buildings going up in Washington, D.C. They would be simple boxes with exterior windows but no interior court or wings.[28] Public buildings located according to the dispersal plan included the Atomic Energy Commission headquarters at Gaithersburg, Maryland; the Bureau of Standards building five miles from the Atomic Energy Commission building; and the Central Intelligence Agency headquarters at Langley, Virginia.

For the federal buildings located in the central area of the capital city, simplicity and efficiency guided their design. The General Accounting Office, located north of Judiciary Square, was one of the notable buildings of this era. The Public Buildings Administration staff designed the seven-story General Accounting Office building as a solid unit without courts or wings. Except for the corridors, all partitions were movable in order to allow for maximum flexibility of room arrangement. Interior finishes were selected with an eye to easy and inexpensive maintenance and custodial care. All lobbies and corridors were lighted with recessed florescent units. Reynolds cited the General Accounting Office building as illustrative of federal government architectural practices.[29]

With the role of the Public Buildings Service evolving from that of an active participant in the creative work of designing a public building to that of an administrator of this process, concerns were raised about the quality of architecture. During hearings on the GSA's lease-purchase program, Congressmen Frank Thompson Jr. and Henry S. Reuss proposed a plan that would enlarge the scope of the Commission of Fine Arts to include the review of all federal government buildings sponsored by the GSA throughout the nation. Thompson and Reuss suggested that the Commission advise and consult with the agency on "establishing the highest possible standards of architectural design, style, and ornamentation for Federal public buildings, and methods of achieving such standards."[30] Supposedly, the Commission would participate in the selection of private architects for public buildings projects. Although both lawmakers introduced identical bills to carry out this suggestion, nothing came of the effort.

The Public Buildings Construction Act of 1959 authorized a new program of federal buildings. The lease-purchase program for general-use federal buildings had attracted only a handful of investors and viable projects. The time allotted to implement the experimental program had expired, and by 1959 the program was defunct. The 1959 act stipulated that funds for actual construction would require separate legislation. No more than thirty projects could be approved at any one time by the Congress before funds were appropriated for them. The Public Buildings Service estimated an expenditure of $350 million per year for the following five years.[31]

At the same time that the General Services Administration was preparing for its largest public building program since the Depression era, the Post Office Department announced a $1.5 billion building program that would be financed entirely by private investors who would finance and construct the buildings. The post office would then lease the buildings for periods of ten to thirty years. In order to secure the kinds of buildings required, the post office published a brochure of designs:

> applicable to buildings ranging in size from 1,000 to 12,000 sq. ft. This presents 37 schematic plans and elevations in color for each. There are plan descriptions, suggested materials and general notes on each plan. The book also contains sections on space criteria, lot layout, and minor suggested construction detail.[32]

Deputy Postmaster General E. O. Sessions asserted that the program offered the Department, for the first time in its history, a means of obtaining uniform, efficient, and appealing small post offices throughout the nation.[33]

"Guiding Principles for Federal Architecture"

A new era in federal building design was ushered in with the administration of President John F. Kennedy. In August 1961, Kennedy directed that a survey be made of the government's immediate and long-term space needs, with particular reference to the Washington, D.C., area. In order to carry out this work, an Ad Hoc Committee on Federal Space was appointed. The committee members included Luther H. Hodges, secretary of commerce; Arthur J. Goldberg, secretary of labor; David E. Bell, director of the Bureau of the Budget; Bernard J. Boutin, administrator of the General Services Administration, and Timothy J. Reardon Jr., special assistant to the president.[34]

The committee's report, issued the following year, included "Guiding Principles for Federal Architecture." These guiding principles articulated a three-point policy for the federal government. First,

federal buildings should be designed in a style that reflected "the dignity, enterprise, vigor, and stability of the American national government." Regional styles and art works should be considerations in
the design of buildings. "Buildings shall be economical to build, op-
erate and maintain, and should be accessible to the handicapped."
Second, "an official style must be avoided." The committee felt that
the government should be willing to bear the cost of avoiding excessive uniformity in building design. Quality designs would also be a
product of advice garnered from distinguished architects. The third
point emphasized the importance of the site. "Special attention
should be paid to the general ensemble of streets and public places
of which Federal buildings will form a part. Where possible, buildings should be located so as to permit a generous development of
landscape."[35]

The ad hoc committee's guiding principles, as well as its report on
the need to upgrade Pennsylvania Avenue, elicited a favorable response from the architectural press. The AIA *Journal* exclaimed, "It is
heartwarming indeed to see such a clarion call for architectural excellence come from a high development source—it must be hoped
that the Congress which holds the purse-strings will go along with
it!"[36]

Almost coincident with the issuance of the guiding principles was
the resignation of Leonard Hunter to join the firm of John Carl
Warnecke and Associates. In summing up the character of federal architecture during his tenure as head of the federal architecture program, Hunter described it as "good architecture."[37]

In order for the GSA to carry out its new mandate for improved architectural design, Karel Yasko of Wisconsin was appointed to succeed Hunter. Described as an "administrative dynamo" for his work
as Wisconsin state architect, Yasko had achieved noteworthy results
in farming out design work for state buildings to private architects.
Upon his appointment in late 1962, he set about the task of integrat-
ing the guiding principles with his responsibility for supervising the
national building program.[38] While his most important work lay in
recommending able architects to his agency for federal buildings
projects, he also played a key role in advising the executive branch on
all aspects of design, including the preservation of older buildings
and the integration of new buildings in historic, small-scale settings.
The *Architectural Record* noted that Yasko was given far more freedom
than any of his predecessors to obtain quality designs.[39]

The result of this effort to improve the quality of federal architecture was a collection of federal building projects that stand out from their predecessors and successors. They include the office building for the Department of Housing and Urban Development (HUD) designed by Marcel Breuer of Nolen-Swinburne. The sweeping curves of the HUD building recalled Breuer's buildings for UNESCO in Paris and IBM in Nice, France, and was described as unlike anything the General Services Administration had ever put up.[40] The building for the new National Air and Space Museum in Washington, designed by Hellmuth, Obata & Kassabaum, was admired for its forthrightness of architectural expression.[41] The firm of Curtis & Davis designed the long horizontal Forrestal Office Building that faces the south side of the Mall to bridge the new Tenth Street Mall. The *Architectural Record* praised the project as offering amenities such as courtyards and terraces, and a unified circulation pattern that was unique in Washington, D.C., federal buildings.[42]

Outside of Washington, D.C., the Federal Center in Chicago captured the attention and approval of the architectural presses. The center consisted of a thirty-story courthouse and office building, a forty-three-story office building, and a one-story post office. The modernist Ludwig Mies van der Rohe (with three other firms) designed the complex, covering less than fifty percent of the block-and-a-half plot. The plaza provided "badly needed open space in the heart of that city's tightly-packed Loop area." The *Architectural Record* felt that the "serene face and lean elegance of Miesian architecture have great merit in a dense urban situation. The pleasing shapes and sizes, artful proportions and meticulous detailing . . . will add a large measure of visual delight to the Federal Center."[43]

Other notable buildings of the era included the double-slabbed John F. Kennedy Federal Office Building in Boston, designed by the Architects Collaborative. Across the plaza from the federal building was the new City Hall designed by competition winners Kallman, McKinnell and Knowles. Together with other civic buildings, the Boston federal building formed an important part of Government Center, a plaza that some observers compared with St. Mark's Square in Venice and St. Peter's Square in Rome.[44]

Perhaps the most celebrated project of the era was the development of the area around Lafayette Square, the park across Pennsylvania Avenue from the White House. Except for the Treasury Annex and the U.S. Chamber of Commerce building, little had been constructed around the square that conformed to the McMillan commission's concept of an Executive Grouping. President Franklin D.

Roosevelt had already made a stake in the claim for preservation of the residential atmosphere around the square by insuring that the federal government purchased the Blair House. Decatur House, a key building in the northwest corner, became a property of the National Trust for Historic Preservation. Proposed plans in the 1950s for new development on the square, however, called for sleek modern buildings that would replace the low-rise residential quality with a distinctly institutional presence in the area.

Turning aside these plans, President Kennedy sought the advice of architects and designers including John Carl Warnecke. Warnecke advised the president to keep the old houses and place new buildings behind them. Warnecke's ideas appealed to the president and Warnecke was given the job of carrying them out. He tied together the elements of the square by designing new red brick office towers on either side of the square, one for a new Executive Office Building and the other for the Court of Claims. Replicas of older buildings were designed to fill in the gaps where nonconforming buildings of the early twentieth century were taken down.

The overall effect of the old and new architecture served as a watershed in thinking about new development in older areas. When Commission of Fine Arts Chairman William Walton apologized to the president for taking up so much of his time with Lafayette Square matters, the president replied, "That's all right. After all, this may be the only monument we'll leave."[45] While other monuments to the president ultimately were built, Lafayette Square was significant not only to the environs of the White House and the capital city, but as Kennedy saw it, the project also had importance as an example to other cities and communities throughout America.[46]

By the early 1970s, the banner of quality design for federal buildings was taken up by the National Endowment for the Arts under the leadership of its chairman, Nancy Hanks. At the direction of President Richard M. Nixon, Hanks pulled together the nation's leading designers into the Task Force on Federal Architecture. One of the products of the task force's deliberations was the Public Buildings Cooperative Use Act of 1976. This legislation authorized the General Services Administration to accommodate a great many uses that previously had been banned, including commercial establishments and facilities for cultural events.[47] This legislation encouraged the agency to utilize space in its older federal buildings. If a building's continued use was impractical, it could be protected with covenants and turned over to another responsible owner. Thus was inaugurated the greater effort to study older federal buildings and to preserve their historical qualities while accommodating normal office functions.

Despite these high-level efforts at fostering design excellence in public buildings, some critics questioned the commitment of the federal government to this goal. Ada Louise Huxtable noted that several outstanding buildings came out of the General Services Administration pipeline during the 1960s and early 1970s. However, she felt that the effort was *"sturm und drang* all the way, and the only reason there were any results was that Mr. Yasko had that Presidential directive firmly in hand." After Yasko's transfer within the agency to conduct a fine arts inventory, Huxtable concluded that the agency "system" had defeated any effort to continue the program.[48]

The Continuing Debate

The issue of the quality of design for federal buildings continues. Historically, the Supervising Architect's Office was singled out when criticism was raised about public architecture. After all, for many years, the Office was solely responsible for the designs. When private architects participated in the federal architecture program, such as during the Tarsney Act era, efforts were made to contrast the high quality of designs private architects provided with those government architects provided. For the past forty years, private architects have had the upper hand in the design process and the debate about quality endures.

Some critics point to the General Services Administration as the responsible vehicle in fostering excellence in design. Others, even those within the agency "system," point to the private architects and wonder why they do not produce better buildings. As Yasko stated in 1963 to an AIA gathering:

> Then there is the other side of the coin which may even be the most fatal indictment. This is the architect who, given a public project, gives of himself only enough to get by. He is, in a sense, a criminal who has robbed the commonwealth of his talent—if he has it. Especially when the road is clear and the opportunity to create a piece of architecture is laid in his lap. No amateur architects on the public buildings committee to design for him, no bureaucrat to impose rigid rules on him, only people looking to him to produce a fine piece of architecture. They stand before him naked

and innocent and he leaves them dry and unfulfilled. Who can escape bitterness when he is led to expect the moon and instead is given a glass box?[49]

Although the Supervising Architect's Office, as it developed and flourished from the mid-nineteenth century to the mid-twentieth century, no longer exists, many issues that surrounded its evolution are still vital topics for discussion. The imagery or symbolism of public buildings inspires (or defeats) the best efforts of architects. The system to bring about the best results is still examined, punctuated by periodic pledges from various administrations to first-rate designs. The architectural profession that grew to maturity on the issue of who should design federal buildings continues the debate on public buildings through the edifices it creates.

While it is unlikely that an institution like the Supervising Architect's Office will ever be reinstated in the federal government, a study of its past accomplishments can set a framework for future deliberations. What other entity can claim credit for designing thousands of civilian public buildings, many of which later generations appreciated, studied, protected, and preserved? Perhaps the system of designing federal buildings, as administered by the Supervising Architect's Office, ultimately will be judged to have been an exemplary system after all.

NOTES

CHAPTER I

1. There are many books on the U.S. Constitution and the subsequent inter-
    pretation of its provisions. Among the most useful reference works for this
    project are Edward Dumbauld, *The Constitution of the United States*
    (Norman, Okla.: University of Oklahoma Press, 1964); Max Farrand, ed.,
    The Records of the Federal Convention of 1787 (New Haven, Conn.: Yale
    University Press, 1911); John Franklin Jameson, ed., *Essays in the
    Constitutional History of the United States in the Formative Period 1775–1789*
    (Cambridge, Mass.: Riverside Press, 1889); and Joseph Story, *Commentaries
    on the Constitution of the United States* (Boston: Hilliard, Gray, 1833).
2. J. K. Shishkin, *The Palace of Governors* (Santa Fe: Museum of New Mexico,
    1972) offers a summary of the history of this early government building. See
    also Henry-Russell Hitchcock and William Seale, *Temples of Democracy: The
    State Capitols of the U.S.A.* (New York: Harcourt Brace Jovanovich, 1976), pp.
    7–8.
3. Charles E. Hatch, Jr., *America's Oldest Legislative Assembly and Its Jamestown
    Statehouses* (Washington, D.C.: National Park Service, 1956), p. 1.
4. Ibid., p. 14.
5. Marcus Whiffen, *The Public Buildings of Williamsburg, Colonial Capital of
    Virginia* (Williamsburg, Va.: Colonial Williamsburg, 1958), p. 50.
6. For a detailed study of the origins and development of the King's Works, see
    H. M. Colvin, gen. ed., *The History of the King's Works* (London: Her
    Majesty's Stationery Office, 1963–1982), 6 vols.
7. Joshua C. Taylor, *The Fine Arts in America* (Chicago: The University of
    Chicago Press, 1979), p. 47.
8. See discussion Taylor's chapter on "Art and the New Republic," ibid., pp. 29–
    45.

CHAPTER 2

1. Talbot Hamlin, *Benjamin Henry Latrobe* (New York: Oxford University Press, 1955), pp. 295–296.
2. James H. McCulloch to Alexander J. Dallas, 16 July 1816, Correspondence with Customs Collectors, Record Group 56, National Archives, Washington, D.C.
3. Hamlin, *Benjamin Henry Latrobe*, p. 490.
4. Alexander J. Dallas to John Steele, 11 June 1816, Correspondence with Customs Collectors, Record Group 56, National Archives, Washington, D.C.
5. Steele to Dallas, 15 June 1816, Correspondence with Customs Collectors.
6. Steele to William H. Crawford, 30 May 1817, Correspondence with Customs Collectors.
7. Crawford to Steele, 4 June 1818, Correspondence with Customs Collectors.
8. Crawford to Steele, 19 June 1818, Correspondence with Customs Collectors.
9. Crawford to Steele, 10 December 1819, Correspondence with Customs Collectors.
10. Samuel Swartwout to Louis McLane, 30 September 1831, Correspondence with Customs Collectors.
11. Swartwout to McLane, 30 September 1831, Correspondence with Customs Collectors.
12. McLane to Swartwout, 3 October 1831, Correspondence with Customs Collectors.
13. Swartwout to McLane, 2 June 1832, Correspondence with Customs Collectors.
14. Ithiel Town to McLane, 4 March 1833, Records Received Concerning the Construction of the New York Custom House, Record Group 56, National Archives, Washington, D.C.
15. For a complete discussion of the construction of the New York Custom House, see Louis Torres, "Samuel Thomson and the Old Custom House," *Journal of the Society of Architectural Historians*, 20 (December 1961), pp. 185–190; and "John Frazee and the New York Custom House," *Journal of the Society of Architectural Historians*, 13 (October 1964), pp. 143–150. See also Francis R. Kowsky, "Simplicity and Dignity: The Public and Institutional Buildings of Alexander Jackson Davis," in *Alexander Jackson Davis: American Architect, 1803–1892*, Amelia Peck ed. (New York: Rizzoli International Publications, 1992), pp. 42–48.
16. *Report of the Secretary of the Treasury on the State of the Finances for the Fiscal Year Ending June 30, 1853*, Senate, 33rd Congress, 1st Session, Ex. Doc. No. 2, p. 273.
17. Ammi B. Young to the Custom House Commissioners, 13 April 1839, Letters Received Relating to the Construction of Custom Houses and Other Structures, Record Group 56, National Archives, Washington, D.C.
18. Young to the Custom House Commissioners, 13 April 1839, Letters Received Relating to the Construction of the Customs Houses and Other Structures.
19. Daniel Robbins, *The Vermont State House: A History and Guide* (Montpelier: Vermont Council on the Arts, 1980), p. 27.
20. Young to Levi Woodbury, 30 November 1840, Letters Received Relating to the Construction of Custom Houses and Other Structures.
21. See Robert L. Alexander, "Robert Mills," in *Macmillan Encyclopedia of Architects*, 1st ed., vol. 3 (New York: Free Press, 1982), pp. 200–208; and Gene

Waddell and Rhodri Windsor Liscombe, *Robert Mills' Courthouses and Jails* (Easley, S.C.: Southern Historical Press, 1981).

22. Donald J. Lehman, "Treasury Building, Washington, D.C. Part I: The First Treasury, 1800–1833" (Washington, D.C.: General Services Administration, 1967, mimeographed), p. 52.

23. Robert Mills to John C. Spencer, 21 March 1843, Personnel Folder of Notable Treasury Employees, Record Group 56, National Archives, Washington, D.C.

24. Mills to Woodbury, 20 October 1840, Personnel Folders of Notable Treasury Employees.

25. Ibid.

26. Ibid.

27. Newspaper clipping included in Ammi B. Young's 1843 report to the Commissioners, Letters Received Relating to the Construction of Custom Houses and Other Structures.

28. *Report of the Secretary of the Treasury on the State of the Finances for the Fiscal Year Ending June 30, 1853,* p. 272, lists the cost at $886,658 and the furniture at $24,452.

29. John S. Norris to John C. Spencer, 6 July 1843, Letters Received Relating to the Construction of Custom Houses and Other Structures.

30. Norris to Spencer, 27 November 1843, Letters Received Relating to the Construction of Custom Houses and Other Structures.

31. M. V. Jones to George M. Bibb, 13 February 1845, Letters Received Relating to the Construction of Custom Houses and Other Structures.

32. Jones to Bibb, 20 February 1845, Letters Received Relating to the Construction of Custom Houses and Other Structures.

33. Jones to Robert J. Walker, 22 August 1845, Letters Received Relating to the Construction of Custom Houses and Other Structures.

34. Jones to Walker, 21 May 1847, Letters Received Relating to the Construction of Custom Houses and Other Structures.

35. William J. Duane to Mills, 16 September 1833, Personnel Folder of Notable Treasury Employees, Record Group 56, National Archives, Washington, D.C.

36. Mills to Duane, 18 September 1833, Personnel Folder of Notable Treasury Employees.

37. Mills to Woodbury, 2 July 1834 and 5 July 1834, Personnel Folder of Notable Treasury Employees.

38. Woodbury to Mills, 9 July 1834, Personnel Folder of Notable Treasury Employees.

39. Oliver Wolcott to Benjamin Lincoln, 24 May 1799, Correspondence with Customs Collectors, Record Group 56, National Archives, Washington, D.C.

40. Albert Gallatin to Benjamin Lincoln, 6 May 1802, Correspondence with Customs Collectors.

41. Gallatin to Lincoln, 21 June 1802, Correspondence with Customs Collectors.

42. Gallatin to Lincoln, 11 October 1802, Correspondence with Customs Collectors.

43. Richard Rush to H. A. S. Dearborn, 11 August 1826, Correspondence with Customs Collectors.

44. *Report of the Secretary of the Treasury on the State of the Finances for the Year Ending December 30, 1829* (Washington, D.C.: Blair & Rives, 1837), p. 11.

45. *Report of the Secretary of the Treasury on the State of the Finances for the Year Ending December 30, 1836* (Washington, D.C.: Blair & Rives, 1837), p. 686.

46. *Report of the Secretary of the Treasury on the State of the Finances for the Year 1837* (Washington, D.C.: John C. Rives, 1851), p. 108.
47. *Report of the Secretary of the Treasury on the State of the Finances for the Year 1843* (Washington, D.C.: John C. Rives, 1851), p. 617.
48. *Report of the Secretary of the Treasury on the State of the Finances for the Year 1849* (Washington, D.C.: John C. Rives, 1851), p. 24.
49. *Report of the Secretary of the Treasury on the State of the Finances for the Fiscal Year Ending June 30, 1850,* (Washington, D.C.: John C. Rives, 1851) p. 149.
50. Ibid., p. 150.
51. Robert Mills, *Design No. 1 for a Marine Hospital on the Western Waters to Accommodate 100 Patients* (Washington City: P. Haas' Lithography, ca. 1837) and *Design No. 2 for a Marine Hospitals on the Western Waters to Accommodate 50 Patients* (Washington City: P. Haas' Lithography, ca. 1837).
52. *Report of the Secretary of the Treasury on the State of the Finances for the Fiscal Year Ending June 30, 1850,* p. 150.
53. Ibid., p. 151.
54. The five articles written by Fiske Kimball and Wells Bennett, "The Competition for Federal Buildings, 1792–1793," that appeared in the *Journal of the American Institute of Architects,* 7 (1919) and 8 (1920), present a comprehensive study of the competitions and competitors for the President's House and the Capitol.
55. Daniel D. Reiff, *Washington Architecture 1791–1861: Problems in Development* (Washington, D.C.: U.S. Commission of Fine Arts, 1971), p. 20.
56. Ibid., p. 23.
57. U.S. Congress, House, *City of Washington,* H. Doc. 159, 7th Congress, 2nd Session, 1803.
58. U.S. Congress, House, *City of Washington,* H. Doc. 444, 15th Congress, 1st Session, 1818.
59. Lehman, "Treasury Building," pp. 58–69.
60. U.S. Congress, House, *New Executive Buildings,* H. Doc. 90, 23rd Congress, 2nd Session, 1835.
61. U.S. Congress, House, *Additional Buildings for War and Navy Departments,* H. Doc. 85, 27th Congress, 3rd Session, 1843.
62. U.S. Congress, House, *Fire-Proof Public Buildings,* H. Doc. 267, 28th Congress, 1st Session, 1844.
63. Ibid.
64. Lehman, "Treasury Building," p. 7.
65. See Agnes Addison Gilchrist, *William Strickland, Architect and Engineer, 1788–1854* (Philadelphia: University of Pennsylvania Press, 1850).

CHAPTER 3

1. See tables included in *Report of the Secretary of the Treasury on the State of the Finances for the Fiscal Year Ending June 30, 1858* (Washington, DC: William A. Harris, 1858), pp. 114–116.
2. William L. Hodge to M. Hampton, 27 March 1851, Letters Sent by the Secretary Concerning Customhouses and Other Buildings, Record Group 121, National Archives, Washington, D.C.
3. Thomas Corwin to Ammi B. Young, 4 March 1852, Letters Sent by the Secretary Concerning Customhouses and Other Buildings.
4. Lyman Gage to Commissioners of Bangor, Maine Custom House, 14 June 1852, Letters Sent by the Secretary of the Treasury Concerning New Buildings, Record Group 121, National Archives, Washington, D.C.

5. Advertisement for construction of custom house at Norfolk, Virginia, December 1852, Letters Sent by the Secretary of the Treasury Concerning New Buildings.

6. James Guthrie to P. G. T. Beauregard, 21 April 1853, Letters Sent by the Secretary Concerning Customhouses and Other Buildings.

7. P. G. Washington to A. Blackman, 16 May 1855, Letters Sent by the Secretary Concerning Customhouses and Other Buildings.

8. Guthrie to Bogardus & Hoppin, 25 August 1853, Letters Sent by the Secretary Concerning Customhouses and Other Buildings.

9. Guthrie to Alexander H. Bowman, 9 October 1853, Letters Sent by the Secretary Concerning Customhouses and Other Buildings.

10. "Alexander Hamilton Bowman," *National Cyclopedia of American Biography*, vol. 5 (New York: James T. White, 1907), pp. 522–523.

11. Guthrie to I. Letcher, 4 March 1854, Letters Sent by the Secretary Concerning Customhouses and Other Buildings.

12. Bowman to Guthrie, 25 August 1858, Letters Sent, Chiefly by the Supervising Architect, Record Group 121, National Archives, Washington, D.C.

13. "Buildings under the Supervision of the Treasury Department," in the *Report of the Secretary of the Treasury on the State of the Finances for the Fiscal Year Ending June 30, 1854* (Washington, DC: A. O. P. Nicholson, Printer, 1854), pp. 349–350.

14. Guthrie to Hannibal Hamlin, 19 July 1854, Letters Sent by the Secretary Concerning Customhouses and Other Buildings.

15. Guthrie to E. B. Washburne, 5 May 1856, Letters Sent by the Secretary Concerning Customhouses and Other Buildings.

16. Guthrie to George W. Jones, 2 October 1856, Letters Sent by the Secretary Concerning Customhouses and Other Buildings.

17. Ibid.

18. *Report of the Secretary of the Treasury on the State of the Finances for the Fiscal Year Ending June 30, 1857* (Washington, D.C.: Cornelius Wendell, Printer, 1857), p. 27.

19. "Report of the Engineer in Charge of the Office of Construction," ibid., p. 93–94.

20. Guthrie to Washburne, 11 April 1856, Letters Sent by the Secretary Concerning Customhouses and Other Buildings.

21. Guthrie to W. O. Goode, 10 January 1857, Letters Sent by the Secretary Concerning Customhouses and Other Buildings.

22. Guthrie to L. D. Campbell, 2 April 1856, Letters Sent by the Secretary Concerning Customhouses and Other Buildings.

23. Guthrie to Jedekiah Kidwell, 9 January 1856, Letters Sent by the Secretary Concerning Customhouses and Other Buildings, discusses the 3rd Joint Resolution of Congress, dated 11 September 1841, which declared, "no public money shall be expended upon any site or land, hereafter to be purchased by the United States for the purpose of armories, forts, fortifications, navy yards, customhouses, light houses, or other public buildings, until the written opinion of the Attorney General shall be had in favor of the validity of the title and also the consent of the State in which the Land or Site may be, shall be given."

24. "Buildings under the Supervision of the Treasury Department, p. 362.

25. Guthrie to Bowman, 2 October 1854, Letters Sent by the Secretary Concerning Customhouses and Other Buildings.

26. Washington to John T. Hudson, 22 May 1855, Letters Sent by the Secretary Concerning Customhouses and Other Buildings.

27. See "Expenses of the Bureau of Construction," September 1856, Letters Sent, Chiefly by the Supervising Architect.

28. Georgia Willis Read and Ruth Gaines, ed., *Gold Rush: The Journal, Drawings, and Other Papers of J. Goldsborough Bruff, Captain, Washington and California Mining Association,* 2 vols. (New York: Columbia University Press, 1944).

29. For biographical information on Cluss, see Tanya Edwards Beauchamp, "Adolf Cluss and the Building of the U.S. National Museum: An Architecture of Perfect Adaptability" (master's thesis, University of Virginia, 1972), and Adolf Cluss file in Applications and Recommendations for Appointments as Superintendents of Construction, 1853–1904, Record Group 56, National Archives, Washington, D.C.

30. For a thorough discussion of the use of the Italian Renaissance palazzo style in federal government buildings of the 1850s, see Daniel Bluestone, "Civic and Aesthetic Reserve: Ammi Burnham Young's 1850s Federal Customhouse Design," *Winterthur Portfolio,* 25 (Summer / Autumn 1990), pp. 131–156.

31. For a description of the use of lithography in the nineteenth century, see John W. Reps, *Cities on Stone: Nineteenth Century Lithographic Images of the Urban West* (Fort Worth, Tex.: Amon Carter Museum of Western Art, 1976).

32. For biographical information on Köllner, see ibid., and Harry T. Peters, *America on Stone* (Garden City, New York: Doubleday, 1931).

33. Guthrie to August Köllner, 1 May 1855, Letters Sent by the Secretary Concerning Customhouses and Other Buildings.

34. Washington to Köllner, 9 August 1855, Letters Sent by the Secretary Concerning Customhouses and Other Buildings.

35. Guthrie to Köllner, 19 October 1855, Letters Sent by the Secretary Concerning Customhouses and Other Buildings.

36. Guthrie to Köllner, 18 December 1856, Letters Sent by the Secretary Concerning Customhouses and Other Buildings.

37. Howell Cobb to Stephen A. Douglass, 27 March 1857, Letters Sent by the Secretary Concerning Customhouses and Other Buildings.

38. Guthrie to William H. Pettis, 14 February 1856, Letters Sent by the Secretary Concerning Customhouses and Other Buildings.

39. Cobb to Superintendents of Construction, 21 September 1857, Letters Sent by the Secretary Concerning Customhouses and Other Buildings.

40. Bowman to Alexander Vattemaire, 23 January 1858, Letters Sent, Chiefly by the Supervising Architect.

41. Cobb to John Kurtz, 2 August 1858, Letters Sent by the Secretary Concerning Customhouses and Other Buildings.

42. Guthrie to S. M. Clark, 1 December 1856, Letters Sent by the Secretary Concerning Customhouses and Other Buildings.

43. Bowman to Alexander Provost, 22 April 1858, Letters Sent, Chiefly by the Supervising Architect.

44. Thomas U. Walter to John Rice, 23 March 1855, Thomas U. Walter Letters, The Athenaeum, Philadelphia, Pa.

45. Walter to Rice, 2 May 1855, Thomas U. Walter Letters.

46. Walter to Young, 16 January 1854, Thomas U. Walter Letters.

47. Walter to Young, 1 February 1859, Thomas U. Walter Letters.

48. Cobb to Ely S. Parker, 28 March 1857, Letters Sent by the Secretary Concerning Customhouses and Other Buildings.

49. Guthrie to R. M. T. Hunter, 1 February 1853, Letters Sent by the Secretary Concerning Customhouses and Other Buildings.

50. Guthrie to Hunter, 20 February 1857, Letters Sent by the Secretary Concerning Customhouses and Other Buildings.

51. Guthrie to E. B. White, 5 April 1854, Letters Sent by the Secretary Concerning Customhouses and Other Buildings.

52. Cobb to Messrs. George R. Jackson & Co., 10 December 1858, Letters Sent by the Secretary Concerning Customhouses and Other Buildings.

53. Guthrie to William A. Stearns, 25 October 1856, letter included in Original Drawings, Tracings, and Prints, Record Group 121, National Archives, Washington, D.C.

54. Bowman to Sylvanus Thayer, 11 December 1856, Letters Sent, Chiefly by the Supervising Architect.

55. Bowman to R. Clarkson, 12 October 1858, Letters Sent, Chiefly by the Supervising Architect.

56. Ammi B. Young to Ira Young, n.d., Letters Sent, Chiefly by the Supervising Architect.

57. "Report of the Engineer in Charge of the Office of Construction" in *Report of the Secretary of the Treasury on the State of the Finances for the Fiscal Year Ending June 30, 1857* (Washington, D.C.: Cornelius Wendell Printer, 1857), p. 94.

58. Cobb to Mathius Martin, 22 November 1858, Letters Sent by the Secretary Concerning Customhouses and Other Buildings.

59. Cobb to I. Phelps, 23 December 1858, Letters Sent by the Secretary Concerning Customhouses and Other Buildings.

60. Cobb to Bowman, 13 April 1860, Letters Sent by the Secretary Concerning Customhouses and Other Buildings.

61. Young to Solomon Foot, 23 October 1860, Letters Sent, Chiefly by the Supervising Architect.

62. For background information on Franklin, see Frank N. Schubert, ed., *March to South Pass: Lieutenant William B. Franklin's Journal of the Kearny Expedition of 1845* (Washington, D.C.: U.S. Government Printing Office, 1979); and file on "William Buel Franklin," biographical archive of engineers, Mechanical & Civil Engineering Division, National Museum of American History, Smithsonian Institution, Washington, D.C.

63. Young to Charles B. Bechmann, 20 May 1861, Letters Sent, Chiefly by the Supervising Architect.

64. Isaiah Rogers to Salmon P. Chase, 14 June 1862, Isaiah Rogers File, Personnel Folders of Notable Treasury Employees, Record Group 56, National Archives, Washington, D.C.

65. E. P. Walton to Chase, 28 June 1862, Ammi B. Young File, Personnel Folders of Notable Treasury Employees.

66. Chase to Young, 24 July 1862, Ammi B. Young File, Personnel Folders of Notable Treasury Employees.

67. For biographical information, see Denys Peter Myers, "Isaiah Rogers," in *Macmillan Encyclopedia of Architects*, 1st ed., vol. 3 (New York: Free Press, 1982), pp. 599–602. See also Denys Peter Myers, "The Recently Discovered Diaries of Isaiah Rogers, Architect," *Columbia Library Columns*, 16 (November 1966): 25–31.

68. A. B. Coleman to Chase, 19 June 1862, Isaiah Rogers file, Personnel Folders of Notable Treasury Employees.

69. Bartholomew Oertly File, Personnel Folders of Treasury Department Employees, Record Group 56, National Archives, Washington, D.C.

70. William G. Steinmetz File, Personnel Folders of Treasury Department Employees.

71. J. Goldsborough Bruff File, Personnel Folders of Treasury Department Employees.

72. Lawrence Wodehouse, "Alfred B. Mullett and His French Style Government Buildings," *Journal of the Society of Architectural Historians*, 31 (March 1972), p. 23; and obituary for Alfred B. Mullett, *Cincinnati Tribune* L. A. Rixford Scrapbook, 1885–1897, Cincinnati Historical Society, Cincinnati, Ohio, p. 54.

73. Chase to Alfred B. Mullett, 11 June 1861, in *A. B. Mullett Diaries, Etc.* (Washington, D.C.: Mullett-Smith Press, 1985), p. 100.

74. Chase to Mullett, 6 January 1863, Alfred B. Mullett File, Personnel Folders of Notable Treasury Employees.

75. Mullett to Chase, 13 April 1863, Alfred B. Mullett File, Personnel Folders of Notable Treasury Employees.

76. Mullett to Chase, 1 November 1863, Letters Sent, Chiefly by the Supervising Architect.

77. Rogers to A. W. Randall, 27 May 1864, Letters Sent, Chiefly by the Supervising Architect.

78. Rogers to Chase, 30 June 1864, Letters Sent, Chiefly by the Supervising Architect.

79. Mullett to William P. Fessenden, 21 July 1864, Letters Sent, Chiefly by the Supervising Architect.

80. Rogers to Fessenden, 28 July 1864, Letters Sent, Chiefly by the Supervising Architect.

81. Rogers to Fessenden, 16 November 1864, Letters Sent, Chiefly by the Supervising Architect.

82. William E. Chandler to Hugh McCulloch, 19 June 1865, Letters Sent, Chiefly by the Supervising Architect.

83. Alfred B. Mullett, diary entry, 3 August 1865, in *A. B. Mullett Diaries, Etc.*, p. 85.

84. Alfred B. Mullett, diary entry, 4 August 1864, in *A. B. Mullett Diaries, Etc.*, p. 86.

85. Mullett to William E. Chandler, 5 September 1865, Letters Sent, Chiefly by the Supervising Architect.

86. Chandler to Edgar Needham, 9 September 1865, Letters Sent, Chiefly by the Supervising Architect.

87. Rogers to McCulloch, 20 September 1865, Letters Sent, Chiefly by the Supervising Architect.

CHAPTER 4

1. "The National Architect," *The Nation*, (3 December 1874), p. 360.

2. A. B. Huston, *Historical Sketches of Farmers' College* (Cincinnati: The Student's Association of Farmers' College, n.d.), p. 22.

3. George S. Ormsby to Isaac J. Allen, 13 April 1854, in *A. B. Mullett Diaries, Etc.* (Washington, D.C: Mullett-Smith Press, 1985), p. 100.

4. *30th Annual Report of the Board of Directors from March 1857 to March 1958* (Cincinnati: Ohio Mechanics Institute, 1858).

5. *Catalogue of the Books and Papers in the Library and Reading Room of the Ohio Mechanics Institute of Cincinnati* (Cincinnati: Marshall & Langtry, 1851).

6. Suzanne Mullett Smith, personal communication, April 7, 1983.

7. "Poems in Stone," *Commercial Times* (23 February 1876). In AIA Scrapbooks, AIA, Washington, D.C. n.p.

8. Alfred B. Mullett, 1860 diary, *A. B. Mullett Diaries, Etc.* (Washington, D.C.: Mullett-Smith Press, 1985), pp. 4–50 cover the period October 13–December 7, 1860.

9. Mullett, diary entry, 1 January 1865, in *A. B. Mullett Diaries, Etc.* (Washington, D.C.: Mullett-Smith Press, 1985), p. 51.

10. *Annual Report of the Supervising Architect to the Secretary of the Treasury for the Year 1866* (Washington, D.C.: Government Printing Office, 1866) p. 188.

11. Ibid., p. 189.

12. Ibid., p. 190.

13. Ibid., p. 199.

14. Ibid., p. 190.

15. *Annual Report of the Supervising Architect to the Secretary of the Treasury for the Year 1870* (Washington, D.C.: Government Printing Office, 1870), p. 292.

16. Ibid., p. 292.

17. *Annual Report of the Supervising Architect to the Secretary of the Treasury for the Year 1868* (Washington, D.C.: Government Printing Office, 1868), p. 17.

18. Mullett to George S. Boutwell, January 1870, Letters Sent, Chiefly by the Supervising Architect, Record Group 121, National Archives, Washington, D.C.

19. William A. Richardson to James H. Platt, May 1874, Letters Sent, Chiefly by the Supervising Architect.

20. Mullett to Boutwell, 8 January 1872, Letters Sent, Chiefly by the Supervising Architect.

21. Mullett to James G. Blaine, 27 July 1868, Letters Sent, Chiefly by the Supervising Architect.

22. Mullett to Blaine, 26 March 1869, Letters Sent, Chiefly by the Supervising Architect.

23. Mullett to Blaine, 11 December 1869, Letters Sent, Chiefly by the Supervising Architect.

24. Mullett to Rodney L. Fogg, 22 May 1871, Letters Sent, Chiefly by the Supervising Architect.

25. Mullett to Fogg, 24 May 1871, Letters Sent, Chiefly by the Supervising Architect.

26. Mullett to E. G. Lind, 11 January 1873, Letters Sent, Chiefly by the Supervising Architect.

27. Mullett to George Fisher, 10 February 1870, Letters Sent, Chiefly by the Supervising Architect.

28. Mullett to Boutwell, 22 July 1870, Letters Sent, Chiefly by the Supervising Architect.

29. Mullett to George D. Whittle, 31 October 1867, Letters Sent, Chiefly by the Supervising Architect.

30. Mullett to Boutwell, 12 March 1869, Letters Sent, Chiefly by the Supervising Architect.

31. Mullett to Boutwell, 8 April 1869, Letters Sent, Chiefly by the Supervising Architect.

32. Mullett to W. P. P. Longfellow, 20 September 1871, Letters Sent, Chiefly by the Supervising Architect.

33. Mullett to Associate Justice Nathan Clifford, 11 June 1867, Letters Sent, Chiefly by the Supervising Architect.

34. Thomas U. Walter to Mullett, 10 November 1869, Thomas U. Walter Letters, The Athenaeum, Philadelphia, Pa.

35. Mullett to Walter, 29 October 1869, Letters Sent, Chiefly by the Supervising Architect.

36. Mullett to Joshua Mix, 14 August 1869, Letters Sent, Chiefly by the Supervising Architect.

37. Walter to Mullett, 15 March 1871, Thomas U. Walter Letters.

38. Walter to G. W. Samson, 26 June 1871, Thomas U. Walter Letters.

39. Mullett to George P. Bowen, 20 December 1873, Letters Sent, Chiefly by the Supervising Architect.

40. Mullett to Hamilton Fish, 29 December 1874, Letters Sent, Chiefly by the Supervising Architect.

41. Mullett to Hugh McCulloch, 29 June 1870, Letters Sent, Chiefly by the Supervising Architect.

42. Mullett to John L. Smithmeyer, 5 June 1869, Letters Sent, Chiefly by the Supervising Architect.

43. Mullett to John Ober, 3 June 1870, Letters Sent, Chiefly by the Supervising Architect.

44. "My Own Story," Notes by Edward W. Donn Jr., AIA Archives, Washington, D.C., p. 6.

45. "Poems in Stone," *Commercial Times* (25 February 1876). AIA Scrapbooks, AIA Archives, Washington, D.C., n.p.

46. Mullett to John F. Morse, 24 November 1869, Letters Sent, Chiefly by the Supervising Architect.

47. Mullett to James C. Rankin, 18 October 1873, Letters Sent, Chiefly by the Supervising Architect.

48. Mullett to Jonas Gies, 28 August 1871, Letters Sent, Chiefly by the Supervising Architect.

49. Mullett to Boutwell, 26 August 1872, Letters Sent, Chiefly by the Supervising Architect.

50. *Annual Report of the Supervising Architect to the Secretary of the Treasury for the Year 1866*, p. 189.

51. *Annual Report of the Supervising Architect to the Secretary of the Treasury for the Year 1867*, (Washington, D.C.: Government Printing Office, 1867), p. 3.

52. *Annual Report of the Supervising Architect to the Secretary of the Treasury for the Year 1868*, p. 4.

53. *Annual Report of the Supervising Architect to the Secretary of the Treasury for the Year 1866*, p. 189.

54. *Annual Report of the Supervising Architect to the Secretary of the Treasury for the Year 1867*, p. 1.

55. Ibid., p. 1.

56. Ibid., p. 2.

57. Mullett to Henri Lovie, 28 January 1874, Letters Sent, Chiefly by the Supervising Architect.

58. Office of Archeology and Historic Preservation, National Park Service, *The Old San Francisco Mint 1869–1874: Summary Report for the Advisory Council on Historic Preservation* (Washington, D.C.: National Park Service, July 1969), p. 17.

59. Untitled *New York Tribune* article, dated 9 February 1867, quoted in Hobart Upjohn, "The American Institute of Architects: The Early Years" (unpublished MS, n.d.), pp. 146–147.

60. "Plans for the New Post-Office," *New York Evening Post* (12 June 1867). AIA Scrapbooks, AIA, Washington, D.C., n.p.

61. "Poems in Stone," n.p.

62. Upjohn, "American Institute of Architects," p. 152.

63. "Poems in Stone," n.p.

64. "The Old Assay Office in Boise," Idaho Historical Society, Reference Series, No. 359, May 1965.

65. Walter to Mullett, 15 March 1871, Thomas U. Walter Letters.

66. Richard Upjohn et al. to Bvt. Lt. Col. T. J. Treadwell, 6 December 1866, AIA Scrapbook, AIA, Washington, D.C.

67. Walter to Samson, 16 November 1869, Thomas U. Walter Letters.

68. Mullett to Justin S. Morrill, 14 March 1870, Letters Sent, Chiefly by the Supervising Architect.

69. Mullett to Fish, 17 March 1870, Letters Sent, Chiefly by the Supervising Architect.

70. Walter to Edward Clark, 15 March 1871, Thomas U. Walter Letters.

71. Walter to Samson, 20 June 1871, Thomas U. Walter Letters.

72. Walter to Samson, 26 June 1871, Thomas U. Walter Papers.

73. *Annual Report of the Supervising Architect to the Secretary of the Treasury for the Year 1868*, p. 11.

74. Donald J. Lehman, *Executive Office Building: General Services Administration, Historical Study No. 3* (Washington, D.C.: Government Printing Office, 1970), p. 60.

75. Report of Alfred B. Mullett on State, War and Navy Building, March 1872, Letters Sent, Chiefly by the Supervising Architect.

76. *Annual Report of the Supervising Architect to the Secretary of the Treasury for the Year 1867*, p. 6.

77. *Annual Report of the Supervising Architect to the Secretary of the Treasury for the Year 1868*, p. 9.

78. Mullett to Commissioners of the New Jail, October 1873, Letters Sent, Chiefly by the Supervising Architect.

79. *Annual Report of the Supervising Architect to the Secretary of the Treasury for the Year 1873*, (Washington, D.C.: Government Printing Office, 1873), p. 30.

80. Mullett to Columbus Delano, 7 November 1874, Letters Sent, Chiefly by the Supervising Architect.

81. Mullett to John Coburn, 2 March 1871, Letters Sent, Chiefly by the Supervising Architect.

82. Mullett to Salmon P. Chase, 3 December 1868, Letters Sent, Chiefly by the Supervising Architect.

83. Mullett to George Bliss, 9 January 1874, Letters Sent, Chiefly by the Supervising Architect.

84. Mullett to T. J. Robertson, 25 November 1869, Letters Sent, Chiefly by the Supervising Architect.

85. Mullett to S. M. Cullum, 18 October 1869, Letters Sent, Chiefly by the Supervising Architect.

86. Mullett to A. M. Clapp, 18 January 1870, Letters Sent, Chiefly by the Supervising Architect.

87. Mullett to J. M. Rice, 25 March 1872, Letters Sent, Chiefly by the Supervising Architect.

88. Mullett to C. P. Dixon, 24 August 1874, Letters Sent, Chiefly by the Supervising Architect.

89. Mullett to Louis Blodget, 11 November 1867, Letters Sent, Chiefly by the Supervising Architect.

90. Richard Upjohn, "Annual Address of the President," *Proceedings of the 3rd Annual Convention of the American Institute of Architects*, Nov. 16 & 17, 1869 (NY: Office of the New York Evening Post, 1870), p. 5.

91. Richard Upjohn, "President's Address," *Proceedings of the First Annual Convention of the American Institute of Architects*, Oct 22 and 23, 1867 (New York: Raymond & Caulon, Printers), 1867, p. 7.

92. Walter to Mullett, 18 June 1869, Thomas U. Walter Letters.

93. "Civis," "The Office of the Supervising Architect: What It Was, What It Is, and What It Ought to Be" (New York, n.p. 1869), 8 pp.

94. Ross Allan Webb, *Benjamin Helm Bristow: Border State Politician* (Lexington, Ky.: University of Kentucky Press, 1969), p. 137.

95. Mullett to William J. McPherson, 17 June 1874, Letters Sent, Chiefly by the Supervising Architect.

96. Mullett to David Coey, 2 December 1874, Letters Sent, Chiefly by the Supervising Architect.

97. Mullett to James C. Rankin, 2 December 1874, Letters Sent, Chiefly by the Supervising Architect.

98. "The Mighty Mullett," newspaper clipping, AIA Scrapbook, September 1, 1874, n.p.

99. Ibid.

100. John L. Smithmeyer to A. J. Bloor, 21 October 1874, Bureau of Architecture File, AIA Archives, Washington, D.C.

101. "Resignation of Supervising Architect Mullett," *New York Tribune* (24 November 1874), AIA Scrapbook. n.p.

102. Mullett to Benjamin Helm Bristow, 21 November 1874, Letters Sent, Chiefly by the Supervising Architect.

103. Bristow to Mullett, 23 November 1874, Alfred B. Mullett File, Personnel Folders of Notable Treasury Employees, Record Group 56, National Archives, Washington, D.C.

104. Mullett to Asa Snyder, 4 December 1874, Letters Sent, Chiefly by the Supervising Architect.

105. Mullett to William L. Burt, 26 December 1874, Letters Sent, Chiefly by the Supervising Architect.

106. "Mullett," *The Baltimore Sun* (25 November 1874), AIA Scrapbook, AIA Archives, Washington, D.C., n.p.

107. "Why Mullett Resigned," Loose article, 24 November 1874, copies of Alfred B. Mullett Papers, Washington, D.C., Historical Society of Washington, D.C.

108. Mullett to Coburn, 2 March 1871, Letters Sent, Chiefly by the Supervising Architect.

109. Mullett to John Sherman, 20 March 1877, Personnel Folders of Notable Treasury Employees.

110. Alfred B. Mullett to John Sherman, 20 March 1877, Personnel Folders of Notable Treasury Employees.

111. Walter to Edward Clark, 1 August 1876, Thomas U. Walter Letters.

112. Mullett to Sherman, 20 March 1877, Personnel Folders of Notable Treasury Employees.

113. Walter to Mullett, 18 March 1882, Thomas U. Walter Letters.

114. Alfred B. Mullett, Memorandum of Civil Commissioner, 10 December 1883, Washington, D.C.

115. Obituary of Alfred B. Mullett, *Cincinnati Tribune*, L. A. Rixford Scrapbook, 1885–1897, Cincinnati Historical Society, Cincinnati, Ohio., p. 54.

116. Records of the Washington Chapter, AIA Archives, Washington, D.C.

117. *Proceedings of the 24th Annual Convention of the American Institute of Architects* (Chicago: Inland Architect Press, 1891), p. 107.

118. Obituary of Alfred B. Mullett.

119. "Western Architects," *Cincinnati Times-Star* (18 November 1887), AIA Scrapbook.

120. P. B. Wight, "Government Architecture and Government Architects," *American Architect and Building News,* 1(18 March 1876), p. 92.

CHAPTER 5

1. Thomas U. Walter to William Stickney, 5 December 1874, Thomas U. Walter Letters, The Athenaeum, Philadelphia, Pa.

2. "Poems in Stone," *Commercial Times* (23 February 1876). AIA Scrapbooks, AIA Archives, Washington, D.C., n.p.

3. "Government Architects: Mullett's Opinion of His Successor," *Evening Times* (Albany) (17 June 1875). AIA Scrapbooks., n.p.

4. "Poems in Stone," n.p.

5. Horace C. Jacobs to William A. Potter, 8 May 1875, Letters Sent, Chiefly by the Supervising Architect, Record Group 121, National Archives, Washington, D.C.

6. Sarah Bradford Landau, *Edward T. and William A. Potter: American Victorian Architects* (New York: Garland Publishing, 1979), p. 303.

7. "Poems in Stone," n.p.

8. "The Architectural Exhibition at the Centennial: Government Architecture II," *American Architect and Building News* [hereafter referred to as *AABN*], 1 (8 July 1876), p. 219.

9. Potter to Edward T. Avery, 29 June 1875, Letters Sent, Chiefly by the Supervising Architect.

10. "Architectural Exhibition at the Centennial," p. 219.

11. "Poems in Stone," n.p.

12. "Architectural Exhibition at the Centennial," p. 219.

13. "Poems in Stone," n.p.

14. Ibid. n.p.

15. "Architectural Exhibition at the Centennial," p. 219.

16. Peter B. Wight, "Government Architecture and Government Architects," *AABN*, 1 (18 March 1876), pp. 92–93.

17. *Annual Report of the Supervising Architect to the Secretary of the Treasury for the Year 1875*, (Washington, D.C.: Government Printing Office, 1875), p. 15.

18. A. J. Bloor, ed., *Proceedings of the 9th Annual Convention of the American Institute of Architects*, (New York: Committee on Publications of the AIA, 1875), p. 11.

19. P. B. Wight to A. J. Bloor, 11 December 1875, Bureau of Architecture Files, AIA Archives, Washington, D.C.

20. Walter to Bloor, 8 January 1876, Bureau of Architecture Files.

21. John L. Smithmeyer to Bloor, 13 December 1875, Bureau of Architecture Files.

22. "A Bill to Establish a Bureau of Architecture," H. R. 1834, 44th Congress, 1st Session, 7 February 1876.

23. "A Talk with Architects," *Real Estate Record and Builder's Guide*, 17 (12 February 1876). AIA Scrapbooks, p. 111.

24. "The Proposed Bureau of Architecture," *Real Estate Record and Builder's Guide*, 17 (19 February 1876). AIA Scrapbooks, p. 129.

25. "The Bureau of Architecture," *The Evening Post* (New York) (14 February 1876), and "The Architectural Bureau Bill," *The Evening Post* (9 February 1876), AIA Scrapbooks. AIA Scrapbooks, n.p.

26. "Bureau of Architecture." AIA Scrapbooks, n.p.

27. "Proposed Architectural Bureau."

28. "Bureau of Architecture."

29. W. H. Bishop to Bloor, 3 March 1876, Bureau of Architecture Files.

30. Walter to Bloor, 30 March 1876, Bureau of Architecture Files.

31. Smithmeyer to Bloor, 22 June 1876, Bureau of Architecture Files.

32. Ross Allan Webb, *Benjamin Helm Bristow: Border State Politician* (Lexington, Ky.: University Press of Kentucky, 1969), p. 335.

33. Walter to Edward Clark, 21 July 1876, Thomas U. Walter Letters.

34. Walter to Clark, 1 August 1876, Thomas U. Walter Letters.

35. Potter to Lot M. Morrill, 13 July 1876, Head of Bureaus File, Record Group 56, National Archives, Washington, D.C.

36. "Correspondence," *AABN* 1 (12 August 1876), p. 263.

37. Ibid.

38. "Summary," *AABN*, 1 (19 August 1876), p. 265.

39. For a complete biographical study of Hill, see Margaret Gordon Davis, "James G. Hill, Victorian Architect, Washington, D.C." (M.A. thesis, University of Virginia, 1981).

40. *Report of the Supervising Architect to the Secretary of the Treasury for the Year 1876* (Washington, D.C.: Government Printing Office, 1876), p. 11.

41. "Summary," *AABN*, 2 (January 6, 1877), p. 1.

42. "Summary," *AABN*, 2 (April 28, 1877), p. 129.

43. "Architects for Public Buildings," *AABN* 7 (17 January 1880), p. 19.

44. "Summary," *AABN*, 3 (23 February 1878), p. 61.

45. "Summary," *AABN*, 7 (17 January 1880), p. 18.

46. "Summary," *AABN*, 9 (29 January 1881), p. 49.

47. "Summary," *AABN*, 47 (30 March 1895), p. 129.

48. Alfred B. Mullett to John Sherman, 20 March 1877, Personnel Folders of Notable Treasury Employees, Record Group 56, National Archives, Washington, D.C.

49. "The New York Post Office Disaster," *AABN*, 2 (19 May 1877), p. 156.

50. "Correspondence" *AABN*, 2 (23 June 1877), p. 198.

51. Mullett to Sherman, 1 December 1879, James G. Hill, Personnel Folder, Applications and Recommendations for Positions in the Washington, D.C., Offices of the Treasury Department, Record Group 56, National Archives, Washington, D.C.

52. Walter to Stickney, 25 May 1877, Thomas U. Walter Letters.

53. "Summary," *AABN*, 4 (23 November 1878), p. 169, and 4 (7 December 1878), p. 185.

54. Walter to Elijah E. Myers, 2 December 1878, Thomas U. Walter Letters.

55. "Summary," *AABN*, 5 (24 May 1879), p. 161.

56. "Summary," *AABN*, 5 (21 June 1879), p. 193.

57. Leonard Swett to Sherman, 19 May 1879, James G. Hill File, Applications and Recommendations for Positions in the Washington, D.C., Offices of the Treasury Department.

58. Walter to Hill, 21 May 1879, Thomas U. Walter Letters.

59. Mullett to Sherman, 1 December 1879, James G. Hill File.

60. "Summary," *AABN*, 11 (7 January 1882), p. 1.

61. "Summary," *AABN*, 10 (3 December 1881), p. 201.

62. Hill to Charles J. Folger, 11 January 1882, James G. Hill File.

63. "Summary," *AABN*, 13 (9 June 1883), p. 265.

64. James Coleman, *The Investigation of James G. Hill, Supervising Architect of the Treasury. Argument of James Coleman Before the Investigating Committee* (n.p., August 1883), p. 96.

65. Ibid., p. 100.

66. "Summary," *AABN*, 14 (22 September 1883), p. 133.

67. Hill to Folger, 21 September 1883, Letters Sent, Chiefly by the Supervising Architect.

68. Hill to W. H. Murray, 7 July 1883, Letters Sent, Chiefly by the Supervising Architect.

69. *Annual Report of the Supervising Architect to the Secretary of the Treasury for the Year Ending September 30, 1883* (Washington, D.C.: Government Printing Office, 1883), p. 20.

70. George M. Kober, *Report on the Housing of the Laboring Classes in the City of Washington, D.C.* (Washington, D.C.: Government Printing Office, 1900), includes floor plans prepared by Hill.

71. Davis, "James G. Hill," p. 75, credits Hill with more than 150 architectural projects in Washington, D.C.

72. Walter to A. C. Harmer, 29 October 1883, Thomas U. Walter Letters.

73. Ibid.

74. "Summary," *AABN*, 14 (10 November 1883), p. 217.

75. *Annual Report of the Supervising Architect to the Secretary of the Treasury for the Year Ending September 30, 1884* (Washington, D.C.: Government Printing Office, 1884), p. 3.

76. "Summary," *AABN*, 19 (17 April 1886), p. 181.

77. *Annual Report of the Supervising Architect to the Secretary of the Treasury for the Year Ending September 30, 1884*, p. 7.

78. "Among the Architects," *Chicago Tribune*, 21 October 1887). AIA Scrapbook.

79. *Annual Report of the Supervising Architect to the Secretary of the Treasury for the Year Ending September 30, 1884*, p. 11.

80. Mifflin E. Bell to Carl R. Graves, 12 March 1884, Letters Sent, Chiefly by the Supervising Architect.

81. Bell to Robert Bunce, 30 October 1884, Letters Sent, Chiefly by the Supervising Architect.

82. "Summary," *AABN*, 21 (7 May 1887), p. 218.

83. John Moser Letter, "The Design for the Detroit Post Office," and the "Response of Editors, American Architect," *AABN*, 21 (7 May 1887), pp. 250–251, and "Key to a Design entitled, 'Suggestions of a Facade for the A.I.A. Building, New York City,' by Mr. John Moser, Anniston, Alabama," *AABN*, 15 (19 January 1884), pp. 31–32.

84. M. E. Bell Letter, "The Design for the Detroit Post Office," *AABN*, 21 (7 May 1887), p. 250.

85. Bell to William E. Chandler, 13 March 1884, Letters Sent, Chiefly by the Supervising Architect.

86. O. P. Hatfield, "Proposed Law for the Erection of Public Buildings," *AABN*, 18 (24 October 1885), p. 199.

87. Rufus H. Thayer, *History, Organization, and Functions of the Office of the Supervising Architect of the Treasury Department with Copies of Reports, Recommendations, etc.* (Washington, D.C.: Government Printing Office, 1886), p. 39.

88. As quoted in Thayer, *History, Organization, and Functions,* p. 45.

89. Walter to Bloor, 12 May 1885, Thomas U. Walter Letters.

90. Walter to Bloor, 19 September 1885, Thomas U. Walter Letters.

91. Mifflin E. Bell File, Applications and Recommendations for Positions in the Washington, D.C., Office of the Treasury Department.

92. Will. A. Freret File, Applications and Recommendations for Appoint-ments as Superintendents of Construction, Record Group 56, National Archives, Washington, D.C.

93. "Summary," *AABN*, 22 (30 July 1887), p. 45.

94. "Summary," *AABN*, 25 (5 January 1889), pp. 1–2.

95. "More Light on Freret: Investigating the Supervising Architect," *New York Tribune* (8 February 1889). AIA Scrapbooks. p. 159.

96. *Annual Report of the Supervising Architect to the Secretary of the Treasury for the Year Ending December 31, 1888* (Washington, D.C.: Government Printing Office, 1889), pp. 3–5.

97. Ibid., p. 6.

98. Percy Clark, "New Federal Buildings," *Harper's Weekly* (19 May 1888), pp. 367–368.

99. John C. Poppeliers, "The 1867 Philadelphia Masonic Temple Competition,"

Journal of the Society of Architectural Historians, 26 (December 1967), pp. 279–284; and "James Hamilton Windrim," in *The National Cyclopedia of American Biography* (New York: James T. White & Co., 1893).

100. "Summary," AABN, 25 (30 March 1889), p. 145.
101. "Summary," AABN, 32 (11 April 1891), p. 17.
102. "A New Supervising Architect Appointed," *The Inland Architect,* 17 (April 1891), p. 30.
103. "Appointment of a new Supervising Architect," *The Inland Architect,* 13 (April 1889), p. 49.
104. *Proceedings of the 25th Annual Convention of the AIA* (Chicago: Inland Architect Press, 1892), p. 27.
105. List of Candidates to Fill Vacancy Occasioned by the Resignation of James H. Windrim, Letters Received from the Supervising Architect, Record Group 56, National Archives, Washington, D.C.
106. Francis William Wynn Kervich, *Architecture at Notre Dame 1898–1938* (Notre Dame, Ind.: University of Notre Dame, 1938), n.p.
107. List of Candidates to Fill Vacancy Occasioned by the Resignation of James H. Windrim, Letters Received from the Supervising Architect.
108. "Reorganization of Supervising Architect's Office Probable," *The Inland Architect,* 17 (May 1891), p. 42.
109. "Summary," AABN, 32 (18 April 1891), p. 33.
110. Willoughy J. Edbrooke to Charles Foster, 7 September 1891, Letters Sent, Chiefly by the Supervising Architect.
111. Edbrooke to Herbert M. Greene, 26 September 1892, Letters Sent, Chiefly by the Supervising Architect.
112. *Annual Report of the Supervising Architect to the Secretary of the Treasury for the Year Ending September 30, 1891* (Washington, D.C.: Government Printing Office, 1891), p. 10.
113. Ibid., p. 12.
114. *Annual Report of the Supervising Architect to the Secretary of the Treasury for the Year Ending September 30, 1892* (Washington, D.C.: Government Printing Office, 1892), pp. 8–9.
115. Edbrooke to John G. Carlisle, 20 April 1893, Letters Sent, Chiefly by the Supervising Architect.
116. Jeremiah O'Rourke File, Applications and Recommendations for Appointments as Superintendents of Construction; and biographical files compiled by Donald W. Geyer of Newark, N.J., originally in Karel Yasko Files, GSA, Washington, D.C., copy now at Historical Society of Washington, D.C.
117. "Summary," AABN, 40 (15 April 1893), p. 33.
118. "Inexcusable Blunder by the Government," *The Inland Architect,* 21 (April 1893), pp. 31–32.
119. Jeremiah O'Rourke, "On Architectural Practice of the United States Government," Supplement, *World's Congress of Architects* held in conjunction with the 27th Annual Convention of the AIA at Chicago, commencing July 31, 1893. (Chicago: Inland Architect Press, 1893), p. 280.
120. *Annual Report of the Supervising Architect to the Secretary of the Treasury for the Year Ending September 30, 1893* (Washington, D.C.: Government Printing Office, 1893), p. 4.
121. St. Julian B. Dapray to Jeremiah O'Rourke, 27 July 1893, Letters Sent, Chiefly by the Supervising Architect.
122. O'Rourke to Alfred Stone, 17 January 1894, Letters Sent, Chiefly by the Supervising Architect.
123. O'Rourke to Daniel H. Burnham, 16 February 1894, Letters Sent, Chiefly by the Supervising Architect.

124. Burnham to John G. Carlisle, 9 March 1894, Letters Sent, Chiefly by the Supervising Architect.

125. Carlisle to Burnham, 12 March 1894, Letters Sent, Chiefly by the Supervising Architect.

126. *Annual Report of the Supervising Architect to the Secretary of the Treasury for the Year Ending September 30, 1893*, p. 4.

127. Obituary of Jeremiah O'Rourke, *Newark Evening News* (24 April 1915), p. 6.

CHAPTER 6

1. Richard Guy Wilson, "Architecture, Landscape, and City Planning," *The American Renaissance 1876–1917* (New York: The Brooklyn Museum, 1979), p. 92.

2. Leland M. Roth, *McKim, Mead & White, Architects* (New York: Harper & Row, 1983), p. 116.

3. Ibid., p. 130.

4. Thomas S. Hines, *Burnham of Chicago: Architect and Planner* (New York: Oxford University Press, 1974), p. 97.

5. Ibid., p. 87.

6. Ibid., p. 86.

7. Ibid., pp. 120–121.

8. Daniel H. Burnham, as quoted in Hines, *Burnham of Chicago,* p. 129.

9. William Windom, as quoted in James Windrim, "Architecture and the U.S. Government," *Proceedings of the 25th Annual Convention of the American Institute of Architects, 1891* (Chicago: Inland Architect Press, 1892), p. 25.

10. Windrim, "Architecture and the United States Government," p. 25.

11. "The Government Architecture Reorganization Bill," *The Inland Architect*, 19 (February 1892), p. 2.

12. "The Government Buildings Bill," *American Architect and Building News* [hereafter referred to as AABN], 39 (11 February 1893), p. 88.

13. "Summary," AABN, 39 (25 February 1893), p. 114.

14. "The Government Architecture Reorganization Bill," *The Inland Architect*, 20 (December 1892), p. 48.

15. As quoted in "Summary," AABN, 39 (4 March 1893), p. 129.

16. Ibid.

17. Charles Foster to Senate Committee on Public Buildings and Grounds, 4 February 1893, Letters Sent, Chiefly by the Supervising Architect, Record Group 121, National Archives, Washington, D.C.

18. Willoughby J. Edbrooke to Foster, 18 February 1893, Letters Sent, Chiefly by the Supervising Architect.

19. Alfred Stone to AIA members, 6 March 1893, Scrapbook of the Western Association of Architects, AIA Archives, Washington, D.C.

20. Edward H. Kendall, "President's Address," *Proceedings of the 27th Annual Convention of the AIA, 1893* (Chicago: Inland Architect Press, 1893), pp. 9–10.

21. Daniel H. Burnham, "President's Address," *Proceedings of the 29th Annual Convention of the AIA, October 15, 16 & 17, 1895* (Providence: E. A. Johnson, & Co., Printers 1895), p. 9.

22. Jeremiah O'Rourke to G. G. Vest, 13 January 1894, Letters Sent, Chiefly by the Supervising Architect.

23. "Supervising Architect's Bill Passed," *The Inland Architect*, 22 (January 1894), p. 52.

24. "Consideration of the Correspondence Relative to the Tarsney Bill," *The Inland Architect*, 23 (April 1894), p. 26.

25. "Washington" column, AABN, 43 (31 March 1894), p. 150.

26. Glenn Brown, "Government Buildings Compared with Private Buildings," *AABN*, 44 (7 April 1894), p. 9.
27. "Summary," *AABN*, 44 (14 April 1894), p. 13.
28. "Summary," *AABN*, 43 (24 March 1894), p. 133.
29. Alfred Stone to members of the AIA, 21 May 1894, Western Association of Architects Scrapbook.
30. "Buildings for the U.S. Government," Scrapbook of the Western Association of Architects, n.d.
31. "Report of the Legislative Committee on Government Architecture," *Proceedings of the 30th Annual Convention of the AIA*, October 20, 21, and 22, 1896, (Providence: E. A. Johnson & Co., Printers, 1896), p. 29.
32. "The Public Buildings Bill," *AABN*, 45 (11 August 1894), pp. 53–54.
33. O'Rourke to William M. McKaig, 14 August 1894, Letters Sent, Chiefly by the Supervising Architect.
34. "The New Government Architecture Bill," *The Inland Architect and News Record*, 23 (July 1894), pp. 62–63.
35. "Why the McKaig Bill Did Not Pass," *The Inland Architect*, 25 (March 1895), p. 13.
36. Jeremiah O'Rourke, discussion following "Report of the Legislative Committee on Government Architecture" *Proceedings of the 30th Annual Convention of the AIA, October 20, 21, & 22, 1896* (Providence: E. A. Johnson & Co., Printers, 1896), p. 37.
37. "Summary," *AABN*, 47 (2 February 1895), p. 49. See also the John M. Carrère papers, Library of Congress, Manuscript Division.
38. "M'Kaig Bill Smothered," *The Sun*, n.d., AIA Scrapbook, AIA Archives, p. 210.
39. "Summary," *AABN*, 47 (23 March 1895), p. 117.
40. "W. M. Aiken Appointed Supervising Architect," *The Inland Architect*, 25 (April 1895), p. 25.
41. "Summary," *AABN*, 47 (30 March 1895), p. 129.
42. Burnham, "President's Address," p. 9.
43. "Chicago," *AABN*, 48 (22 June 1895), p. 119.
44. Henry Ives Cobb File, Applications and Recommendations for Appointments as Superintendents of Construction, Record Group 56, National Archives, Washington, D.C.
45. *Proceedings of the 30th Annual Convention of the AIA, 1896*, p. 35.
46. Ibid., pp. 34–36.
47. Ibid., p. 41.
48. Ibid., p. 36.
49. "Summary," *AABN*, 34 (12 December 1896), p. 85.
50. "Summary," *AABN*, 55 (6 March 1897), p. 73.
51. "Secretary Gage and the Supervising Architect's Office," *The Inland Architect*, 29 (March 1897), p. 11.
52. "Legislative Committee on Government Architecture," *Proceedings of the 31st Annual Convention of the AIA, September 29, 30 and October 1, 1897* (Providence: E. A. Johnson & Co., Printers, 1897), pp. 28–29.
53. Ibid., p. 11.
54. U. S. Congress, House, *Erection of Public Buildings*, H. Report 1078 to Accompany H.R. 8152, 52nd Congress, 1st Session, 1892.
55. O'Rourke to John G. Carlisle, 13 January 1894, Letters Received from the Supervising Architect, Record Group 56, National Archives, Washington, D.C.
56. O'Rourke to McKaig, 14 August 1894, Letters Sent, Chiefly by the Supervising Architect.
57. Daniel H. Burnham, "Suggestions toward the Best and Speediest Methods

for Harmonizing and Utilizing All the Architectural Societies in the United States," *Proceedings of the 21st Annual Convention of the AIA, October 19th, 20th and 21st, 1887*, pp. 115–116.

58. O'Rourke to Carlisle, 13 January 1894, Letters Received from the Supervising Architect.
59. Will. A. Freret to Charles S. Fairchild, 19 June 1888, Letters Sent, Chiefly by the Supervising Architect.
60. O'Rourke to McKaig, 1 August 1894, Letters Sent, Chiefly by the Supervising Architect.
61. O'Rourke to McKaig, 14 August 1894, Letters Sent, Chiefly by the Supervising Architect.
62. *Proceedings of the 31st Annual Convention of the AIA, 1897*, p. 11.
63. Statement of George B. Post, *Proceedings of the 30th Annual Convention of the AIA, 1896*, p. 36.
64. U.S. Congress, House, *Erection of Public Buildings*.
65. Ibid.
66. "United States Government Architecture," *Cedar Rapids Daily Republican*. AIA Scrapbook, AIA Archives, Washington, D.C., p. 244.
67. U. S. Congress, House, *Erection of Public Buildings*.
68. Statement of George B. Post, *Proceedings, 1896*, p. 36.
69. Richard Morris Hunt, "President's Address," *Proceedings of the 22nd Annual Convention of the AIA, October 17, 18, & 19, 1888* (New York: Oberhauser & Co., Printers, 1889) p. 5.
70. "Summary," *AABN*, 45 (21 July 1894), p. 21.
71. John M. Carrère, "The Influences against the McKaig Bill," *AABN*, 47 (23 February 1895), p. 84.
72. "Report of the Legislative Committee on Government Architecture," *Proceedings of the 30th Annual Convention of the AIA, October 20, 21, and 22, 1896* (Providence: E. A. Johnson & Co., Printers, 1896), p. 39.
73. "The McKaig and Chicago Post Office Bills," *The Inland Architect*, 27 (February 1896), p. 1.
74. Windrim, "Architecture and the United States Government." p. 25.
75. C. H. Read, "Government Architects," *The Southern Architect*, p. 89 AIA Scrapbook. p. 237.
76. John M. Carrère, AIA Circular, 11 December 1894, AIA Scrapbook.
77. George B. Post et al. to Carrère, 24 March 1896, AIA Scrapbook.

CHAPTER 7

1. Glenn Brown, "The Tarsney Act," *The Brickbuilder* (May 1906), p. 12.
2. "Summary," *American Architect and Building News* [hereafter referred to as *AABN*], 61 (20 August 1898), p. 57.
3. Richard W. Longstreth, "Academic Eclecticism in American Architecture," *Winterthur Portfolio*, 17 (Spring 1982), pp. 55–82.
4. Theodore Wells Pietsch, "What the Beaux Arts Training Means to American Architects," *The Inland Architect*, 32 (January 1899), p. 54.
5. "W. M. Aiken Appointed Supervising Architect," *The Inland Architect*, 25 (April 1895), p. 25.
6. William Martin Aiken, "National Architecture," *The Inland Architect*, 28 (November 1896), p. 32.
7. *Annual Report of the Supervising Architect to the Secretary of the Treasury for the Year Ending September 30, 1896* (Washington, D.C.: Government Printing Office, 1897), p. 6.

8. Frank L. Averill File, Applications and Recommendations for Positions in the Washington, D.C., Office of the Treasury Department, Record Group 56, National Archives, Washington, D.C.

9. Francis B. Wheaton File, Applications and Recommendations for Positions in the Washington, D.C., Office of the Treasury Department.

10. "A Government Representative Sent to Brussels," *The Inland Architect*, 29 (July 1897), p. 52.

11. Edward A. Crane File, Applications and Recommendations for Positions in the Washington, D.C., Office of the Treasury Department.

12. Edward A. Crane File, AIA Membership Application, AIA Archives, Washington, D.C.

13. William Martin Aiken to Director, Bureau of Ethnology, 21 April 1897, Letters Sent, Chiefly by the Supervising Architect, Record Group 121, National Archives, Washington, D.C.

14. Aiken to Charles E. Kemper, 9 May 1895, Letters Sent, Chiefly by the Supervising Architect.

15. "Summary," AABN, 54 (12 December 1896), p. 85.

16. "Summary," AABN, 56 (8 May 1897), p. 42.

17. "Summary," AABN, 64 (7 December 1901), p. 73.

18. "In Memoriam—William Martin Aiken," AABN, 94 (23 December 1908), p. 214.

19. "Summary," AABN, 57 (10 July 1897), p. 14.

20. "Supervising Architect's Examination Proposed," *The Inland Architect*, 29 (July 1897), p. 52.

21. Articles relative to the Tarsney Act can be found in *The Inland Architect*, 30 (August 1897), pp. 4, 5, and 9.

22. "The New Supervising Architect of the Treasury," *The Inland Architect*, 30 (November 1897), p. 37.

23. Robert Allen Jones, "Cass Gilbert, Midwestern Architect in New York" (Ph.D. diss., Case Western Reserve University, 1976), p. 63.

24. For biographical information on Taylor, see: Jones, "Cass Gilbert"; Patricia Anne Murphy, "The Early Career of Cass Gilbert: 1878–1895" (M.A. thesis, University of Virginia, 1979); and Mark Reinberger, "James Knox Taylor— The Academic Revival in Federal Architecture" (paper written for seminar on federal architecture, Cornell University, Spring 1979).

25. Cass Gilbert to Clarence Johnston, January 1897, as quoted in Murphy, "Early Career of Cass Gilbert," p. 136.

26. James Knox Taylor to Jeremiah O'Rourke, 5 September 1893, Applications and Recommendations for Positions in the Washington, D.C., Offices of the Treasury Department.

27. Taylor to O'Rourke, 27 September 1893, Applications and Recommendations for Positions in the Washington, D.C., Offices of the Treasury Department.

28. "Summary," AABN, 58 (30 October 1897), p. 37.

29. "The New Supervising Architect of the Treasury Department," *Inland Architect*, 30 (November 1897), p. 38.

30. "The New Supervising Architect of the Treasury," p. 37.

31. Byron R. Newton to Thomas P. Gore, 28 March 1913, General Correspondence, 1910–1939, Record Group 121, National Archives, Washington, D.C.

32. Oscar Wenderoth to Newton, 4 April 1914, General Correspondence, 1910–1939.

33. "Supervising Architect's Examination Thesis," *The Inland Architect*, 30 (November 1897), p. 38.

34. "The New Supervising Architect of the Treasury," p. 37.

35. "United States Governmental Work and Workers," *The Inland Architect*, 31 (April 1898), p. 25.
36. "Summary," *AABN*, 78 (4 October 1902), p. 2.
37. Ibid.
38. "Summary," *AABN*, 64 (22 April 1899), p. 25.
39. "United States Government Architectural Work and Workers," p. 26.
40. Ibid., p. 27.
41. "Washington" column, *AABN*, 71 (2 February 1901), p. 38.
42. "Summary," *AABN*, 64 (13 May 1899), p. 49.
43. Jones, "Cass Gilbert," p. 82.
44. Ibid., p. 85.
45. Ibid., p. 94.
46. "Cass Gilbert's New York Customhouse Design," *The Inland Architect*, 35 (February 1900), pp. 6–7.
47. "Washington" column, *AABN*, 71 (2 February 1901), p. 38.
48. "The New Baltimore Custom House," *AABN*, 94 (29 July 1908), p. 35.
49. "The New Supervising Architect of the Treasury," p. 38.
50. *Annual Report of the Supervising Architect of the Treasury Department for the Fiscal Year Ending June 30, 1899* (Washington, D.C.: Government Printing Office, 1899), p. 4.
51. "Correspondence regarding Government Competition," *The Inland Architect*, 38 (August 1901), p. 7.
52. "List of Buildings and Extensions for Which Drawings Were Prepared by Private Architects," 1 July 1912, General Correspondence, 1910–1939.
53. Franklin MacVeagh to Taylor, 23 January 1911, Letters Sent, 1888–1912, Competitions, Record Group 121, National Archives, Washington, D.C.
54. MacVeagh to Green & Wicks, 28 March 1911, Letters Sent, 1888–1912, Competitions.
55. Percy Ash File, Applications and Recommendations for Positions in the Washington, D.C., Offices of the Treasury Department; and biographical files, Penn State Room, Pennsylvania State University, University Park, Pa.
56. Edward W. Donn Jr. File, Applications and Recommendations for Positions in the Washington, D.C., Offices of the Treasury Department.
57. Theodore W. Pietsch File, Applications and Recommendations for Positions in the Washington, D.C., Offices of the Treasury Department.
58. Nathan C. Wyeth File, Applications and Recommendations for Positions in the Washington, D.C., Offices of the Treasury Department.
59. Taylor to Miss A. E. Brown, 12 May 1905, Letters Sent, Chiefly by the Supervising Architect, 1888–1912.
60. "The Washington (D.C.) Atelier's Annual Banquet," *AABN*, 96 (7 July 1909), p. 1A.
61. *The Washington Atelier, 1904 Year Book*, AIA Archives, Washington, D.C.
62. Editorial, *AABN*, 95 (10 March 1909), p. 88.
63. Editorial, *AABN*, 95 (10 March 1909), p. 88.
64. Arthur Young & Co., "Office of the Supervising Architect, Report No. 14," 28 September 1910, General Correspondence, 1910–1939.
65. R. O. Bailey to Wenderoth, 4 December 1912, General Correspondence, 1910–1939. The telegram states, "Secretary wishes you to know that resignation takes effect June fifteenth, but one month's leave granted after that, which makes a delay to middle of July before salary here will be available."
66. "Tarsney Act," *Journal of the AIA*, 1 (January 1913), pp. 6–7.
67. Milton B. Medary Jr., "Committee on Government Architecture," *Journal of the AIA*, 1 (January 1913), p. 35.

68. "New York Chapter," *Journal of the* AIA, 1 (January 1913), pp. 43–44.
69. Reinberger, "James Knox Taylor."
70. For biographical information on Wenderoth, see Sherman Allen to Thomas P. Gore, 28 March 1913, General Correspondence, 1910–1929; and "Oscar Wenderoth," *Who Was Who in America with World Notables,* Vol. V, 1969–1973 (Chicago: Marquis Who's Who, Inc., 1973), p. 768.
71. Oscar Wenderoth to Paul Gerhardt, 24 July 1912, General Correspondence, 1910–1939.
72. Wenderoth to MacVeagh, 27 August 1912, General Correspondence, 1910–1913.
73. Second draft of Annual Report of the Supervising Architect's Office for the Fiscal Year Ending June 30, 1913, General Correspondence, 1910–1939.
74. Memorandum regarding Outside Architects, 20 December 1912, General Correspondence, 1910–1939.
75. Second draft of Annual Report of the Supervising Architect's Office for the Fiscal Year Ending June 30, 1913, General Correspondence, 1910–1939.
76. Report on Standardization of Buildings, 21 September 1912, General Correspondence, 1910–1939.
77. Second draft of Annual Report of the Supervising Architect's Office for the Fiscal Year Ending June 30, 1913, General Correspondence, 1910–1939.
78. Wenderoth to Thomas Hastings, 23 October 1912, General Correspon-dence, 1910–1939.
79. Wenderoth to William G. McAdoo, 16 November 1914, General Corre-spondence, 1910–1939.
80. Wenderoth to McAdoo, 30 November 1914, General Correspondence, 1910–1939.
81. Newton to C. O. Lobeck, 25 February 1915, General Correspondence, 1910–1939.
82. Wenderoth to W. B. Kilpatrick, 12 September 1915, General Correspon-dence, 1910–1939.
83. Obituary of James A. Wetmore, *The Federal Architect* (April 1940), p. 8.
84. Ibid.
85. Report on Standardization of Buildings, 21 September 1912, General Corre-spondence, 1910–1939.
86. Obituary of James A. Wetmore, p. 8.
87. Newton to Chairman, Committee on Public Buildings and Grounds, House of Representatives, 4 May 1916, General Correspondence, 1910–1939.
88. As quoted in Beth Grosvenor, *How to Apply National Register Criteria to Post Offices* (Washington, D.C.: National Park Service, 1984), p. 14.
89. McAdoo to Newton, 15 August 1915, General Correspondence, 1910–1939.
90. Newton to Chairman, House Committee on Public Buildings and Grounds, 4 May 1916, General Correspondence, 1910–1939.
91. *Annual Report of the Supervising Architect of the Treasury Department for the Fiscal Year Ended June 30, 1916,* (Washington, D.C.: Government Printing Office, 1916), p. 4.
92. *Annual Report of the Supervising Architect of the Treasury Department for the Fiscal Year Ended June 30, 1917* (Washington, D.C.: Government Printing Office, 1917), p. 4.
93. Newton to Assistant Secretary J. H. Moyle, 11 November 1917, General Correspondence, 1910–1939.
94. James A. Wetmore to Courtland M. Fenquay, 7 November 1923, General Correspondence, 1910–1939.

95. "The Institute and Government Architecture," *Proceedings of the 50th Annual Convention of the AIA, December 6, 7 & 8, 1916 (Washington, D.C.: American Institute of Architects, 1917),* p. 42.

96. Breck Trowbridge, "Government Architecture," *Proceedings of the 50th Annual Convention of the AIA, 1916,* p. 44.

97. John Elfreth Watkins to Wetmore, 15 December 1915, General Correspondence, 1910–1939.

98. Sue A. Kohler, *The Commission of Fine Arts: A Brief History, 1910–1976* (Washington, D.C.: The Commission of Fine Arts, 1983), p. 1.

99. Bureau of Fine Arts File, AIA Archives, Washington, D.C.

100. Glenn Brown, "A Bill for a National Advisory Board on Civic Art and a Plea Showing the Demand and the Necessity for Such a Board," Bureau of Fine Arts File, AIA Archives.

101. Theodore Roosevelt to Glenn Brown, 19 January 1909, Bureau of Fine Arts File, AIA Archives.

102. For a history of the Commission of Fine Arts, see Kohler, *Commission of Fine Arts.*

103. "A Bill for the Creation of a Proposed Government Bureau of Buildings and Grounds, with a Report Showing How Such a Law Would be a Public Benefit," *Journal of the AIA,* 1 (November 1913), p. 498.

104. Ibid., p. 500.

105. "Government Architecture," *Journal of the AIA,* 2 (December 1914), p. 590.

106. Cass Gilbert, "President's Address," *Proceedings of the 43rd Annual Convention of the AIA, December 14, 15 and 16, 1909* (Washington, D.C.: Gibson Bros., Printers & Publishers, 1910), pp. 9–10.

107. Milton B. Medary, Jr. "Address of Chairman of Committee on Public Works," *Proceedings of the 57th Annual Convention of the AIA, May 21, 22 and 23, 1924* (Washington, D.C.: Gibson Bros., Inc., 1924), p. 30.

108. Lt. Col. C. O. Sherrill, "Public Works and Public Buildings in Washington," *Proceedings of the 57th Annual Convention of the AIA, 1924,* p. 31.

109. J. H. Moyle to Dreher Construction Company, 10 January 1918, General Correspondence, 1910–1939.

110. Newton to Moyle, 11 November 1917, General Correspondence, 1910–1939.

111. L. S. Rowe to C. J. Thompson, 28 May 1919, General Correspondence, 1910–1939.

112. Andrew W. Mellon to Henry Cabot Lodge, 9 July 1921, General Correspondence, 1910–1939.

113. Mellon to John W. Langley, 31 December 1921, General Correspondence, 1910–1939.

114. Wetmore to Fenquay, 7 November 1923, General Correspondence, 1910–1939.

115. Milton B. Medary, Jr. "The Committee on Public Works—the Public Buildings Bill," *Proceedings of the 59th Annual Convention of the AIA, May 5, 6, 7, 1926,* (Washington, D.C.: American Institute of Architects, 1926), p. 25.

116. "The New Program for Public Buildings in Washington," *Journal of the AIA,* 6 (January 1918), p. 20.

117. "The Discussion in the United States Senate of an Amendment to the Bill for the New Treasury Department Building Providing that the Plans Therefore Should be Submitted to the Commission of Fine Arts," *Journal of the AIA,* 5 (August 1917), supplement, pp. 1–8.

118. "Shadows and Straws," *Journal of the AIA,* 7 (January 1919), p. 3.

CHAPTER 8

1. A. Ten Eyck Brown to Thomas M. Bell, 22 February 1926, General Correspondence, 1910–1939, Record Group 121, National Archives, Washington, D.C.
2. McKenzie Moss to Bell, 3 March 1926, General Correspondence, 1910–1939.
3. Ibid.
4. "Report of the Committee on Public Works," *Proceedings of the 60th Annual Convention of the AIA, May 11, 12, 13, 1927* (Washington, D.C.: American Institute of Architects, 1927), p. 144.
5. *Proceedings of the 60th Annual Convention of the AIA, 1927*, pp. 145–146.
6. "Committee on Public Works," *Proceedings of the 63rd Annual Convention of the AIA, May 21, 22, 23, 1930* (Washington, D.C.: American Institute of Architects, 1930), p. 86.
7. National Capital Planning Commission and Frederick Gutheim, *Worthy of the Nation: The History of Planning for the National Capital* (Washington, D.C.: Smithsonian Institution Press, 1977), p. 172.
8. Horace W. Peaslee to Charles S. Dewey, 3 January 1927, General Correspondence, 1910–1939.
9. Peaslee to Benjamin F. Betts, 4 April 1931, Horace W. Peaslee Papers, AIA Archives, Washington, D.C.
10. Peaslee to Dewey, 3 January 1927, General Correspondence, 1910–1939.
11. Milton B. Medary Jr. to Andrew W. Mellon, 9 July 1926, General Correspondence, 1910–1939.
12. Louis A. Simon, "Development of the Proposed Federal Building Group at Washington," *Journal of the AIA*, 16 (February 1928), p. 61.
13. Peaslee to Betts, 4 April 1931, Horace A. Peaslee Papers.
14. Personnel Classification Board, Classification Sheet for Edward H. Bennett, General Correspondence, 1910–1939.
15. "Linked Buildings Proposed in New Triangle Program," *Washington Evening Star*, 2 May 1927, p. 1, 12. Included in General Correspondence, 1910–1939.
16. W. E. Reynolds to General Accounting Office, 3 June 1937, General Correspondence, 1910–1939.
17. "Report of the Committee on Public Works," *Proceedings of the 61st Annual Convention of the AIA, May 16, 17, 18, 1928* (Washington, D.C.: American Institute of Architects, 1928), p. 120.
18. "Report of the Committee on Public Works," *Proceedings of the 62nd Annual Convention of the AIA, April 23, 24, 25, 1929* (Washington, D.C.: American Institute of Architects, 1929), p. 146.
19. Louis A. Simon, "The Federal Building Program in Washington," *Journal of the AIA*, 15 (December 1927), p. 397.
20. Louis A. Simon, "Federal Triangle," *The Federal Architect*, 6 (October 1935), p. 16.
21. Simon, "Federal Building Program in Washington," p. 368.
22. "Public Buildings and Other Improvements Recently Completed, Under Way or Planned for Washington," 5 November 1931, General Correspondence, 1910–1939.
23. James A. Wetmore to Ralph W. Yardley, 6 July 1926, General Correspondence, 1910–1939.
24. John T. Doyle to Wetmore, 13 May 1926, General Correspondence, 1910–1939.

25. George O. Von Nerta to U.S. Civil Service Commission, 29 August 1929, General Correspondence, 1910–1929.

26. Andrew C. Borzner to Doyle, 29 July 1926, General Correspondence, 1910–1929.

27. V. A. Matteson to Doyle, 28 July 1926, General Correspondence, 1910–1939.

28. Henry H. Kendall to Doyle, 29 July 1929, General Correspondence, 1910–1939.

29. Wetmore to Civil Service Commission, 12 October 1927, General Correspondence 1910–1939.

30. Mellon to R. P. Lamont, 10 January 1930, General Correspondence, 1910–1939.

31. Ferry K. Heath to Harry J. Allen, 22 March 1930, General Correspondence 1910–1939.

32. S. Lowman to John F. Miller, 19 April 1930, General Correspondence, 1910–1939.

33. Heath to William Adams Delano, 22 October 1930, General Correspondence, 1910–1939.

34. Lowman to Delano, 22 November 1930, General Correspondence, 1910–1939.

35. Resolution Adopted by the Board of Directors of the AIA, 13 November 1930, included in General Correspondence, 1910–1939.

36. Heath to Felix Hebert, 22 January 1932, General Correspondence, 1910–1939.

37. Arthur Woods to F. T. Miller, 26 March 1931, General Correspondence, 1910–1939.

38. James J. Davis to Ogden Mills, 9 March 1932, General Correspondence, 1910–1939.

39. Miller to Woods, 26 March 1931, General Correspondence, 1910–1939.

40. Edwin Bateman Morris, editorial, *The Federal Architect*, 1 (July 1930), p. 3.

41. Edwin Bateman Morris, editorial, *The Federal Architect*, 1 (April 1931), p. 3.

42. Heath to Woods, 8 April 1931, General Correspondence, 1910–1939.

43. W. D. Lovell to Hendrick Shipstead, 12 February 1932, General Correspondence, 1910–1939.

44. Unsigned and undated memorandum, General Correspondence, 1910–1939.

45. Betts to William H. Woodin, 4 March 1933, General Correspondence, 1910–1939.

46. Betts to Woodin, 4 March 1933, General Correspondence, 1910–1939.

47. Betts to Lewis W. Douglas, 9 March 1933, General Correspondence, 1910–1939.

48. Franklin Delano Roosevelt to Woodin, 21 March 1933, General Correspondence, 1910–1939.

49. Executive Order 6166, 10 June 1933.

50. Edwin Bateman Morris, editorial, *The Federal Architect*, 4 (October 1933), p. 5.

51. Edwin Bateman Morris, editorial, *The Federal Architect*, 4 (January 1934), p. 5.

52. Harold L. Ickes to Woodin, 2 August 1933 and 25 August 1933, General Correspondence, 1910–1939.

53. Ickes to C. J. Peoples, 15 May 1934, General Correspondence, 1910–1939.

54. Peoples to Ickes, 23 May 1934, General Correspondence, 1910–1939.

55. Peoples to the Surgeon General, 30 June 1934, General Correspondence, 1910–1939.

56. Peoples to Henry I. Harriman, 27 October 1934, General Correspondence, 1910–1939; and Reynolds to Everett M. Dirksen, 20 August 1934, General Correspondence, 1910–1939.

57. Henry Morganthau Jr. to Fritz G. Lanham, 27 May 1938, General Correspondence, 1910–1939.

58. Reynolds to Dirksen, 20 August 1934, General Correspondence, 1910–1939.

59. W. O. Mullgardt to John J. Cochran, 29 October 1934, General Correspondence, 1910–1939.

60. Reynolds to E. P. Platt & Bros., 14 January 1935, General Correspondence, 1910–1939. The temporary hiring of private architects, referred to as the "prima donnas," is described in the essay, "Washington Concentration Camp," *Architectural Forum*, 62 (February 1935), pp. 148–155.

61. James A. Wetmore, "His Name on Another Building," *The Federal Architect*, 6 (April 1936), p. 37.

62. "Letter from Judge Wetmore," *The Federal Architect*, 10 (July 1939), p. 6.

63. Obituary of James A. Wetmore, *The Federal Architect*, 10 (April 1940), p. 8.

64. For biographical information on Simon, see his AIA Fellowship Application, AIA Archives; Obituary of Simon, *Cosmos Club Bulletin*, 77 (September 1958), p. 2; "The Simon Era in the Supervising Architect's Office," *The Federal Architect*, 12 (January–March 1942), pp. 8, 13; and *The Federal Architect*, 12 (April–June 1942), pp. 8, 9.

65. Simon, AIA Fellowship Application, AIA Archives.

66. Ibid.

67. Aymar Embury II, "Louis A. Simon: A Great Public Servant," *The Federal Architect*, 9 (January 1939), p. 19.

68. "Simon Era in the Supervising Architect's Office," pp. 8, 13.

69. LeRoy Barton to Reynolds, 24 September 1934, General Correspondence, 1910–1939.

70. Reynolds to Board of Consulting Architects, 20 February 1935, General Correspondence, 1910–1939.

71. Simon to Reynolds, 21 February 1935, General Correspondence, 1910–1939.

72. Reynolds to John S. Edward, 6 November 1936, General Correspondence, 1910–1939.

73. "A Statement of the Representatives of the American Institute of Architects in Conference with the Representatives of the Secretary of the Treasury," General Correspondence, 1910–1939.

74. Frank Lloyd Wright, speech to the Association of Federal Architects, published in *The Federal Architect*, 9 (January 1939), p. 23.

75. Francis P. Sullivan, Report of the Committee on Public Works of the American Institute of Architects, 28–31 May 1935, General Correspondence, 1910–1939.

76. Sullivan to Morganthau Jr., 20 August 1935, General Correspondence, 1910–1939.

77. Morganthau Jr. to Sullivan, 31 October 1935, General Correspondence, 1910–1939.

78. Report of Selection of Architects for Service under the Treasury Department, p. 2, n.d., General Correspondence, 1910–1939.

79. Ibid.

80. Peoples to Reynolds, 17 April 1937, General Correspondence, 1910–1939.

81. Morganthau Jr. to Sullivan, 27 April 1937, General Correspondence, 1910–1939. A handful of post office buildings of this period were designed in the Art Deco, International, or Moderne styles, including the Forest Hills Station Post Office, Queens, N.Y. (1937–1938), designed by Lorimer Rich. See Susan Tunick, *Terra Cotta Skyline: New York's Architectural Ornament* (Princeton, N.J.: Princeton Architectural Press, 1997), p. 111.
82. Peoples to Reynolds, 17 April 1937, General Correspondence, 1910–1939.
83. "Federal Building Program Curbed," *Los Angeles Times* (27 July 1937), p. 1, included in General Correspondence, 1910–1939.
84. James D. Head to Peoples, 28 July 1938, General Correspondence, 1910–1939.
85. Peoples memorandum, 16 March 1939, General Correspondence, 1910–1939.
86. Treasury Department press release, 23 May 1938, General Correspondence, 1910–1939.
87. Peoples memorandum, 16 March 1939, General Correspondence, 1910–1939.
88. Morganthau Jr. to Fritz G. Lanham, 27 May 1938, General Correspondence, 1910–1939.
89. Reynolds to Ernest J. Bohn, 2 October 1939, General Correspondence, 1910–1939.
90. Treasury Department news release, 19 March 1939, General Correspondence, 1910–1939.
91. Charles D. Maginnis to Morganthau Jr., 9 June 1938, General Correspondence, 1910–1939.
92. Charles F. Cellarius to Charles Butler, 1 August 1939, General Correspondence, 1910–1939.
93. Peoples to Morganthau Jr., 18 March 1939, General Correspondence, 1910–1939.
94. Reynolds to Charles W. Eliot, 1 July 1939, General Correspondence, 1910–1939.
95. Reynolds to Robert Gray Allen, 8 August 1939, General Correspondence, 1910–1939.
96. Letter by Wetmore, *The Federal Architect*, 10 (January 1940), p. 6.

EPILOGUE

1. Jess Larson, "A Statement on Public Construction," *Public Construction*, No. 72 (July 1949), p. 3.
2. Federal Works Agency, *First Annual Report* (Washington, D.C.: Government Printing Office, 1940), pp. 9–10.
3. Ibid., p. 70.
4. "The Simon Era in the Supervising Architect's Office," *The Federal Architect*, 12 (April–June 1942), p. 9.
5. Helen Howe West, *George Howe: Architect, 1886–1955* (Philadelphia: William Nunn, 1973), p. 55.
6. Federal Works Agency, *First Annual Report*, p. 70.
7. Ibid.
8. Ibid., p. 76.
9. Ibid., p. 75.
10. Ibid., pp. 80–81.
11. Federal Works Agency, *Third Annual Report* (Washington, D.C.: Government Printing Office, 1942), p. 2.

12. Ibid., p. 31.

13. "The Simon Era," p. 8.

14. Federal Works Agency, *Third Annual Report*, p. 37.

15. Federal Works Agency, *Fourth Annual Report* (Washington, D.C.: Government Printing Office, 1943), pp. 17–18.

16. "The Public Buildings Administration and Its Work as of June 30, 1948" (Unpublished manuscript, Public Buildings Administration), p. 34.

17. Jess Larson, "Statement on Public Construction," p. 1.

18. "The Public Buildings Administration and Its Work as of June 30, 1948," p. 43.

19. Commission on the Organization of the Executive Branch of the Government, *Department of Works: A Report with Recommendations* (Washington, D.C.: Government Printing Office, 1949), pp. 50–51.

20. U.S. Congress, House, *Federal Property and Administration Services Act of 1949*. Pub. Law 81–152, 81st Congress, 1st session., 1949, H.R. 4754.

21. W. E. Reynolds, "Federal Building Practices Do Improve," *Public Construction*, no. 73 (August 1949), p. 1.

22. Ernest Mickel, "Washington News," *Architectural Record*, 107 (April 1950), pp. 20, 22.

23. Ernest Mickel, "Washington News," *Architectural Record*, 107 (January 1950), p. 16.

24. "Branch Post Office, Denver Colorado," *Architectural Record*, 112 (August 1952), p. 152.

25. Ernest Mickel, "Washington Topics," *Architectural Record*, 114 (November 1953), p. 38.

26. Ernest Mickel, "A Washington Report," *Architectural Record*, 116 (November 1954), pp. 12–13.

27. Ernest Mickel, "Washington Topics," *Architectural Record*, 116 (September 1954), pp. 38, 304.

28. Ernest Mickel, "Washington Report," *Architectural Record*, 109 (January 1951), p. 16.

29. W. E. Reynolds, "Current Construction Activities of the General Services Administration in the District of Columbia," *Public Construction*, no. 76 (November 1949), p. 1.

30. Ernest Mickel, "Washington Report," *Architectural Record*, 121 (April 1957), p. 32. *Architectural Record*. Copyright 1957 by The McGraw-Hill Companies. All rights reserved. Reproduced by permission of the publisher.

31. Ernest Mickel, "Washington Topics," *Architectural Record*, 116 (September 1954), p. 48.

32. Ernest Mickel, "A Washington Report," *Architectural Record*, 126 (December 1959), p. 50. *Architectural Record*. Copyright 1959 by The McGraw-Hill Companies. All rights reserved. Reproduced by permission of the publisher.

33. Ibid.

34. "New Hope for Federal Architecture," *AIA Journal*, 39 (August 1962), p. 48.

35. "Guiding Principles for Federal Architecture," *AIA Journal*, 39 (August 1962), p. 49.

36. "New Hope for Federal Architecture," p. 48. Reprinted with permission from *Architecture* (formerly *AIA Journal*), August 1962, copyright 1962, BPI Communications, Inc.

37. "People in the News," *Architectural Forum*, 117 (September 1962), p. 15.

38. "People in the News," *Architectural Forum*, 118 (January 1963), p. 13.

39. "A Bold Solution to a Difficult Problem," *Architectural Record*, 137 (March 1965), p. 137.

40. "Home for HUD," *Architectural Forum*, 127 (September 1967), p. 72.
41. "A Museum for the Space Age," *Architectural Record*, 137 (March 1965), p. 142.
42. "Office Complex Bridges New Mall," *Architectural Record*, 137 (March 1965), p. 145.
43. "Mies Designs Federal Center," *Architectural Record*, 137 (March 1965), p. 128. *Architectural Record*. Copyright 1965 by The McGraw-Hill Companies. All rights reserved. Reproduced by permission of the publisher.
44. "A Great Plaza for Boston's Government Center," *Architectural Record*, 135 (March 1964), pp. 192–195.
45. As quoted in Jonathan Barnett, "Those New Buildings on Lafayette Square," *Architectural Record*, 143 (April 1968), p. 154. *Architectural Record*. Copy-right 1968 by The McGraw-Hill Companies. All rights reserved. Reproduced by permission of the publisher.
46. John F. Kennedy to Bernard L. Boutin, 15 October 1962; letter reprinted in "Lafayette Square—The Final Word," *AIA Journal*, 39 (January 1963), p. 36.
47. Bill N. Lacy, introduction to *The Federal Presence: Architecture, Politics, and Symbols in United States Government Building*, ed. Lois Craig (Cambridge, Mass.: The MIT Press, 1977), n.p.
48. Ada Louise Huxtable, "Must Bad Buildings be the Norm?" *The New York Times*, 11 March 1973, pp. 23–24. Copyright © 1973 by *The New York Times Co*. Reprinted by permission.
49. Karel Yasko, "What (and Who) Determines Quality?" *AIA Journal*, 40 (July 1963), p. 65. Reprinted with permission from *Architecture* (formerly *AIA Journal*), July 1963, copyright 1963, BPI Communications, Inc.